CW00420298

Also available at all good book stores

9781785315527

9781785316272

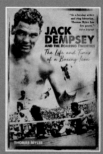

9781785316371

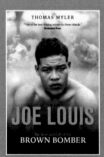

9781785315367

9781785315374

9781785315626

9781785315404

9781785315350

9781785313912

HATS, HANDWRAPS AND HEADACHES

HATS, HANDWRAPS
AND HEADACHES

A LIFE ON THE INSIDE OF BOXING

PADDY FITZPATRICK
WITH LEE 'TEACH' SIMPSON

First published by Pitch Publishing, 2020

Pitch Publishing
A2 Yeoman Gate
Yeoman Way
Worthing
Sussex
BN13 3QZ
www.pitchpublishing.co.uk
info@pitchpublishing.co.uk

© 2020, Paddy Fitzpatrick with Lee Simpson

Every effort has been made to trace the copyright.
Any oversight will be rectified in future editions at the
earliest opportunity by the publisher.

All rights reserved. No part of this book may be reproduced,
sold or utilised in any form or transmitted in any form or by
any means, electronic or mechanical, including photocopying,
recording or by any information storage and retrieval system,
without prior permission in writing from the Publisher.

A CIP catalogue record is available for this book
from the British Library.

ISBN 978 1 78531 642 5

Typesetting and origination by Pitch Publishing
Printed and bound by TJ International, Padstow, UK

Contents

Paddy:

I would like to dedicate this book to my mam and dad, the most beautiful, loving parents and guides any son could have. My sister, who has always been a light in my life. And to my beautiful 'chocolate' wife, Kerry, and my children.

I would also like to dedicate this book to the memory of one of my closest friends 'Big' Richy Curtis – 'I miss our talks already. Be cool brother – I love you.'

Lee:

I would like to dedicate this book to my beautiful wife Kate and my daughter Evie – the most precious things in my life.

Paddy's thanks go to:

Tommy G and Miss Lynn, for always being there. Freddie Roach for giving me quite possibly my last opportunity to change my life. Dave Amos, thank you for everything, 'simples'. To my Youth – I need you as much as you need me. And to Teach, for how this whole process has developed our friendship into one I really appreciate.

One Love.

Lee's thanks go to:

My wife Kate, without your belief, constant love and support, this book could *not* have been written. Dominic Salles, a mentor and friend – your advice, encouragement and enthusiasm is always appreciated and valued. Simon Lawson, for listening to me talk endlessly about boxing, and even seeming to enjoy the conversations! You're a top man. To everyone who has contributed to this book and given me their time – I appreciate you. To the Pitch team for all the advice and for believing in this project. And to Paddy, for allowing me into his fascinating life, his friendship, and increasing my peace!

Foreword

*'Relentless' Lamon Tajuan Brewster,
world heavyweight champion 2004–
2006 and holder of the fastest knockout in
a heavyweight championship fight at 53
seconds versus Poland's Andrew Golota.*

TODAY IS 10 April 2020.

I am writing this on the 16th anniversary of the night of 10 April 2004, when *we* defeated the great heavyweight champion of the era, Wladimir Klitschko, at the Mandalay Bay Hotel, Las Vegas, Nevada, which resulted in me becoming the WBO heavyweight champion of the world.

I first met Paddy at Freddie Roach's Wild Card gym in Los Angeles during the late 1990s.

I used to go into the Wild Card every day to train and there was just something about Paddy that was different. I'm a big 'energy' person and after being around someone for a while, you start to notice their energy. His energy felt calming to me. I was comfortable with him and his energy made me want to open up to him. Seeing the way he handled people and his positive attitude helped me to take to him as a person, even before I worked with him as a coach. I was living in Los Angeles at the time, and I didn't have any family out there, so the people I met in my life were like my family and Paddy had a beautiful spirit.

I had watched him working with other fighters too. He worked with Laila Ali, who is like a sister to me, and I liked what I saw. So, when the time came for me to fight for the world heavyweight championship, I wanted to make sure that I could put as much gas in my tank as possible to give me the fuel I needed to win this huge fight. Paddy was one of the people who I heavily depended on.

Physically, Paddy really pushed me in my preparations for this fight. He helped me to gain physical strength in a way that improved my mental strength too. He was a coach who focused on the mental side and that was important to me. Mentally, Paddy helped me to open doors that otherwise I might not have opened. Sometimes in life you have to be able to shift into much higher gears in order to accomplish your goals. Paddy made me believe in him and then through this I believed that I could achieve my own goal.

He's a great *life* coach too. He'd say such wonderful things. He had my back and he would get on top of me when I was slacking! He helped me be a better version of myself. And when you have somebody who can do *that*, well, you can't lose!

This is a book about Paddy's life and let me tell you, he hasn't had it easy. He's been up and he's been down. He's been rich and he's been poor. He's been a friend and he's been a foe. That's powerful because if I'm going to go into anything in life, I'd rather go with someone who is truly experienced. I want to go with someone who has been on the battlefield. I want someone who knows what it feels like to get knocked down and then have to get right back up again. I want to be with someone who knows what it feels like for others *not* to believe in you – and yet you still persevere.

Paddy is my brother *forever*. It don't matter if he's on the other side of the world or if he is right next to me. It don't matter if I see him today or 20 years from now. Paddy is my brother.

Being asked to write the foreword to his book is like being asked to be the godfather of a child. That's how important this story is to me. For me to have this role is an honour because I know how many greats Paddy has worked with – and because Paddy is my friend. It is my hope and my prayer that this book is successful because I want people to understand what perseverance truly is. No matter how down he has been, how much pressure has been put on him, or how hard the challenges life throws at him, Paddy has always come out the other side smiling. This dude is a true warrior.

We made history, me and Paddy. We knocked out a man in Wladimir Klitschko who *everyone* was afraid of. I didn't go into the ring by myself. Paddy was right there with me. Every muscle movement, every vein in my body, every breath I took, he was with me. Every time I hit that man, he was hitting him there with me. And every time I had to stand up to his punches, Paddy was standing up to them with me.

Paddy helped Lamon Brewster become heavyweight champion of the *entire* world. Not the western hemisphere, but the world: every continent, every single mountain, every valley and ocean. I became the world champion because the team believed in me. Paddy sacrificed everything for us to achieve this goal. He supported me with my mental headaches when I was down, tired or didn't want to keep working. Paddy kept pushing me shouting, 'Come on T! You can do it T! Think about your family T!' 'T' is what he always calls me.

Paddy taught me to achieve something that most people will never achieve. Few people on Earth can say that they were heavyweight champion of the world – but Lamon Brewster can.

Thank you, Paddy!

I hope you enjoy reading about my friend and his sometimes crazy, other times difficult and often brilliant life.

Peace and God bless you all.

Introduction

Becoming 'Teach' and writing this book

Fitzpatrick's Boxing Gym – March 2017.

The first punch that connects with my face lands on my jaw, exactly between where the mandible connects with the skull bone.

It hurts – *a lot.*

A bloke called Casper did it. *Casper* – like the *friendly* ghost. Later, I learn that what hit me with such force was a right cross – and it was my own fault. I deserved it. One of the best things about boxing, as I quickly found out, was that each painful experience was the fighter's *own* fault. This was one of the simple beauties of boxing. Because if I was making the mistake and getting hit, I could also learn from the mistake and make an adjustment to prevent getting hit in the first place. Casper had warned me not to let my left hand drop, regardless of how tired I was becoming, and to punctuate his fistic point – he hit me.

'Experience', he says, talking to me at the side of the ring as his next sparring partner gets his gear on, 'is the best way to learn. You won't forget so easily. One of the best things about boxing is that you learn to make adjustments. If you don't, you get hit. It's good motivation, and it helps the fighter not to forget. If you make a mistake in boxing, you're punished. And the punishment is pain.'

I didn't forget his lesson. The ache in my jaw lasted for several days afterwards.

I have barely recovered from the physical and emotional onslaught that is squaring up to a fighter a lot more skilful than I am when I hear Casper shout, 'Hey Teach, don't get too comfortable. You're up again next.'

I take a deep breath. Casper is *way* better at boxing than I am. Even if he is pulling his punches for me, it doesn't feel like it. And getting hit in the face is getting hit in the face. No one *likes* it.

The question is: *why am I doing this?* I'm in my 40s. I'm married. I have a very demanding job. Shouldn't I just take it easy?

But I love coming to this gym.

And that's partly the point of this book really. There are plenty of boxing gyms in Swindon. But this gym, Fitzpatrick's, is something *special*. At least it's special to me and to the wide variety of characters here. My name is Lee Simpson. But no one knows this at the boxing gym. 'Teach' is what they call me – on account of the fact that in my day job, I am a teacher.

Paddy Fitzpatrick, the Irish coach who owns and runs the gym, thinks up a nickname for everyone. My nickname is not original. But I am pathetically pleased with it. It feels like acceptance.

The nicknames vary from person to person. There's 'The Duke', who has won the Irish national cruiserweight title and the Commonwealth cruiserweight title; there's 'Sniper', 'Sky-High' (a very tall lad), and 'Heavy' too who, as you have probably worked out, is carrying a bit of weight around the stomach. And there's a guy called 'Danger', who just keeps on smiling, no matter how many times someone hits him in the face.

After I complete conditioning circuits and hit the heavy bags for a few rounds, I hear my name.

'Hey Teach!' shouts Paddy, 'You're up on the speed ball now, dude – get your gloves off!'

The speed ball.

This is an apparatus I have been looking forward to using since I started coming to the gym. It's that small, teardrop-shaped ball that hangs from the roof in front of a board. The skilled user will bounce it from the board with a consistently fast rattle, like an automatic machine gun. From the beginning, this is one of the things I have wanted to be able to do well since taking boxing up. The elegant *duh-duh-duh, duh-duh-duh, duh-duh-duh* at such effortless high speed.

Unfortunately, the dream image I have of myself stroking the leather of the speed ball is a long way from the reality.

When I get to the speed ball, Paddy is waiting for me. Unsurprisingly, he is striking the ball with such rapidity that it appears as a blur.

Suddenly, he stops and puts his arm around my shoulder. 'OK Teach, I'm gonna show you how to do this *exactly*. You watch me do it right, imitate what I do and then work towards speed. The key is rhythm. Get the rhythm right and then you can build up the speed.'

He looks me in the eye. 'Understand me?'

Not quite, I think. But the thing is, I want to understand, which is why, several years since I started coming to the boxing gym as a novice boxer in my 40th year, I am still coming here. And I am by no means the first man to do this.

Perhaps most famous is the story of F.X. Toole, the pen name of Jerry Boyd, a writer spoken of now in the same breath as greats like Raymond Carver and Ernest Hemingway and best known for being the writer of the original story *Million Dollar Baby*, which was made into the film by Clint Eastwood.

In his late forties, Toole walked into the Broadway Gym in South Central Los Angeles, meeting a weathered and gnarled old trainer called Dub Huntley. Huntley thought that Toole was lost, until Toole asked Huntley to train him. It was a shock to Dub, but he took on the ageing Toole thinking that the old guy would drop off pretty quickly if he trained him hard.

But Toole didn't drop off and he kept coming back, week after week, training and sparring in the gym with men a lot younger and a lot fitter than he was.

F.X. Toole has become a bit of a hero to me. In interviews, he explains how age and poor eyesight at 48 years old caused him to take more shots than he needed to, lacking both hand speed and a young man's reactions. While sparring, Toole had teeth cracked, his nose broken and developed a jaw problem that forced him to quit the physical act of boxing.

And yet, he had fallen in love. In fact, the connection that F.X. Toole made with boxing, and Dub Huntley in particular, saved his life according to his daughter Erin. As Erin tells it, divorce and the subsequent loss of his children took the life out of her father. Boxing, and the sense of family and community that he found in the Broadway Gym, brought some of it back.

In amongst the hopes and dreams of the boxers, Toole re-found his heart – because fighters *have* to have a whole lot of heart. And to Toole, this felt like home. 'God has blessed me with the Sweet Science,' is what Toole used to say when asked about boxing. And when, in his early 70s, Toole finally realised his ambition of becoming a writer, he dedicated his first book of short stories called *Rope Burns* to 'God and ... Dub Huntley'.

When I first contacted Paddy about learning to box, I had fully expected him to put me off the idea. But he didn't. He encouraged me. And I couldn't detect a single patronising note in the tone he used with me from the first time I met him.

I was reassured, and relieved, because at 40 years old I had entered what I now know was a dark place for me. In truth, I had entered that dark place many years before this point in my life but as I turned 40, I had acknowledged the fact. I recognised that this dark place was affecting me and the people I loved.

And I hoped that boxing could help.

I hadn't entirely realised until that time but I wasn't the person that I wanted to be. Regardless of how successful I looked on the outside, I wasn't dealing effectively with the stresses in my life. I was coping in a very stereotypical way for a male. Allowing the stresses to build up, pretending I was fine, and keeping a lid on the stress pot until nothing more could fit inside it.

And then there would be an explosion as the pressure cooker of my emotions looked for some kind of release.

I knew at this point that I couldn't allow this to continue. And that's when I turned to boxing.

Naively, I thought that boxing would help with anger and frustration. Hitting things must be good therapy is what I reasoned. It seemed simple.

And I was right, but only on the *simplest* level possible.

The physical act of exerting myself at a tough sport that requires the participant to develop every muscle and fibre of his body helped me massively. I was pushing myself physically more than I ever had before, and just the act of focusing on this single sport for a two-hour session until my T-shirt was so wet with sweat that I had to change it, was having an immediate impact upon my equilibrium.

The more I took part, the better I got. And the better I got at boxing, the better I felt physically – and *psychologically.*

I have become fascinated with what A.J. Liebling, the famous writer for the *New Yorker,* described as 'The Sweet

Science'. The mechanics of how to fight efficiently and effectively; the science behind how to capture the greatest amount of power in a punch and how to evade an opponent with the smallest margin of distance between you and him in order to ensure an immediate counter-attack.

I have even improved my own ability to teach effectively in my day job through observing the coaches at the gym and studying the way Paddy communicates how to learn efficiently to students others would find hard to reach.

I have also benefited from being part of the community that Paddy's gym fosters and he calls his 'boxing family'.

Most importantly, I am benefiting from the peace that boxing has brought to me as an individual, and by extension to my life and those around me.

Peace may seem a strange by-product of a combat sport that has caused me to have a painful jaw, to bleed from the nose, and to hold my ribs for weeks after a sparring session. But peace is exactly what boxing, and Paddy's coaching and friendship, has helped me to find.

I am convinced that choosing *this* gym has made the difference. I don't think this could have happened just anywhere. Boxing at this gym has helped me to find a peace that I have not known before and did not expect to find – least of all in the sweat and violence of combat sport.

Over the last few years, I have developed a friendship with Paddy and learned about his extraordinary life in boxing, which is what this book is really about. This is *his* story spanning his early fights in Limerick, training champions in

LA and being a key part in the winning of a world heavyweight championship with Lamon Brewster in Las Vegas.

As Paddy would say, I hope that this book keeps you smilin'.

This is his story and I am glad to help him tell it.

1

It's Over

August 2015

This should have been the best of times.

By rights, 'Saint' George Groves and his coach Paddy Fitzpatrick should have been a team almost at the peak of their potential for success. They were fighting for one of the most valuable possessions in elite-level sport – a world title belt from one of the four major governing bodies of world boxing – in Las Vegas. A world title belt that would finally have meant they had achieved their ambition – their dream – at the third time of asking.

It was September 2015. Groves, Paddy's most high-profile fighter at the time, was boxing for the WBC super middleweight title at the MGM Grand Garden Arena on a show promoted by multiple world champion and Mr Vegas himself, Floyd Mayweather Jr.

George's opponent was 'The Ripper', Badou Jack, a tough Swedish fighter who had taken the title from Anthony Dirrell in a 12-round contest that resulted in a majority decision in favour of Jack.

After losing two titanic world title fights against 'The Cobra' Carl Froch, George and Paddy had re-grouped as Team Groves and won the European super middleweight title and WBC silver belt with a convincing win over the skilled and durable Frenchman Christopher Rebrasse.

For years, they had been mixing with the best in the boxing community, narrowly missing out on world titles, but coming back stronger each time. Their eyes were determinedly focused on the fistic prize they knew George was so patently capable of achieving – a major world title belt.

This should have been the best of times.
George had enjoyed his most outstanding training camp to date in the time they had been together, improving upon his personal bests for cardiovascular performance and every other measure of his fitness. George's sparring had been excellent – efficient and *seriously* damaging. For the first time in their work together, he had hurt *every* sparring partner.

He was ruthless.

He was ready.

Together, George and Paddy had scaled the pinnacle of the boxing pyramid. Winning an elite-level European belt and fighting in front of 80,000 spectators at Wembley Stadium, London for a world title in what was the biggest sporting event of its kind in Britain since the 1940s.

They had achieved all of this.

And yet in his heart, four weeks before George was due to fight Badou Jack, even with the tantalising possibility of George becoming the champion of the world and so many potential opportunities opening up for them, Paddy knew that their relationship was over.

He knew that whatever the outcome of the fight, he would leave George's team.

Leave and never go back.

2

Paddy

YOU HAVE to know where Paddy's gym is if you are going to find it.

There is nothing outside that gives you any indication you have arrived, except for a single old-style sign weighted down next to a door in a side street off the main terraced road. The sign spins around in the wind. On one side in large capital letters are the words 'BOXING' and on the other 'GYM', which leaves you in no doubt about where you are.

What you notice immediately when you are outside the gym are the noises you can hear coming from inside. A staccato beat, like someone at a snare drum, repetitive thuds, muffled grunts and the shrill bleep of a timer set to sound after every three minutes.

I had agreed to meet Paddy to talk about his life before boxing really took hold of him after a training session at the gym. I was running late, so the session had already started when I arrived.

Paddy's boxing gym is old school: simple, effective, no frills. The gym has four distinct sections: an area with weights, machines and apparatus to improve cardiovascular performance; a variety of heavy bags and double end bags hanging from joists in the roof; four speed balls to improve rhythm, coordination and reactions; and a ring at the back of the gym set up for sparring.

The space that holds the gym is not as big as you might expect. It's roughly half the size of a large tennis court. Fitzpatrick's gym brings to mind a description of the famous Teofilo Al Brown gym in Colon, Panama, used by Panamanian boxing legend 'Manos de Piedra' or 'Hands of Stone' Roberto Duran. This was a boxing gym named after Panama's first world boxing champion that bred champions. It was affectionately known as the 'Box of Matches' gym by its members, including such greats as Luis Ibarra, Ismael Laguna and Eusebio Pedroza. The name referred to the fact that the young boxers who trained at the gym were crowded in so tightly that they had to rub shoulders to punch the bags.

In Paddy's gym, there are pictures and cuttings framed in display cases showing the professionals he has coached or worked with throughout his career. These pictures have fascinated me since I started coming to this gym. Famous names like James 'Lights Out' Toney, the four-time world champion; 'Saint' George Groves, the super middleweight world champion; Eamonn 'King Kane' O'Kane, the IBF intercontinental champion; and Laila Ali, Muhammad Ali's daughter, who retired from the sport as an undefeated world champion.

Mixed in with these greats are newspaper clippings celebrating the successes of a new group of fighters Paddy is nurturing: welterweight Ryan Martin, *Ultimate Boxxer*'s Sam 'The Sniper' Smith, and Luke 'The Duke' Watkins, who held both the Irish national and Commonwealth cruiserweight belts until recently. There is also a picture of the legendary Ali holding Paddy's son D.J. in his arms and another of Paddy and Laila paying homage to her father in a photograph in which they stare directly at each other imitating the wide-mouth expression he held in one of the many famous images that became iconic around the globe.

Other walls around the perimeter of the gym are chalked with words and phrases designed to inspire young boxers, like 'Attitude is Everything' and 'Perfect Practice creates Perfect Reactions'. In between the messages are promotional posters advertising boxing events that Paddy has put on, showing the new generation of fighters what they can achieve if they continue to work hard.

Accompanying all of the hard work is music. Music in a boxing gym is hardly unusual. It is the *choice* of music in Paddy's gym that struck me when I first started to train there, *not* the fact there is music playing. There are pictures of the reggae legend Bob Marley on the walls, and it is this music that dominates as we train. Marley's music encourages peace and harmony, tranquillity and understanding of others – and while we listen to his message, we practise and learn how to more efficiently and effectively inflict pain on our fellow man.

Maybe this strange cognitive dissonance between the message of the music and our fistic purpose in the gym shouldn't work – but to my mind it does. I have never felt more peaceful, empathetic or understanding than when I have completed a session at the gym and sparred a few rounds.

As I organise myself and wrap my hands, I notice Paddy circulating through the heavy bags, his signature fedora hat cocked at a slight angle, a smile on his face and singing enthusiastically along with Bob. All the while, his eyes are focused on the lads practising footwork, head movement and combinations on the bags. Intermittently, he stops to give some immediate feedback to one of the lads, models an improvement, and leaves the lad to adjust his work.

I catch Paddy's eye. He heads over to me with the usual, 'Hey Teach!' He bumps my fist in the traditional boxer's greeting and reminds me not to forget to warm up.

It is February and the evenings are cold. The gym has no heating and just like the other lads, I am wearing several layers of training clothes.

Regardless of the temperature outside, though, the lads are already moving around and sweating as they hit the bags or shadow box. Heat visibly rises from their bodies like a mist. The glass in the window of the door is steamed up with condensation and even the walls and concrete floor seem to perspire.

I know I need to warm up, especially at my age, so I grab a tennis ball and begin bouncing it from the gym's concrete floor. I move around in a crouch, wide-legged in my boxing stance, bouncing the ball carefully as I shuffle, stalk, and pivot around the punch bags that hang from the roof. By the time the session is over, I have worked out for almost two hours.

As we warm down, I reflect that boxing is not for the faint-hearted or the partly committed. You have to *want* to take part in this – it's just too hard to sort of want to do it. You don't *play* boxing, like you play football or rugby.

I dry off as best I can with an old blood-stained towel that I keep in my gym bag. My hair is sticking up at strange angles from the pressure applied when wearing my head guard, so I flatten it down until I decide I am acceptably presented. I change my T-shirt, which feels like it has been left out in the rain.

The gym empties and Paddy makes sure he talks to each person as he or she leaves, asking what they have learned during the session and pointing out an area of their boxing that they can improve on.

Paddy switches off the lights in the gym and locks up.

We cross the patio between the boxing gym and his house. He offers me a drink and we sit down at his kitchen table to talk about beginnings.

3

Before Professional
Boxing Takes Hold

BEFORE HE entered professional boxing and trained world title contenders, what did Paddy do? Who was he? How did a lad from southern Ireland end up, at 27 years of age, apprenticed to Freddie Roach as his assistant trainer at the Wild Card gym, Los Angeles – one of the most famous boxing gyms in the world?

He laughs when I ask him about what appears to be a chance meeting with Roach in the Channel Islands when he is, in his own words, at a real 'low point' in his life.

It is a meeting that seems to come at a crossroads, at a time when he needed a change, something to hang on to and believe in. Something to provide a purpose in what seemed like a purposeless world. And then, suddenly, boxing is there. Freddie Roach is there, with the possibility of working as his apprentice in LA. A whole new world of opportunity presents itself to offset the dark clouds that have been enveloping and consuming him in the previous months. It seems too good to be true, I say to him. You're down on your luck. You're in the Channel Islands with no direction or purpose and just about to sign up with the French Foreign Legion – and then wham, like a stiff jab you didn't expect, Freddie Roach is there, just when you need something different. And the flight path of your life literally changes?

Paddy is still smiling. 'I know,' he says. 'Luck? Providence? Someone looking out for me? Sure Teach, I don't know who or what it was – but it's the truth. And I went to LA and things did change for me.'

Alright, so that's the beginning of the journey to training world title contenders professionally. But what about the *real* beginning, I ask. What about the 27 years that led up to that moment?

'I grew up in Parteen, County Clare, which is about ten minutes from the centre of Limerick city. My experience of being a child was that where I grew up was nice. When you're a kid, you see things like a kid. You don't know any better, do you?'

He pauses.

'There was plenty of niceness in my childhood. But there were also difficult experiences for me. There was suffering too, misery and torment. I was bullied for quite a bit back then, from around 12 to when I was 15, at secondary school.'

There's maybe a pattern there, I say to him. I've read about fighters who say that they experienced bullying as young men – even world champions of such stature as 'The Fighting Marine' Gene Tunney.

'Yeah, well, that's the age when kids are testing each other, testing themselves – and finding themselves. Some kids try to find themselves by not knowing what the hell they're supposed to be doing. Some kids are finding themselves by thinking that they have to take ownership of other people. And because of the bullying, I was miserable for quite a period of that time. And sometimes back then, I wanted so badly to kill myself, but I didn't have the balls to do it.

'It's hard for a kid. It's like mind games in boxing. When a bully gets in your head, they get in your head. When you're 12, and you've limited experience of the world outside, when the bullies are in your head, they're in your head – full stop. What's important to a child is different to an adult. Your world is small, so those bullies seem massive inside that small world.

'As an adult, when you have that experience of what someone is trying to do to you, you say OK, they're just trying to get in my head. I can deal with that. But when you're 12, dude, it ain't good. At the time, I would have given anything to have the balls to kill myself – just to get away from it all. But it was too hard to do. So I just carried on.'

Paddy's voice trails off. I can see the memories are causing him distress. He is visibly upset, so I change my angle of questioning.

Did anyone know about how you felt?

'No, I just kept it to myself. I sort of told my brother but you know what men are like, and he told me to just get on with it. So I did.

'My parents would have loved to have got involved. But I didn't want to tell them because as a kid you worry, don't you, that it'll get worse.'

Did you ever make a cry for help?

'Around 12 years of age, I faked the symptoms of appendicitis just to get out of going to school. My brother's appendix had burst, so I knew what to say and do to make it seem like I had the same problem. Back then, you would get around six weeks off school for the operation and the recovery. It wasn't until after the medical staff had completed the operation that they told my parents I hadn't needed it. But by then, it was too late. I needed to recover and the plan had got me out of school.'

I can see that in talking about his feelings, Paddy is not remembering them but *reliving* them, which is much more painful.

Is that when you got into boxing, when you were feeling victimised? When you were feeling this pain?

'No, I was into judo [a Japanese martial art] at the time. And I'm not sure that the pattern is that kids who are bullied will gravitate towards boxing – just that they are looking for *something*.'

We pause briefly as Paddy reflects on the past. Then without prompting he says, 'I tried to kill myself when I was 20 years old too. But that didn't work either. I guess I was as shit at suicide as I was in my own professional fighting career!'

He laughs. It is loud and a little too explosive, like he's trying to blast something away – maybe the pain?

I try to turn our conversation to Paddy's career as a boxer. Firstly, I ask about his experiences as an amateur in Ireland.

'Well, as a youth, around 14 to 16, I was a Limerick league champion and a silver medallist in the Munster championships. But all of that's pretty small when you consider the small geographical area. I trained at St Francis boxing gym in Limerick. I used to train with two guys called Bimbo and Ken. In fact, Ken is now the head coach and Bimbo is a coach and referee – almost 40 years on. St Francis boxing gym will always have a place in my heart because it was my first introduction to a boxing gym.

'It wasn't where I first started boxing because that was in my living room where my old dad had got me this roll of lino. He'd wrapped it tight and then he'd tied it so that it wouldn't unroll. I used to hit it and that's what started me learning how to box.

'But St Francis was my first *gym* – and introduced me to the culture and attitude that surrounds the boxing community. You always remember your first of anything, don't you? And a gym's no different, I suppose.

'The gym was underground and down by the docks in Limerick. It was small and to access it you had to walk down a slope. Now I think back, there wasn't that much to the gym physically. There was a ring in there but not a great deal more – apart from the people. I loved it in that gym. There were other gyms, but that was the right gym for me. I didn't really know that at the time. When I look back, I can see what going to that gym did for me.

'It's funny, I remember just before I went to St Francis gym, I knew this family down the road. There were brothers in this family and they would stand out on their front lawn of an evening beating the shit out of each other with boxing gloves on – for entertainment! I used to watch them going at it and one day they gave me some boxing gloves, which I still have to this day.'

Paddy gestures to a pair of gloves sitting on his shelf. They are a faded brown colour, worn and scuffed. The way the gloves have aged and weathered, along with the deflated padding, punched flat by years of use, reminds me of the gloves you see worn in the black and white pictures of greats like Jack Dempsey. They sit there, amongst other boxing memorabilia, including the white Adidas boxing boots given to him by Muhammad Ali's daughter Laila after they shot the famous video where she boxed impossibly against her father when he was in his prime.

'The brothers gave me a set of boxing gloves and a pair of boots. And because of their generosity, and me being a gullible type, I made such a rookie mistake when I first went to St Francis. I took the new gear with me on my first night and I arrived at the door and told the coaches that I wanted to start boxing.

'They said, "Have you boxed before?" and I told them honestly, that I hadn't – other than pummelling that roll of lino in my living room.

'So they told me to get ready. I put the gloves and boots on and started the training session. And then they say to me, OK kid, get your sparring gear on and get in the ring.

36

'I remember thinking that was a bit strange because it was my first time in the gym and surely you would build up to sparring? I didn't know what to expect, so I followed their instructions. I got in with Bimbo, and he would have been around 19 back then, and he handed me my ass. As it got to the end of the third round of this pasting, I was thinking, "What the feckin' hell's going on?" Then the coach says to me a bit shocked, "So you haven't boxed before then?" And I'm a bit frustrated by this and say, "No I haven't feckin' boxed before, I told you I hadn't boxed before!"

'By now he's really laughing at me, but I haven't recognised my mistake yet so he says, "Never walk into a boxing gym with all that gear saying you've never boxed. I thought you were a smart-arse, and that maybe you did know a thing or two and were trying to pull the wool over my eyes, so I tested you out."

'They had thought I was some kind of smart fella, rocking up in their gym, pretending I didn't know much so I could take a few scalps and make myself feel good.

'By then though, they had realised that I was the *real* novice deal and they're saying, "Oh, you *really* haven't boxed before," when what they really mean is, "Boy, you *are* shit at this. You *really* have just walked through this door for the first time. What the hell are you coming in with gloves and boots for, acting like the big bollocks? And they're just pissing themselves [laughing] at my expense!

'That was boxing lesson number one.

'It's not there any more, the gym,' he says to me a few seconds later, like he's been transported back in time as he tells the story and then snaps back into the present. 'There's a car park and a shopping centre now. But St Francis still exists. It's just moved. I've been back to visit and I still keep in touch once in a while.'

I'm laughing now at how shocked the young Paddy must have looked after this first lesson. I can imagine the scene, with this pale, skinny young Irish kid getting belted around a ring under the artificial lighting of a basement gym.

So, how long did it take you to get yourself into a position where you were able to compete seriously as a schoolboy amateur?

'Well, as strange as it sounds when you consider how badly I got knocked about on that first time at St Francis, I was hooked. I was hooked and I was determined. And I had a little bit of natural talent, which I was able to stretch out a long way.

'It didn't take me a huge amount of time to get to a standard where I could compete. It was a matter of months really. I had good coaching at St Francis, you know. And listen, if a kid has any rhythm about him at all, if he has any desire *to learn* at all, well, then the technical side of boxing is not the hardest thing to pick up. I had rhythm and I had desire. I listened. I applied myself to the coaching and instruction I was given. I practised and practised – improving my skills day by day – until they could see how much I had improved.

'The thing is, it's not the technical side of boxing that is the biggest challenge for the learner – it's the *emotional* side of boxing. I remember the day before my first fight. I pulled up outside of the gym expecting to train as usual, and one of the coaches is standing there holding his kit bag and he stops me going in and says, "We're boxing tomorrow." I remember not processing this at the time and thinking, "Shit man, what are you talking about, we're *boxing*." And then the realisation hit me and I just sort of stared at him until he said, "We're not training tonight, you're boxing *tomorrow*."

'My first amateur fight was at St Munchen's amateur boxing club, just across the river in Limerick. I went to the fight with my dad. No one else came, just me and my dad – and I got the shit beat out of me for three rounds.

'It was so bad, I remember thinking about halfway through the fight that someone was going to stop it, with a bit of luck – but no one did. He fairly whupped my ass.

'I look at amateur fights these days and compare the stoppage decisions with my fights back in the day and I know that if I had that fight now, it would have been stopped in the second round to protect me.'

Unlike earlier, Paddy is talking comfortably and enthusiastically now about his life as a young boxer.

He tells me the story of his past in a broad southern Irish accent that is engaging and expressive, though I can't help noticing that he occasionally slips in the odd Americanism, probably due to the amount of time he has spent working as a trainer in Los Angeles. These American words and phrases are delivered with the sounds, inflections and intonations associated with a west coast Californian, rather than a working-class lad from Limerick, before his vocabulary and tone slip quickly back into his native southern Irish English.

'Later on in my amateur career, I met the same kid who had taught me such a brutal lesson in that first fight, when I was boxing in the Limerick championships. This time around, though, things had changed. I boxed him really well, and gave him standing counts. Technically, I had improved but mostly I had improved my composure and the emotional side of my boxing.

'The emotion management side of boxing, the psychological element, is the most difficult thing to teach a fighter. All the greats knew this: Cus D'Amato, Angelo Dundee – trainers and managers at that elite level.

'Sure, perfect practice, combined with repetition, creates perfect physical reactions for a fighter. I don't think any trainer would disagree with that. But the emotional side, well, that's not as straightforward, is it? And because each man is different, it takes time to get right.

'The emotions are a difficult thing to master. We sometimes think an event, like a fight, creates stress – and that a fighter is stressed and emotional because of the event. But it's not that at all. It's the individual who creates the stress and *applies* that stress to the event.'

How long did it take you to work that out, I ask? Or did someone teach you that cause-and-effect way of looking at the stress a fighter experiences?

'I had to work it out through experience – 100 per cent, Teach. And it took me decades to do it, too. The fact is it's not the *event* that creates the stress. If it was, then every time a person took part in that event, assuming the conditions surrounding the event were the same, then the event would be equally stressful, and the individual's reaction would be equally as stressed each time.

'But that's not how it works. The brain takes over and as you develop experience, your brain tells you that you've been here before. It's OK. It's cool. You've got this. And then you perform more successfully and realise that it's not the event that was the problem – it was *you*: your preparation and your reactions. Change your mindset – change the result.

'Due to little or no knowledge of a situation, a fighter puts a lot of stress on himself. Once he knows a bit, at least he can understand the stresses and plan to react to these appropriately. When he has more experience and more understanding, then he is going to be at his emotional best. He will react better. There will always be stress. Nerves will not go away. And nerves are healthy. But as an individual, I can choose to control myself more effectively than I have before now – once I have more knowledge and understanding.

'Teach, the best fighters in the world will tell you that they knew it was time to retire on that last ring walk when they didn't feel nervous.'

Really, I say, because that seems counter-intuitive to me. Surely having no nerves means you have mastered a situation? If you have no fear, then nothing can beat you, right?

'Trust me, Teach, the amount of fighters I've spoken to about this – it's true. Even Freddie Roach told me that. And from him, it was personal experience. He knew it was time to hang up his gloves when he didn't feel the emotions any more. Nerves, stress, anxiety are a good thing for a fighter.

They are all relevant to the event of a fight. All part of the experience.'

Angelo Dundee, the great trainer of Muhammad Ali, always said fear was a fighter's friend. The emotion encouraged a fighter to think carefully about the risks he was taking in the ring – and act accordingly, I say.

'A lot of coaches feel that biologically, nerves are there to super-charge the thought system and switch a fighter on so he makes good decisions quickly. *If*, and this is crucial, *if* he can control those nerves.

'Nerves tell the fighter that what he is doing is serious – and that he needs to react accordingly. What happens when these nerves go, and the corresponding thoughts leave too? Is that when a fighter starts to take too many risks? Is that when things become too dangerous? Because if it is, we know when a fighter should hang up his gloves, don't we?

'When you don't understand that the emotions are a part of being a fighter, and should be used to your advantage, then you have this erroneous idea that you have to get rid of your emotions and feelings like fear and nervousness. That these feelings are *problems* that need to be overcome if you're to be a success.

'The new fighter experiences fear or nerves in or around the ring, and he starts thinking, "Feckin' hell, what am I doing? This isn't for me. I shouldn't be feeling like this if I was going to be good at something. I'm not gonna be able to do this. There's no way I can feel like this and then control myself."

'But then you realise that everyone feels like this at first and that it's not about getting rid of the nerves, it's about accepting them, and then channelling them to the fighter's advantage.'

So after a decent-*ish* career as an amateur, I say to Paddy, what was it that made you turn over and start out as a professional fighter?

'Well, I didn't plan it – and maybe that's part of why it turned out so badly for me.

'When I left Ireland, and left the amateurs, I thought that I was finished with boxing really. But the second I arrived in England, my uncle in Swindon, where I was living, told me that my mam had encouraged him to get me to a boxing club, so I said I would look into it.

'The thing is, I was only 16 when I moved to England. And at that time in a young man's life, you don't know what you want to do, do you? Or what's good for you. So, as I was a long way from home, rather than stick at boxing, I was having a go at everything and anything that I would have been embarrassed to try back in County Clare, near my parents.'

I notice that Paddy is again giving off signals that he is becoming a little distressed by where the conversation is leading. I ask whether he left Ireland to find work opportunities.

'No, not really. Work wasn't my issue. This was back in the mid-eighties. I had spent the time between the ages of 12 and 15 pretty miserable, due to all of the bullying I had experienced. Now I found myself at 16, away from home, with more freedom than I had ever had – and I didn't know what to do with myself.

'Listen, I had been through times in my early teens wanting to kill myself but unable to see it through. Then I move to an entirely new setting. At the beginning I thought to myself, "I've got this. I can find my way here." I got work quickly. I always knew that I was a worker. I was raised right, to learn that a man had to work. He had to earn and he had to stand up for himself. I didn't leave Ireland for work. I could have found work wherever I was.

'The truth is I wanted to travel. Since I was 11 years old, I would thumb my way around Ireland on my own. I used to travel from Limerick to Kilkee as I had some cousins there. At 14 years old, I was driving from Limerick to Wexford. My dad would be beside me, my mother in the backseat, and I would drive the car. When we went through a town I'd say, "Dad, we're going through Tipperary," and he'd sit up straight and wave at people as if to say everything was OK.

'The day after I arrived in England, I got a job with a man called Tom Gallagher, who has since then played every role in my life from a father figure to a brother, a friend and a confidant. I would work hard, have a few pints after work, smoke some hash, function well at work the next day – and then repeat the routine. The weekends – they were often just a blur.'

I ask about boxing.

'I wasn't really boxing at all then, just dropping in and out of gyms at random – nothing committed. And maybe that contributed to my problems. Boxing has always grounded me and given me stability and purpose – when I've allowed it to.

'It was during this period of my life, when things were all over the place in my head, that I made the decision to go into the pro boxing ranks.

'I was around 18 or so when I turned over, and I kind of just fell into it really. I'd fallen out with someone and it had ended up in a pub fight where I had come out of it pretty well and someone mentioned that there was a gym down the road and I should look into it. So I did. Compared to now, I didn't know anything about being a professional fighter – absolutely nothing. I had no idea about a trainer and I was totally naive about the role of a manager.

'I shouldn't have gone pro at all. I mean, how could it have worked? I had no chance. For the previous two years in England, most of the time I was high on hash, speed or acid and once me and a buddy even crushed up travel sickness tablets and snorted those. Hardly the conditioning programme required for a professional athlete, is it?

'I took a pro fight pretty soon, which didn't make sense at all, but nothing in my life at this time did, so why would my boxing decisions have been any different? I was fighting at light-welterweight then, being a skinny 18-year-old, but no matter what I did, I just couldn't get anything that had worked for me in the amateurs to come off in the pro ranks.'

That must have really frustrated him. Teenagers aren't known for their patience or resilience when things are going badly, so I ask him how did he cope with losing?

'It took me a while to work it out in all honesty. No one likes to lose, and I had my pride, so each time I would lose I would think, "Train harder, run further, spend more time in the gym." I'd do it and then I'd lose again and think the same thing again. And the more time I spent in the gym, training and running, the less sleep I was having too. I just couldn't work out why I wasn't improving when I was working harder than ever? The thing is, Teach, I am glad that I got back into boxing. My life has always been much more stable when I've been involved in boxing. Just not in the way that I did when I was 18.'

I think of the amount of misguided hopefuls there must be in this sport – there must be plenty of amateurs who make the same judgement error and turn pro with limited knowledge of the business.

'I say it how it is to my guys *before* they make a decision. I tell them everything that is *wrong* with boxing, and with the *business* of boxing, in that last meeting that we have before they make the decision of whether to turn pro or not. I make sure that they know about the fundamental importance of money and ticket sales. A new prospect has to get the right opponents in front of him in order to develop. The opponents, often journeymen travelling up and down the country, they have to be paid, and they ain't selling tickets. So the money for the opponent comes out of the prospect's ticket sales. And the prospect's team also need to pay the promoter of the show. Normally, the promoter isn't making massive money in the small hall shows, but he'll still have his costs to cover if he's putting on the show, so you have to cover that too.

'Look, the basic facts are that the prospect will need to sell enough tickets to cover all of those costs, and his team's, and hopefully make a few quid for himself. I tell them that most professional fighters retire before they've even had ten fights – it's that hard to make a living in boxing.

'They all listen to me saying, "Yes coach, yes coach," and then after a few months as a pro and trying to get their first fight off the ground, they normally come to me complaining when the reality doesn't match up with the dream. And I say, "Surprise, surprise – I told you that much."'

So how did the professional scene work out for you, I ask? Ten fights too?

'Hey, listen Teach, it was less than ten fights for me. When you know you're shit, you know you're shit, and you work it out sooner than ten fights!'

Paddy bursts out laughing at this point. He shakes his head with a huge grin on his face. 'I should never have become a pro. But, there was a positive in going back to boxing. At a time in life where I was teetering on the edge, boxing stabilised me a little, and I'm thankful for that – even if it was only for a short while.'

So Paddy the pro boxer doesn't work out. What happens then? Is there a pause from boxing?

'I boxed as a pro between 1988 and 1990. When that didn't work out, I ended up doing door security on nightclubs and pubs. Sometimes I'd be drunk when I did it. Other times, I'd be off my face and full of acid tablets. By the time I was 26, I had built up my own little security firm called Pro-Guard Security. I had 16 guys working for me on the doors of pubs and clubs in Swindon.

'There was this one place I worked the door myself in a town near Swindon. There was just me working the whole evening, and I would arrive for a night's work after being on the drink all day, full of acid tablets and speed – and yet I would run the door without any problems. At that stage, I was making money. Some people might have called me a success. I was running my own business. But life didn't make sense to me at that time. I wasn't proud of the way I was living my life back then.

'That's when I decided enough was enough. I needed space. I knew things were getting out of control and I had to get away from everything. I walked away from my business, from my family, and decided to go to the Channel Islands.

'I was 26.

'When I needed some space to think, I had left and returned to Swindon a few times before. I had even been to the Channel Islands once before too – but this time was significant. It felt different. It felt more final. I still went to boxing gyms in the Channel Islands, trained and sparred, because I knew I needed the connection with boxing to maintain some stability in my life. But I had had it with the pro game – and maybe with everything else. I didn't really know *what* I was going to do. I only knew I needed to get away.'

And it's in the Channel Islands, for the second time, that Freddie Roach enters Paddy's story – and changes his life forever.

4

El Novio de la Muerte?

IT WAS the second time you went to the Channel Islands that you met Freddie Roach, wasn't it?

Paddy nods. 'Around 1996.'

I smile and say to him that it seems very lucky that he just happens to bump into one of the world's most famous boxing trainers when he's in a gym in Jersey. It just seems too good to be true. Did it really happen like that?

'Imagine a kid bumping into Santa Claus,' says Paddy. 'That's what it was like for me. It was luck because things weren't going good for me then. Turning pro hadn't worked for me. I had gone to the Channel Islands for the first time a while back and then come back to Swindon. My head still wasn't screwed on correctly when I got back to Swindon after that first time, so things didn't really change for me. I wasn't living the way I should have been. I was as low as I had ever been.

'At this time in my life, when I returned from the Channel Islands for the first time, I was struggling with people in general. Ever since I was a child, I have been a fiercely loyal person. And in life, I have met people who haven't met up to these same standards. I've always found that really hard to deal with. And back then, I couldn't get my head around it. I questioned how it was possible for other people not to be loyal. It just didn't make sense to me. In my mind, I thought if you were decent to people, they would be decent in return. That's quite naive, isn't it?'

I don't answer.

'So to cut a long story short, I had had enough of people and didn't think they were worth the effort. So I decided that if the world didn't meet my standards, then I didn't want to remain a part of it.

'I went to the doctor and told him I couldn't sleep and I needed something to help me. I knew he'd have a million questions if I told him the truth. So he gave me 12 sleeping tablets, and I supplemented this prescription with 24 paracetamol and four pints of beer from a pub round the corner.

'It was the middle of the day and while I drank the pints, I had the tablets sitting in my pocket. I remember chatting away as if there was nothing wrong, and all the while knowing what I planned to do. I was biding my time and building up the courage to actually go through with the act. I left the pub, stopped at an off-licence and bought a couple of bottles of cider.

'I went back to where I was staying in the spare room of my sister's house in Swindon, and I wrote letters to me Mam, Dad, Tom and Lynn Gallagher and their three daughters explaining everything as best I could.'

He stops as his voice breaks slightly and tears fill his eyes at what must be a painful memory. 'I couldn't even do that right,' he says with a bittersweet smile on his lips. 'I took 36 tablets, drank four pints of beer and two three-litre bottles of cider. I thought that would have finished the job, wouldn't you?'

I nod, though I have to confess to never having considered what concoction of prescription medication and alcohol would be necessary to put me to sleep forever.

'Eventually, my brother-in-law found me because my sister was asking, "Where's Gavin?", which is my real name. I mean, this was two days I hadn't been around but my brother-in-law knew me well enough that he thought I was an asshole, so it wasn't unusual that they didn't know where I was. Eventually, though, after two days, my sister tells my brother-in-law to check the spare room.'

He laughs.

'Two days I'd been in there. And as my brother-in-law shook me, I gradually came around – stoned off my face. I remember thinking, "Shit, I can't even kill myself right."'

Listening to Paddy for the last 30 minutes or so as he struggles with these memories, I can see and feel something of what he must have experienced in that period and I say, 'So would you say that was definitely a low point, then?'

He almost spits out the wine he is sipping and laughs a real belly laugh as I reflect on my understatement.

'Yeah, I'd say that was a low point. It's not just a rough day at work, is it?'

I feel a bit stupid and ask whether this was the point when he left Swindon for the Channel Islands a second time.

'No, I stuck around in Swindon for a while after that because I had met the girl who became my first wife around that time. I had tried to kill myself while I was seeing her. She had no idea, of course. I didn't tell her, like I didn't tell anyone else. She used to work for my sister and when I met her, she was seeing a dude who wasn't doing the right thing by her. His behaviour towards her wasn't right.

'I decided to get involved in the situation. Partly because having been bullied myself, I hate other people being bullied; and partly for my own ego where I thought, "No one is ever going to bully me again," and to prove this to myself, I would interfere in other people's lives to stop them being bullied.

'It had nothing to do with me really, but I got involved and he moved on. My first two children were born to her. She is a great girl and a fantastic mother. It's just that on reflection, we should never have got married. There were too many things I was dealing with at that time. Everything seemed to be snowballing, and the pressures of marriage were part of the problem.

'The fact was, the marriage, and my life at that point, weren't working. I needed to get away. I wasn't able to change into something that I needed to be in order to find my peace by waking up constantly in the same environment, with the same problems and issues. So I had to get away from the environment that I had created in order to make a change. That's how I ended up in the Channel Islands for the second time.'

Why the Channel Islands again, I ask?

'I had been before, and there was a girl, Simone, who was a family friend who I knew would help me out over there. I had known her since I was 12 and she had dated my brother once upon a time. Still to this day, she's close to my family – a fantastic friend.

'We weren't close then, but I knew I could trust her, and so I went over to the Channel Islands adamant that I wasn't going to go through a suicide attempt again and thinking that there had to be something that I could do that would give my life greater purpose and direction. I just had to find it.

'Simone put me up and gave me a place to stay and after a while, having told her how I felt, she advised me to go and see someone – a professional. I was dead against the idea. When I was a kid, I had been taken to see a priest who was a kind of psychologist too, because I used to get scared about how, if I was a good boy, I would live forever and never die – in Heaven like a good Catholic.

'I couldn't conceive of that. What do you mean live forever? That idea scared the shit out of me. So I used to swear at God. I used to go into the church and swear at him because in my mind, if I was a bad boy, then I wouldn't live forever. We were taught this whole host of mad stuff like we would be able to go fishing in little boats – forever? Can you imagine that? Doing the things you like to do over and over and over until you hated them? And that's Heaven?

'My little 12-year-old brain just couldn't compute that idea of Heaven. It was terrifying. So I used to swear at God each day in my head thinking, "I don't want to be good. I don't want to live forever."

'When Simone was saying to me to go and see a professional, I had visions of this priest psychologist who I had seen back in the day. It didn't work out then was how I saw it, so why would it work out now?

'Eventually, Simone talked me into it. She found me a guy in Jersey and said she'd come with me, so I went. In the first session, I broke down, started crying and losing my temper. It wasn't going well. But the psychologist was cool. He just stayed calm. He let me act up, let Simone cool me down.

'After four or five sessions, Simone didn't have to come with me any more, and I was beginning to look forward to the sessions. He was amazing. He lived in France and flew to Jersey in his own plane every session. He even invited me over to his family home in France.

'I will *always* remember that trust.

'But regardless of the progress I was making, the demons that I had were still there. I was moving forward but I still felt the way that I did – and I couldn't see how my circumstances were going to change, even if I was beginning to understand what my circumstances now were through the help of my psychologist.

'So, I had pretty much decided to join the Foreign Legion.'

I'm genuinely taken aback by this revelation. The *Foreign Legion*, I say, still feeling a bit rocked. How long had you been considering joining up to something as extreme at that – and why?

'Why does anyone think of joining the Foreign Legion, Teach?' he says, looking straight into my eyes. I suppose I knew the answer already.

There is more than one Foreign Legion. Those I am most familiar with are the French Foreign Legion and *Los Novios de la Muerte* or *The Bridegrooms of Death* in the English translation for the Spanish Foreign Legion, which was established as an equivalent to the well-known French version.

Men who signed up to be a part of a Foreign Legion were joining something unlike any other military unit. For most volunteers, and the men were all volunteers, the legion would be the end of a road that had been beset with problems – and mostly problems that couldn't be solved. In fact, when describing General Francisco Franco's soldiers when he was the commanding officer of the Spanish Foreign Legion, his biographer Paul Preston considered them 'a motley band of desperados, misfits, and outcasts'.

What the volunteers would find out swiftly was that the legion was more than the traditional patriotic army unit. It was a religion and a family. The motto of the French iteration of the legion is *Legio Patria Nostra* or *The Legion is our Fatherland*, explicitly making the volunteer who could be of any nationality aware that he was joining a *new* family – and in return for an absolute sense of belonging and a brutal form of love, demanding his *absolute* loyalty in return.

And if the French version of the legion was not explicit enough, its younger equivalent, the Spanish Legion, left nothing to the imagination. Each recruit was given the name of *El Novio de la Muerte* or *Bridegroom of Death*. Presumably, these soldiers felt that their lives were so bad that the thought of losing them held little to scare them.

You must have felt that there was nowhere left for you to go if you were considering volunteering for the legion, I say?

'Yeah, well, I was about to join the legion because I had tried to kill myself, and that hadn't worked. My life was a mess. My marriage wasn't working and I just thought, "Shit happens in the legion so maybe the legion could decide for me how I would live – or even if I would continue to live."'

And so this is the point when Freddie Roach comes into your life, I ask him? You're 26; you've got no direction or purpose in life; you're sleeping at a friend's house so you can get some time away from everything that England represents; and, you're seeing a psychologist to get some understanding and guidance?

And that's when Roach, an internationally renowned boxing trainer from Los Angeles, just *happens* to be in the same gym as you while you're working the pads with someone?

'Yeah, Teach, and I know how it sounds. But Freddie was there, just like I say, and that's when my life changed because I had to decide: did I go with Freddie to LA or did I join the Foreign Legion?'

5

Freddie Roach and Santa's Grotto

WE'RE SITTING in Paddy's living room in the house he has built right next to his boxing gym. You step out of the gym's office, take three or four steps across a patio and you're in Paddy's house. His life and his boxing gym are that close. Outside of his family, boxing is Paddy's over-riding passion – the obsession of his life.

Passion is how Paddy describes the love he has for this sport, and the world of the 'fight game'. This comes across powerfully and immediately when you talk with him about boxing. It is this passion and his substantial knowledge and articulacy about coaching boxing, all of it conveyed with a glint in his eye and an Irish raconteur's charm, that drew me to *his* story.

In the living room, Paddy's wood burner is belting out heat. It is always too hot for me, though I never say anything. Even though I am sitting on his sofa, Paddy is moving around the room checking his wood is organised on the hearth, squaring piles of magazines so they are symmetrical and tidying away the occasional toy that Junior, his youngest boy, has left downstairs. 'People come to see me and as they start to talk to me, I get up and start moving around and looking for things to organise. What must they think?' he says, laughing at himself.

Eventually, he joins me on the sofa opposite, though he continues to move and fidget throughout our conversation, which I bring back around to Freddie Roach and the Wild Card gym.

'When Freddie offered me the chance to go to LA with him, I didn't need to think about it too much. Listen, I wasn't going to join the Foreign Legion because it was a dream I had had since I was a boy or anything. Who dreams of joining the Foreign Legion? I was lost, simple as that.

'Freddie *knew* boxing and here he was offering me to go from zero straight to the top. He was inviting me in as an assistant trainer with his professionals. I wasn't even being asked to come in and coach the amateurs first and work my way up. I was being brought straight into a stable of world champions in what seemed like a heartbeat.'

What do you think was going through Freddie's head at that point, I ask him? Do you think he saw something in you?

'I ain't got a clue. Freddie's been around enough and looking back on it now, I think he knew I was pretty lost. But he must have seen enough in me to think I was worth it too, because it wasn't like he said if I was ever over in LA, I should drop into the gym. He invited me to come and work for him as his assistant coach and he paid my fare over to America.

'I once heard him say in an interview to a Japanese TV station when I was the assistant coach to him, as he trained the Japanese cruiserweight Yosuke Nishijima, that I reminded Freddie a lot of himself when he was younger. Maybe that was the reason Freddie liked me? But he obviously felt that there was enough about me that he could mould into something good, and I'm grateful for that. He gave me a reason to try again.'

I decide to lighten the mood a little at this point. The conversation so far has been difficult at times, dredging up hurtful memories. It has been moving too and at other times profound. I'm conscious that this must be a bit exhausting for Paddy, so I change the direction of my questions.

How about the hat? Were you wearing the fedora at 27 in LA? Because it's become kind of your thing now, hasn't it?

'On and off, yes. It all started because when I was a kid. I used to see my dad and uncles getting up to go out of the house of a morning, and putting on their crombies. My dad would wear a flat cap and my uncles wore fedoras. I used to think that they were smart-looking dudes. So when I left home for England I left with a brown fedora, which I've worn on and off since then.'

The fedora has come to be connected with Paddy. There is a large graffiti work, produced by local kids in the area, on the wall of his house as you walk to the boxing gym's entrance. The fedora is prominent in the artwork. I have also noticed that in press conferences and video interviews, Paddy wears the fedora. It makes him immediately recognisable. It's the type of hat you don't see every day on the street – and especially not in a boxing gym. I ask if Paddy has experienced any problems with his slightly eccentric dress sense. He laughs.

'Well, when I first moved back to England from the States there were some problems. In the States, you can work a man's corner in a pair of Timberland boots and jeans. And that's exactly what I did when I first came back and I was training Robert Lloyd-Taylor, a welterweight from London. So, having been in the States as long as I had been, I dressed how I liked – including my fedora.

'After a fight, as I'm going from Robert's corner to the changing room, two elderly gentlemen approach me and ask if they can speak to me. I didn't know who they were. They begin the conversation by saying we don't do that and looking me up and down. I don't really follow, so I ask them what it is they don't do. They look me up and down again, and repeat, we don't do *that*. But this time, they say the last word like they're pointing a finger at me, you know.

'I said, "You've lost me, boys. You're gonna have to give me a bit more to go on. *What* don't you do?" "We don't dress like that," is what they say. So, I'm cool with that and I say "No problem, boys – don't dress like me. This is how I dress."

'And I still don't know who they are yet and they're *still* saying, "No, we don't dress like that." "We're the British Boxing Board of Control (BBBof C)," they finally say, "and we don't dress like that."

'As one of them says this, he points at me and kind of flourishes his finger up and down my whole body.

'I smile and say, "No problem, boys. You don't have to dress like this. This is how I dress."

'They're not happy and they tell me "no" again. And this time they add that I can't return to a fighter's corner unless I'm wearing a tracksuit – and to get rid of my hat.

'To be honest, I didn't know exactly what to say. It didn't seem like a big deal to me, but these two old boys from the BBBofC were really steamed up about it.

'I left it at that and thought, "OK, I'll look into this later." As a consequence, I replaced my boots with trainers and my jeans with a tracksuit.

'A while later, I've got the then-welterweight Jamie Cox up in Liverpool for a fight. This would have been back in 2009.

'Before the fight, this dude comes up to me and says, "Take that off your head." The 'that' in question being my fedora. I say, "Who are you?" He just repeats his demand. I repeat mine. He says, "I'm in charge of boxing in this area." I say to him, "Pleased to meet you. Now, what's wrong with my hat?"

'"You ain't wearing that hat in the corner," he tells me.

'"Why not?" I ask. "No hats allowed in the corner," was his answer.

'I looked over his shoulder to the other corner and there's a dude stood there wearing a flat cap. I said, "Look behind you, there's a guy with a hat on."

'Then he's like, "Forget that, I'm talking to you about your hat."

'I say, "No, that's not fair. Don't talk to me about something that's only personal to me. Talk with me about a rule that applies to *everyone*. You're telling me no hats in the corner and there's a dude stood there in the opposite corner, right now, with a hat on. You can't just tell *me* not to wear a hat.

'He looks at me then and he says, "I ain't. He's got a flat cap on." "Look," I tell him, and I'm getting a bit annoyed by now. "I don't give a shit about taste in hats. He's got a hat on. I've got a hat on. You stop everyone wearing hats and I'll stop wearing my hat. If you don't, I'll wear whatever hat I want to. I'm gonna be in this ring, in this corner, tonight. And unless you stop everyone wearing hats, I'll be wearing my hat."

'That's the last I heard about the hat. But they surely didn't like it for some reason.'

But it has come to be your signature thing, though, I say. It certainly helps you be more recognisable, doesn't it?

'Yeah, it's become kind of synonymous with me now. So much so that sometimes it takes people a few seconds to remind themselves who I am if I'm *not* wearing it. But I didn't have a grand marketing and presentation plan with the hat. I mean, I didn't consciously use it to help me get recognised. I've been wearing a fedora since I was 15. It just became part of my persona over my lifetime, and even if I didn't plan it, I guess it works too.'

So, you meet Freddie Roach in circumstances that seem to be something out of a film script and you've just experienced the luck of the Irish, I say, returning to Jersey?

'I tell you what, Teach, I have been lucky all my life. I've been lucky beyond what I deserve.

'In order to make some money at the time, I was doing door work on the island in clubs and pubs. I had met a brother and sister, and the brother was interested in fitness and so he had asked me to train him in the style of a boxer, which I did.

'It was midway through 1996 and it happened that his sister knew Steve Collins, the WBO middleweight and super middleweight world champion, and he was in Jersey at his training camp for his fight against Nigel Benn, defending the WBO super middleweight title. Steve had Freddie training him.

'So, Freddie was in the gym when Steve had finished his session, and I was in there with my friend who I was training, and we got talking. Freddie was cool with me, and I saw him a few more times in the gym in 1996 when Steve was training for the Frederic Seillier fight. Each time we talked and I got to know him.

'Steve Collins is probably my favourite Irish fighter of all time, and there have been lots of great Irish fighters. It's a really deep pool but part of the joy of boxing is that you always connect to a certain fighter for certain reasons. Steve is a gentleman. He always has been. He was never great at a specific element of boxing, but he was damn good at everything that makes a complete fighter: excellent chin; fantastic fitness; he could brawl with you; box intelligently; counter-punch; he understood the psychology of boxing too; he had grit and determination and a never-give-up mentality. He did everything very well.

'I had gotten to know Freddie a little through our conversations and he invited me up to Steve's training camp to watch him train. I wasn't involved with Steve. I was just watching, learning and talking with Freddie. Freddie had watched me training some people in the gym I went to and he must have seen something in me, because he asked me if I wanted to come out and work with him in LA.'

What did Freddie say to you, I ask?

'Freddie doesn't waste his words and he just said to me, "How would you feel about working with me in LA?" I mean, that was like Santa Claus asking a kid if he wanted to come to his grotto in the North Pole and play with all the toys! It was the Wild Card gym – I jumped at the chance.

'The way it worked was that once I had agreed to go over to LA, Freddie said, "OK, I've booked you a ticket, meet me at the airport." It was as simple as that. I'd be lying if I said I didn't think about why Freddie was doing this for me. I didn't know him, so why was he throwing me a bone? I've met someone who is excellent at what he does – one of the best – and it turns out he's cool and humble too, just chatting with me and then he says, "Do you want to come and work with me? And I'll buy your ticket?" You have to digest that. It's not like he was saying if ever you're in LA, drop into the gym, is it? So I thought I'd go to the airport in London that he'd invited me to meet him at, and he probably wouldn't be there, and that would be that. But when I get there, Freddie's there saying, "Great, I'm glad you made it." He gives me my ticket and I go to LA'.

'Why did Freddie throw me a bone?'

I turn over this phrase in my mind for a little while as Paddy checks on Junior. I reflect for a moment on the idea that because of the society we live in, we are sometimes suspicious of people when they do something that seems to have little or no benefit for them that we can see. It's sad, but we almost always question the motive rather than recognising that simply doing a good thing may well be a benefit in itself. Perhaps what Freddie was doing was no more complicated than that and inviting Paddy to LA was just that – a good thing to do.

So what happened when you arrived in LA?

'A guy called Jerry Rosenberg met us at the airport. He had this great name – "The Jewish Bomber" – and it was pretty accurate because sometimes where you found Jerry you'd find an explosion of some sort too. Someone was there to pick up Freddie and Freddie says, "Hey Jerry, this is Paddy. Paddy, this is Jerry," and could Jerry take me to his place for the night and then get me to the gym in the morning. So we drove up to this typical one-storey LA house, and there's all this commotion and barking because Jerry's got all these dogs – vicious dogs too, but he loves them.

'Thing is, Jerry's what we would call a "wideboy" in Britain. He was into everything. He was a nice dude, but as bold as brass. He would chance his arm at anything. Look, he was the kind of guy who would tell you he was about to steal your wallet and then converse with you until you were so enchanted by what he was saying, you'd almost forgotten what he first told you. Then, when he was gone, you'd laugh as you remembered what he said about your wallet. And you'd think, "Yeah, you didn't get me," while you fished for the wallet in your pocket – but sure enough, it would be gone!'

Paddy is laughing right from deep in his belly as he remembers Jerry. And regardless of how much of a chancer

Jerry must have been, it is clear that Paddy liked him from the look on his face.

I want to know what the famous Wild Card gym was actually like from someone who had seen it, smelled it, breathed it and *lived* in it. Paddy shuts his eyes briefly, concentrating as he summons the images and memories from this time in his life.

'Next morning, after a night at Jerry's, I'm up early and straight to Vine and Santa Monica to Freddie's Wild Card gym to start work. The gym was above a laundromat [launderette] then, but I think Freddie's got that now and extended the gym. The gym was around 1,300 square feet, which is not massive. There was only one ring for sparring, three heavy bags, two double end bags, and three speed balls. There was a small area where two dudes could jump rope too. It wasn't a big gym.

'To the side, were some steel stairs that led up to a three-foot square area which acted as the entrance to the gym. On the left as you entered was a small little counter with a tiny little office behind it. You couldn't swing a cat in there, man. On the right, there was a small toilet. The female changing rooms were the size of the toilet cubicle. The male changing rooms were three times the size of the toilet cubicle. And this was a gym that trained world champions. Not because of its size, but because of Freddie.

'Normally, the gym would be buzzing. But I had got there early in the morning. Freddie was always there early too, around about 8am. At first, we would just hang out and chat about boxing. Bit by bit, people would come into the gym and start doing a bit of training. Freddie would introduce me to the people using his gym and he'd be like, "This is Sam Simon and he manages Lamon Brewster," an undefeated heavyweight who was 19-0 at the time. He'd had a lot of knockouts and people were really hot on Brewster then – really talking about him. And man, there were so many names at the gym, it was unbelievable really.'

How did Freddie prepare you for your role as his assistant trainer?

'There was no preparation as such. But I didn't feel like at any stage there was any pressure either. It wasn't really what I thought it would be. I thought I would start at the bottom and hang out at the gym until Freddie had confidence in me. But it wasn't like that. Freddie taught me to wrap hands and then said, "I've seen you wrap hands correctly, so go and wrap hands. I've seen you work the mitts, so go and work the mitts." Straight away when I go there, "Sugar" Shane Mosley was getting ready for his first world title challenge against a guy called Philip Holliday.

'Freddie got me involved in the sparring preparing the fighters for their bouts. He wouldn't say, "I want you to work on such and such." He would just tell you what he had been working on with the fighters and let you go off and work with them. It wasn't a direct form of instruction. Freddie told you what he was working on and gave you the freedom to work on it how you felt was right. Obviously he was watching, but he must have been happy with my work because he never said, "No, no, not that," and corrected me. My learning built up from that very first day as I was immersed in Freddie's gym.'

Did you find anything hard about working at Freddie's gym, I ask?

'Very quickly, I realised that if I was going to operate successfully in my job, I couldn't be surprised. I couldn't be a *fan*. I had to concentrate. There were a lot of great people training in Freddie's gym: James Toney, middleweight and super middleweight world champion, Justin Juuko and Lucia Rijker just to name a few. These were big names. I had to approach everything with the confidence that Freddie was giving me because the gym was sometimes full of famous people and I couldn't afford to be star-struck and let this interfere with my work.

'When someone allows you to work with his world champions, and he's one of the most successful coaches in boxing, that does help with your confidence. Freddie trusted me, so I trusted myself. There was no way Freddie was going to let me work with his champions if he thought that I would wrap their hands incorrectly or work the mitts badly and bust up their hands. He was obviously cool with me. And that gave me credibility. If Freddie thought I was OK, then his fighters thought, "Alright, I'll listen to him."

'Freddie was clear with me and I liked that. "This is my gym," he said. "Here's the rules and I'm the boss. Do the work because I know you're capable but don't get a swelled head because right now, you ain't done shit."

'And he was right – I hadn't. I was just beginning that part of my journey. There was so much craziness and so much learning to come in LA. I just had no idea how rapidly I would progress and how much madness there would be!'

6

'Saint' George Groves

'I've only got 9 weeks before the biggest
fight of my life and I don't have a trainer.'

WE'RE SITTING opposite each other, talking across
Paddy's kitchen table, when the phone rings. Paddy excuses
himself to answer it.

Junior, Paddy's youngest son at four, is running around
the table with Paddy's dog Fagan when he stops, rummages
in a cupboard and fishes out a cereal box. Quickly, Junior fills
his cereal bowl and then comes to join me at the table. He
puts the filled bowl on the table, climbs on a chair and then
hoists himself up on to the table's surface.

Only right now, Junior isn't wearing any pants, and he sits
there, bare bum on the kitchen table, grinning sweetly at me.

I know this might be a problem. Paddy is very keen on
cleanliness and order in his kitchen – everywhere I suppose.
Other evenings when I have been around his home, he has

often interrupted our conversation to sweep away crumbs he can see on a work surface, to mop up a minor spillage or to organise some implements that appear to him to be in the wrong place.

'Hey, Captain Hygiene!' he shouts at Junior. 'Get your backside off that table!'

He isn't angry really and he moves Junior gently before adding milk to his cereal and letting him wander off to munch away at his snack while he watches TV. Paddy rejoins me at the table. We are both in T-shirts having done a two-hour session at the gym. This seems to me a good time to talk about Paddy's tattoos. There are a lot of them on his arms and to me they look like they've been done at different stages of his life. Some are very typical, like my own tattoo of my football team that I had done when I was 16. Others seem far more intriguing, words and quotations, rather than images. What's the story behind your tattoos, I ask?

'I got my first tattoos when I left home and I started with some pretty obvious ones. My first was a mum and dad tattoo which I got when I was 16 and there are some others from around that earlier part of my life too. They were just done for the sake of getting a tattoo, you know?'

Moving on from the tattoos of your youth, how about the others? Do they have significant meaning to you?

'Yeah, well, around 15 years ago, I was doing some research and I came across this Japanese dude called Dr Masaru Emoto. He claimed that positive or negative changes could be made to water crystals just by attaching written words to the containers that the water was being held in.

'So Emoto hired photographers to take pictures of water on a microscopic level after being exposed to words that he had selected because they had either positive or negative connotations attached to them. After the exposure to the words, the water was then frozen to allow crystalline structures to form.'

I look into this experiment. What happened seemed stunning. The water contained in the test tubes with the words 'Hitler' and 'You Make Me Sick' written on them produced blurred, dark, chaotic and ugly structures. The water contained in the test tubes with the words 'Mother Teresa' and 'Love and Appreciation' written on them produced clear, strong, ordered and beautiful crystals – like snowdrops magnified. The experiment was then repeated with words like 'Happiness' and 'Thank you' and the same pattern was replicated.

'Basically, Emoto's research showed that human vibrational energy – thoughts, words, ideas and music – affected the molecular structure of water. The very same water that comprises 80 per cent of the human body and covers the same amount of our planet. If the words and thoughts that come out of us have this effect on water crystals, thought Emoto, it's amazing to think of the effect that they must have on the people who come into our lives.

'Emoto showed that the words we say and write have a vibration to them. You could see that as religious, like the Holy Spirit in action; or as scientific, like in frequencies. Regardless of the point of view, this made sense to me. The idea that positive or negative frequencies had information attached to them made sense to me.

'I decided that if my body was made of 80 per cent water, and that this was the best water possible because it came from whoever made us, and I believe this to be God, then I would attach words to myself in order to influence myself positively.

'I know that there is no proof other than Emoto's research that tattooing my body with positivity will have a positive effect on me. But, there have been plenty of negative experiences in my life, so I am all for helping the positive along in any way I can.'

I ask Paddy to show me the words and phrases he has chosen to be committed to his body.

"Humility," he says, "One Love, One Blood, One People" because we all come from the same thing and go back to the same thing when we die. "Man's Greatest Desire is his Greatest Weakness – To Resist is to Strengthen One's Character." Great men have fallen by allowing their base desires like the love of money, or women, to tell them how they should act – rather than that they should choose to act in the right way because it is the right thing to do. I want to do that.

'I also have *Vaya con Dios*, or go with God; "Peace, What a Man Sows so Shall he Reap" – by Bob Marley. I chose these words and phrases to act as a guide for my life, and hopefully to influence the water that is inside of me to be more beautiful and produce greater happiness for me and those who are around me.'

Tell me about how you met and started working with 'Saint' George Groves, I say to Paddy. Only nine weeks before he was contracted to fight 'The Cobra' Carl Froch, he knocked on your door in Swindon. Is that right?

'More or less. I received a text the day before he came here from George, which was very vague. There had been interactions between us before that, because I had worked with him for the James DeGale fight. I worked his corner, but not in the gym, for the Paul Smith fight too.

'Every now and then, I would get a text from George just asking me how I was doing, but we weren't closely connected.

'And then he sent me a text just before the [first] fight with Froch was made. It was on the same day of the press conference announcing that the fight would happen, I think. The text just said, "Would I be at home the following day?" I replied "yes", and that was it.

'So the next day I get a knock on the door and George was there. I said, "What's on your mind?" and he said, "I suppose by now you know I'm fighting Carl."

'I said, "Yeah, that's a good shout." And he replies, "Well, I've got two questions. Do you think I can beat Carl? And if you do, will you train me for the fight?"

'As a reply to his question, about whether he could beat Carl, I said, "Yes – and here's how I think that you should go about doing it." And in reply to his second question, "Yes," I said, "I will train you for it."'

How did George seem to you in that moment, I ask?

'When George came to my home, he looked lost. Adam Booth had been his trainer for years, but they were no longer working together. At that moment, he didn't seem to have a plan B if I was plan A – though I'm sure he would have thought of something.'

What did you say to convince him that you knew how he could beat an experienced two-belt world champion like Carl Froch?

"'Here's how you beat him,' I said. "You can't compete with him on the inside. So you need to shut him down on the inside and prevent him winning those close exchanges. Carl can't compete with you on the outside. But if you do what you normally do, and when the bell goes you start prowling around the outside of the ring, he'll take that free ground and in rounds five or six you'll be living against the ropes – and that's gonna be a hard night's work against Carl Froch.

"'Carl can't compete with your jab on the outside. So imagine a train coming down a track and you put a large rock on the track. If that train is going at full speed, it's going to crush that rock on the track into dust. But, if the train is stationary, you could put a rock half the size under its wheel and the train won't be able to get going. It's about momentum. So when the bell goes, we've gotta go and meet the man and be just one step outside. And every time Carl steps forward, your jab acts like putting the rock underneath the train with no momentum – bup,'" Paddy punctuates his point with a shadow boxed jab and a sound effect, "'Carl won't be able to live with you on the outside.

"'The key is to stop Carl's momentum with your excellent jab. On the inside, Carl is gonna be the better man. You're not someone who targets sitting inside and going to the body. The only fight where you sat inside and traded to the body was against Kenny Anderson and you were on your ass and you looked sloppy in that fight.

"'So if we know we can't beat him on the inside, we stop him winning inside. Here's what we do. As soon as he gets inside, you're gonna take Carl's left glove and jam it underneath your right arm. You then keep your right glove tucked to your chin as if you're still holding shape, because your arm and elbow with be taking care of Carl's hand. And your left hand you'll keep really tidy and just keep nudging Carl with it, hitting him to the chin, hitting him to the belly.

"'The most important thing is that you're preventing Carl from using his advantage and being dominant on the inside while also simultaneously appearing to the judges that you're quite comfortable with the inside work because you're the one that they see firing the punches that are connecting. And on the outside, you are going to dominate, so you should look good to the judges in both ways.

"'But you will have to be ready to execute that. This is not going to be a 12-round fight, but 12 three-minute fights. Every round will have to be a separate fight. Bank that fight, on to the second fight. Bank that fight, on to the third fight and so on. Don't think of it as being a 12-round fight. Don't pace yourself. Don't pace the fight, pace the round. If you pace the fight, you risk giving away rounds through taking it easy and thinking you can gain the rounds back later on. That's a lot of pressure to put on yourself. And if you give away six rounds, you're gonna have to win the next six – no mistakes.'

And how about the gameplan overall? That's the approach to the actual fight, but there was so much more surrounding the Froch v Groves fights. That's why so many people who might not normally classify themselves as fight fans got so interested, isn't it?

'Of course, 100 per cent. So I say to George, "OK, here's the gameplan. You're no longer working with Adam [Booth]. Everyone in boxing sort of thinks that you're lost and directionless now. Let's allow the public and Carl's team to think that you're lost. To think that you aren't in the right place for this. Don't come across like now you're down here with me everything's cool and Paddy has all the answers. That won't work to our advantage. Let's just underplay this. Tell the press you're OK. That you think, you *think*, you've got this and that you're down here and Paddy's just helping you out a little bit. Let's let them believe the illusion."

'Mentally, I wanted George to play up to the idea that he was lost and on his own, which was a direct contrast to the strength and togetherness of Carl's well-established and successful team. If I could get Carl and his team to underestimate the threat we represented, then that would be to our advantage on fight night.

'Even when Sky came to my gym in Swindon, I acted really laid back and I'd say I'm just helping George out, doing a bit of mitts and that. I would act up that really George was on his own and I was just giving him a hand.'

If getting Froch to underestimate George was what Paddy was after, then he succeeded. In fact, Carl Froch had a pretty low opinion of George Groves as a fighter already.

In his autobiography, Carl Froch states that even though Groves was the IBF's mandatory challenger, he didn't think the fight was big enough for him. He dismisses George as not being very good and definitely not better than domestic level.

Froch goes on to say that he had seen George fight enough times to notice the flaws and weaknesses in his work. And crucially, Carl goes on to pick out one particular weakness he claimed he had seen in Groves – his chin.

We will return to the subject of George's chin later.

Froch acknowledges that he perhaps did not take Groves seriously enough when he reflects on preparations for Froch v Groves II at Wembley. He tells the reader in his autobiography that he did not train hard enough for the first fight, that he wasn't mentally in the right place. Even his trainer, Rob McCracken, agrees.

All of these statements seem to point to the fact that Froch, and possibly his team, had underestimated George in their first fight and that this impacted his performance.

Tell me about George's training camp and his preparation, I say to Paddy.

'The gameplan was ultimately to keep putting the rock underneath the train's wheels and stunt Carl's momentum. George could then look for decent openings to get his shots off while controlling the pace of the fight.

'I told George that his main sparring partner would be Duke [Luke 'The Duke' Watkins, another of Paddy's stable of fighters]. The expression on his face told me he wasn't convinced and he looked at me a bit awkward. He was concerned because at the time, Duke was still an amateur.

'I said, "Listen, Duke's a good amateur, and he's a cruiserweight. He's got a very educated jab and he's strong.

We're not going to beat Carl on the inside, so we don't need someone who's really skilled on the inside for you to work with because your main job is that whenever you get in close, you make sure you tie up Carl's glove and his arm underneath your elbow. That takes care of the inside game.

"'It's the outside game I'm concerned with. Being able to deal with the pressure of a very good dude coming at us. No matter how strong Carl is, and he is strong, Duke is 14 stone to Carl's 12. And Duke is a strong, muscled 14 stone, with a good jab too. And even if Carl can manage to be as strong as Duke, he's not going to be stronger, so you've got the right level of power in front of you with that constant pressure.

"'Of course, Duke doesn't have the education and experience of Carl. But he doesn't need it. You're sparring him in his own gym where he's confident. He's not stressed out here. This is his home. He's not under any pressure either. He's not dealing with any lights or crowds.

"'Duke is comfortable. He's big. He's strong. He's powerful and he's gonna keep coming at you with his jab. If you can deal with Duke, who's stronger and with a better jab than Carl, then you're winning the outside game. And you should be able to win against Carl."

'So I tried to keep the gameplan simple. Stop Carl on the inside. Shut down his momentum on the outside. Dominate Carl with George's jab.'

Those were the fundamentals of the plan. Were there any other strategies that you had in place?

'There were some other things that we said we would pull out of the bag bit by bit because you can't pull everything out at the very beginning of a fight. You have to set things up. Even if you know that every time a man fires his left hook he drops his right hand, that doesn't mean you immediately sit with the man when he's hooking and try to straightaway counter with your left hook. You still have to work out your timing. Understand your opponent's tempo. Feel one or two of his shots to get used to them and think that you're emotionally OK with the shots, you can deal with them. Then you watch for the flaw you know exists, look for an opportunity, and *then* you strike.'

What about making the weight? You told me once that George liked to eat chocolate bars and that sometimes this could compromise his making the weight limit if he wasn't careful.

'I asked George about how do you make the weight and he looked a little bit confused. I told him that the reason I asked was that he had been making the weight up until this point for his fights and if he was good at making weight, then I didn't want to know about it, because we only had nine weeks to train. I didn't want George to hear my voice about every single little thing, because it would diminish the power of my messages in the limited amount of time that we had. I only wanted him to hear my voice connected to the gameplan. So if you make weight, and you're good at that, I'll leave it alone and concentrate on other things. If you have any problems, flag it up to me and we'll take care of it. Other than that, making the weight's on you.

'He told me that he would make weight fine and we were good to go.'

So what happened then? Nine weeks to go until a massive fight for both of you.

'Everything in the gym was going great. I could tell that George believed in the gameplan. You can tell, emotionally, when someone believes in something, rather than they are just telling you that they believe in something. There is no tension. No uncomfortable silences. No challenging my position. So we were on the same page.

'As the weeks went by, I would sit up until four in the morning just studying Carl and I would be sending texts to George as I saw things, so that I wouldn't forget. And every now and again, George must have been up late himself and I'd send a text, and it could be like three in the morning thinking that George's phone would be off and he would be asleep, and George would text back going, "Coach, go to sleep. How well can you know one dude? You've told me everything that we need to know about Carl. We know what we're dealing with – go to sleep."

'And I'd text him back and say, "You can never have enough information. I'm just recording the thoughts as I see them. Don't bother responding to me at night."

'I remember thinking that Carl shared some similarities with the Puerto Rican world champion Felix Trinidad in that he was macho, and his machismo was something he, and others, felt was a great strength. He was that kind of *mano a mano* type of fighter who would meet you and trade with you in the centre of the ring, relying on the power of his punches, and even more importantly, in Carl's case, the strength of his chin and how much punishment he could take in order to win.

'George knew Carl because after George had won the Commonwealth title, he had been one of Carl's sparring partners. At this time, Carl was already a two-belt world champion. His attitude with George was to be complimentary, but not threatened, and say to George that he was good sparring and that he would make it one day.

'Fast forward two years, and now Carl is fighting George, probably still with those memories of sparring in his head. He must have been thinking, "OK, stay in your lane, Groves. You're getting a good chance here to fight the super middleweight champ who helped you out with some sparring when you were only eight fights into your career. You'll do alright. You won't *beat* me. But one day, you might be a champion."

'And this worked to our advantage because to my knowledge, there is no better man, or fighter, when he's up against it than George Groves. I give George's example to any fighter I train on how to manage successfully when the odds seem stacked up against you. In saying that, the converse was true as well. If George felt that he had something in the bag already, that's when you would see the complacent George.

'George performed so well in the first fight with Carl because he was under pressure. I suppose one of the disadvantages that George had in this fight was his limited experience of big world championship fights which, of course, Carl had. Experience counts and what happened in the first round exemplifies this well. I had told George that he was gonna put Carl on his ass. Remember, I had studied Carl in detail, hours and hours of his work, and almost every time

Carl shot his right hand, he picked up his right foot and leant forward a bit – nine out of ten times.'

So Carl's balance and momentum at that point was an opportunity?

'Listen, the fact is that if you have only one foot on the floor and one foot is in the air, you can have a chin made of cast iron, it's your lack of balance that will put you over. Who cares why you go over? If your opponent goes over, it's a point. A fighter can win a whole round with one shot. And plus, George can hit like a damn mule. He's a severe puncher. Carl has an excellent chin. But George was a world-class puncher. If he could catch Carl with his foot in the air and nail him with an excellent shot, then he could have Carl over and in trouble.

'To take advantage of this, I'd have George take a half step back after he jabbed and then meet Carl with his right hand as Carl came forward with his right foot in the air.

'And the more I watched Carl, and saw the way he picked up that right foot, I would think to myself that it wasn't about technique with Carl, it was about this innate grit that he had. This determination and single-minded resolve that says, "I'm gonna get you, no matter what you throw at me." Carl's the kind of dude that you want looking after you when you're walking home late at night. Carl made the absolute best of his best attributes as a fighter – and this resilience and determination was well used by him.

'Carl has to be considered one of the best super middleweights that we've ever had. After Joe Calzaghe, who else dominated like Carl did? Steve Collins maybe?

'Adam [Booth] used to say, "Why try teaching something to a fighter if it didn't suit him?" Look at David Haye. Adam knew that Dave could punch like a mule, had amazing reactions and that he could cover ground in split seconds. So he would have Dave prowling the ring, using his jab and feints to open his man up, and then Dave would take his head clean off. Adam understood that.

'Look at Tyson. Cus D'Amato made being short one of Tyson's greatest attributes, not a weakness, by developing a style that suited Tyson's stature. The art of fighting isn't necessarily proving that you can do something better than the other man, it's making your opponent deal with something that he's not able to deal with by using your own strengths.

'In my view, Carl's team knew his best attributes and exploited these very effectively.'

So what about all the psychology behind the fight? The press conferences and promotional work did a lot to generate interest. Did you plan to execute what happened? How about that now pretty famous line that George used and seemed, by his own admission, to unsettle Carl, 'Everything for a reason'?

'So we were getting closer to the fight and I'm thinking more and more that the macho presentation of Carl is reminding me of Felix Trinidad. At this point, George was naturally conducting himself as a contrast to the "macho" fighter image of Carl, which I thought was right and was down to George, not my lead. The way George presented himself was really getting into Carl's head.'

This contrast between Froch's confident, established macho, and simple man-of-the-people-type presentation of himself, and George's cerebral, cheeky, quick-witted new-kid-on-the-block persona came to a head in a Sky TV preview of their fight in November 2013. Froch found the verbal sparring more challenging as time went on. He also seemed to be finding the exchanges off-putting, perhaps indicating how Groves was getting inside his head.

Froch said, 'This guy [Groves] genuinely believes in what he's saying. Even though when his head hits the pillow at night, he doesn't believe it. And I know that for a fact.'

Groves, smiling, immediately countered, 'But you just said I genuinely believe it. Make up your mind. You're contradicting yourself.'

Round one to Groves, with the added humour of the listener thinking, 'How does Carl Froch know what George Groves is thinking in bed?'

With the pressure appearing to get to Froch, he continued, 'The talking stops now. Eight weeks ago at the press conference, I was engaging in a bit of conflictual [sic] argument. But the fact remains that he's getting a bad whupping.'

Round two to Groves. Is conflictual a *real* word? And when Froch described the 'bad whupping' he said Groves was about to receive, the American slang just didn't sound right coming through Carl's East Midlands accent.

The verbal jousting continued as Froch asked himself the question, 'Do I hate George? Hate's a strong word. There's lots of people that I don't like, but it doesn't mean I *dis*like them.'

And perhaps, in round three of this verbal battle, we have a unanimous decision for Groves as he replies, 'How can you not like someone *without* disliking them?'

Reflecting on their first fight in his autobiography, Froch admits that he couldn't even *say* Groves' name before the fight. He'd let George get under his skin and his performance was affected in a very negative way. He also said he underestimated George and so psychologically he couldn't get pumped up for the fight in the normal way that he would. After all, if this was a fight he would easily win, why did he have to take it as seriously as other fights?

Did Paddy and George get into Carl's head?

You be the judge.

'I was focusing on strategy', says Paddy, 'and because Carl was reminding me of Felix Trinidad, he also reminded me of what the great Bernard Hopkins *did* to Felix Trinidad. When Hopkins fought Trinidad, three months before the fight they had a press conference in Puerto Rico and Hopkins threw the Puerto Rican flag on the floor. Now, you're just asking to get yourself killed grabbing a country's flag and throwing it on the floor in that country. You just don't do it anywhere. But in a macho Latino country, testosterone fuelled and crazy, it's just madness.

'But he did it. And he did that deliberately because he knew that Felix Trinidad was the type of guy to chew the insult over and over and that every time Trinidad walked down the street in Puerto Rico people would be stopping him and saying, "You ain't gonna let him get away with that, are you?"

'Hopkins knew that this would fill Trinidad with a burning energy as he fumed over the insult and walked around like he was chewing a wasp for a whole three months.

'By the time that they fought, Felix Trinidad is so angry that he forgets to go to Hopkins' body and just goes head hunting because his judgement is clouded by Hopkins' mind games. And Hopkins is just bopping him with the jab, rolling underneath the jab, spinning away after his own combinations, which is making Trinidad even more angry.

'You see, Hopkins knew that he had made Trinidad more dangerous, but crucially, he had also made Trinidad's attack more obvious – and therefore easier to deal with.

'I felt that was happening here with Carl too. Carl was getting wound up and accusing George of not showing him respect because George was referring to him in the third person as "Froch". Innocently, George was saying to him, "What would you like me to call you? Carl?"'

What about that really controversial tactic where you broke with convention and actually told Froch how George was going to defeat him, before they fought?

'At that stage, George wasn't even playing mind games. He believed he could beat Carl and he was just telling him that consistently. I remember thinking that Carl was getting really wound up by George telling him that he was going to beat him.

'And that was when it came to me. I was asking myself, "What would wind a man like Carl up even more than he was wound up now?" We'd tell him how we were going to beat him. What could come across as more confident than that? We would tell a man how we were going to beat him because we were impossible to stop. At least, that was the psychology behind the idea.

'I didn't know when I would break this news to George. I wasn't even entirely sure that this was the right thing to do because I knew that it would make Carl more dangerous. A man becomes at his most dangerous just before he feels that everything is about to go wrong. Under these conditions, a man will give everything he has to survive, or in this case, to win. So, all of this was going through my mind.

'But it was also going through my mind that Carl was dangerous anyway. He didn't want to lose his world titles, so what was he going to do? Hit George harder? He was trying to hit him as hard as he could anyway.

'I was wrapping George's hands when I decided to bring up the plan. So I say, "George, there's two weeks to go before the fight. At the next press conference, I want you to tell Carl what we're gonna do in the first round." I deliberately didn't look at George's face as I was saying it. And I tried to deliver the idea in the most matter-of-fact way I could, to play it down.

'When I glanced up, I could see that George had gone red in the face and he says to me, "Why would I tell him what we're gonna do?"

'I said, "Think about it. He's never gonna win the first round against you. He's never gonna have better feet than you or a better, more varied, jab than you. He doesn't have the hand speed of your jab either. So he'll never win the first round against you. So knowing that we're gonna win that round anyway, let's tell him that, and how we're gonna do it."'

Was he convinced?

'George didn't seem entirely convinced so I continued saying, "When you tell him what you're gonna do, only in the first round mind you, and you pull it off, he's gonna have to believe what you said about everything else because you've proved what you said would happen in the first round. Under that pressure, Carl's got to end up thinking, 'My God, he's done what he said he would. What else is going to happen?'"'

Could you refer George to any examples of where this kind of psychological warfare had worked before?

'I did. I told George about Bernard Hopkins v Kelly Pavlik in 2008. Hopkins was nearer to the end of his career at that point and Pavlik was a younger fighter. So Hopkins told Pavlik that Pavlik would win the first five or six rounds and he would hardly touch him because of Pavlik's youth and hand speed. And then he told Pavlik, "In round six I'm going to touch you. In round seven, I'm gonna hit you where I touched you. And then the fight's gonna change. And you're gonna remember this conversation. You're gonna be thinking, 'Wow, what he told me was right.' And then I'm gonna take over the fight and knock you out." And Hopkins went on to follow his gameplan and win the fight by a unanimous decision.

'Hopkins was articulate and very clever with this plan because he turned an obvious disadvantage, the fact that he probably wouldn't win those rounds, into a psychological advantage. Even though he probably wouldn't win those rounds, he presented to his opponent like he was *allowing* his opponent to win those rounds.

'What Hopkins knew, through his experience, was that after five or six rounds of watching, he would work Pavlik out and be able to understand his timing and counter effectively.

'And sure enough, once Hopkins had learned what he wanted to in the fight, in round six he touched Pavlik. When the bell went to end the round, and he was walking back to his corner, Hopkins said something to Pavlik. And you see Pavlik's expression change. And Hopkins will have said something like, "Told you," to Pavlik. And as Pavlik is walking back to his corner his mind will be racing thinking, "Told you? Told you what?" And then it would click. He would remember Hopkins' words, "In round six, I'm going to touch you."

'And then the end begins for Pavlik, because he starts to remember what Hopkins said about round seven and round eight.

'And it worked brilliantly for Hopkins.'

How did you apply this to George?

'I said to George, "You know that your most frequently useful shot will be your jab in the first round. So, let's only throw a maximum of three right hands in the first round. Just tell him that. Say, 'I tell you want I'm going to do, Carl. I'm gonna just dominate you with the jab, keeping it nice and steady, so that you can see that I'm in full control. Then, I *might* drop in a right hand. But, before the bell sounds for the end of the first round, I *am* going to hit you with a good right hand, just to let you know I'm in charge.'

'"During the rest of the press conference, we'll drop in some suggestions about how the rest of the fight's gonna play out – but nothing definitive. We'll just be specific about the first round."

'George still wasn't entirely convinced, and that's where the phrase that became part of our preparations for the fight, "Everything for a reason", came from. George was like, "Why are we gonna tell him?" still. "Because," I said, "you will always win that first round. So, we're not giving anything away by stating the obvious, are we? But we are looking very confident and making Carl question himself. And when we win the round, and do everything we say we are going to do, which is almost guaranteed, then he's got to believe everything else we've said about the fight and it's gonna play with his mind.

'"As Carl is walking back to his corner at the end of the first round, he's gonna feel like Kelly Pavlik when Hopkins said, 'Told you' at the end of the sixth. You understand?

'"And then you'll have Carl where you want him. And don't forget, anything that I ask you to do, and anything that I have you do in the gym, is for a reason. Everything for a reason. Nothing to waste time."

'And that's where "Everything for a reason" came from.'

Did you encourage George to say, 'Everything for a reason' because it really got on Carl's nerves?

'No, but we had talked about how everything we did was for a reason, so I imagine the phrase was quite prominent in George's thinking.

'We left it at that and George told me he needed to think the idea over. I was fine with that and told him that if he wasn't comfortable with the idea, then we wouldn't do it.

'We completed the last bits of George's training with some excellent sparring and then we travelled up to Manchester and we were staying in these flats, rather than a hotel. They looked like a hotel, and there was a reception, but it was an apartment that you rented.

'On the day of the press conference, George told me he was going to wear a suit and asked me if I was OK to do the same. I was fine with that, so I went out into Manchester and bought one, which I thought might go well with the fedora, you know?

'Anyway, I get into the lift on my way down to reception to meet George to go to the press conference, and as I step in, George is in there with Sophie, his wife, because they have an apartment somewhere above mine. George is in his suit, and he can see I have mine on. Then, as we're travelling down, George turns to me calmly and says, "I'm gonna do it."

'"Do what?" I say. "What you told me. I'm gonna tell Carl what we're gonna do in the first round."

'I was pleased with that because I had deliberately played it down. I didn't want to exert too much pressure on George and make it seem like a big deal. I wanted *Carl* to think that.

'I was excited inside but I didn't want George to think that. So I played it calm and said, "Great. Carl won't have a clue what's going on, trust me." And when he delivered the news to Carl, I wanted it to come across as quite matter of fact, rather than a gimmick. This wasn't a gimmick. What Hopkins did wasn't a gimmick, and I had learned from that. This was part of the gameplan.

'We got to the press conference and during the conference I could see George thinking and building up to when he was going to deliver the information to Carl. I mean, I wasn't sure even then that George would tell Carl. It was a brave thing to do and I had to respect that and allow George to choose the right time to say it, if he was going to say it.

'So then when he starts the delivery with, "Carl, in the first round..." I'm really smiling inside thinking "this is great" but not showing it in the press conference. It was confirmation too for me going into the fight that George believed in the whole gameplan. Because if he didn't believe the technical side of the gameplan, why would he voice it now in front of millions on live TV? With two days to go now, I was feeling really secure about us as a team and that George was clearly on the same page as me. I fully believed my gameplan would work. And now I knew that George believed it. We were locked and loaded.'

If the object of Paddy's strategy was a combination of what Bernard Hopkins had done with Felix Trinidad and Kelly Pavlik, to make Froch so angry that his judgement was clouded and his boxing skills compromised, and to plant seeds of self-doubt in Froch's mind, it appeared to have worked.

Describing the early stages of the fight, Froch tells his brother not to worry, promising, 'I'm going to chin this little prick.' From round one, he wanted to land the big shot that ended the contest. In trying to do that, he said he neglected his jab and his head movement, and forgot his footwork. Everything that had made him a world champion.

It seemed that Paddy's psychological preparation for the fight was paying off.

Everything for a reason.

7

Living and Breathing Boxing in LA

– 'Sleeping in the Ring and The Tooth Fight'

IT IS one of those dark autumn nights in November and tonight, Paddy is going to tell me some stories that he thinks will make me laugh – even though they are tinged with danger.

'I actually moved into Freddie's gym within a couple of days because I didn't want to stay at Jerry's. Jerry lived a good distance away from the gym. I didn't have a car and I didn't want to rely on Jerry, so Freddie said I could live in the gym. There's a shower there, a toilet there, a little portable TV attached to the roof – so I moved into the gym. I slept in the ring.'

You actually slept in the boxing ring?

'Yeah, it was my bed.'

And what did your family think? Had you told them where you were going?

'In the first week, I wrote a letter to me Ma just to reassure her not to worry about me. I wanted her to know that I was OK and everything was cool. So I told her that she wouldn't believe how lucky I was because I was sleeping in the biggest four-poster bed in Hollywood! Until recently, that's what she thought too.

'And that was only the beginning of all the crazy situations that LA was going to offer me. In my first week at the Wild Card gym, me and Freddie are in the small office looking out of the window. Freddie leans into the window, puts his chin in his hand and looks sideways at me and he says, "You see this guy coming up the stairs, he owes me gym money."

'And just as Freddie says it, the dude walks in.

'Freddie didn't say any more. That was it. And I just thought, "OK, he owes Freddie gym money." So I wait a little bit and then I go over to the dude and I say, "My man, can I have a chat with you?"

'He says, "Yeah," and looks at me funny.

'I say, "I'm working with Freddie. Do you owe some gym money, dude?"

'And he just says, "What the fuck's it got to do with you?"

'I'm like, "Well, I work at the gym. You owe gym money. I'm just asking for the money."

'Well, that escalated *real* quick.' Paddy starts laughing now. 'If I was a little bit brighter I should have gone, "How are you doing? My name's Paddy," and let him train. I could have dropped over a few times while he was training to say a little more, tried to develop a relationship and then asked him for the money. But no, keen as I was, I just asked him.

'Of course, he got offended because he presumed that I had challenged him and people had heard it. He was shouting his head off at me. I'm like, "Slow down dude," but he was having none of it. It was getting too loud so I said, "OK, let's go outside." And he likes that idea, so he says, "Hell yeah!"

'As we went to the door that led out of the gym, it was just bad timing, but I got there a split second before him. And as he came through the door, and I turned to talk with him, he pulled the door shut and smacked me in the teeth – all in one movement. I got him in a head lock and we went falling back through the door.

'The next thing I know, everyone in the gym is around us trying to break it up and Freddie's standing there rubbing his head thinking, "What's happening in my gym?"

'After a few more seconds, our scuffle gets broken up and the other guy grabs his gym bag and is pacing around ranting and raving, so I go and stand by the counter of our little office. Freddie comes over to me then and he says quietly, "Careful Paddy, he may well have a gun in there." And he gestures at his gym bag. I'm thinking, "What the hell? If you think this dude has a gun in his bag, no wonder you told me he owes you gym money!"

'After a while, the guy stops ranting and leaves. Freddie says to me, "You know who that guy is?"

'I didn't.

'Freddie says, "That's Alex Garcia."

'I say, "Who's he?"

'Freddie replies, "He's ranked number three in the world at heavyweight."

'I think there's reason two that I got told about the gym fees! At that time, Alex was supposed to be getting ready to fight George Foreman, who was on his comeback.'

Suddenly, Paddy opens his mouth wide and with his fingers stretching his lips so I can see, he kind of mumbles, 'See that diamond tooth there. That's because of Alex. When he smacked me in the mouth, he re-arranged the shape of my teeth. It's probably fair to say that he won that little set-to, "The Tooth Fight".

'I didn't see Alex again for around a week. Then this bloke comes up to the top of the stairs and he opened the mesh door and in walks Alex.

'I'm thinking, "Now I know who you are, I definitely don't want to get in a fight with you." Ignorance is bliss, isn't it? Before, he was just a big dude. Who cares? But now I know he's ranked number three in the world – that makes a difference, right?

'He comes over and he just looks at me and says, "What's up?"

'I say, "Ain't nothing."

'He says, "Are you cool?"

'And I say in this really tentative way, "*Yeee-ah*, have you got the gym money?"

'Time sort of stops then and I'm imagining the concussive impact of another heavyweight fist against my jaw. But then he pays the money and we're cool.'

He must have thought you were alright, after the fight?

'Well, I didn't know that at the time, though. Not until I went to this little nightclub that was called The Three of Spades in this mall where the Wild Card gym is situated. Freddie told me that if ever I went there, just to use his name and they would look after me, so I thought I'd pop in.

'There's this dude on the door when I get there and he asks me what I want. I tell him I just want to come in for a drink. He says, "You got any ID?"

'They want ID all the time over there. I say that Freddie sent me down.

'He says, "Freddie Roach?" And I say, "Yeah, I'm his assistant." Well, his tone changes then and I see a glimmer of recognition come across his face. "Come on in," he says, "You that crazy Irish motherfucker?"

'I say what?

'The doorman says, "Do you know Alex Garcia?"

'And I say casually, while I unconsciously rub my chin, "Yeah, we've met."

'He says, "Alex says you're a crazy son of a bitch but you're alright, man." So I got in fine.'

'Let me point out,' says Paddy, 'that Alex calling me a "crazy motherfucker" could have just meant I was simply stupid for taking him on – and not that I was nuts!'

It wasn't the smoothest start to your career as a trainer in LA, then?

'You could say that,' Paddy laughs, 'and it got *worse!*'

'After being with Freddie two or three days, it was kind of like I'd already been in LA a couple of years. There were no airs and graces with Freddie. He just let me get on with my work. But he was cool, and even from early on he'd be like, "If you need a car during the day, take mine if I'm not using it." He had a trust in people.

'Freddie Roach is very much married to boxing. You have to be in order to achieve the levels of success that he has achieved. He'd get to the gym at 8am every morning. I'd wake up at 7am and open up the gym. I'd have done most of the cleaning the night before when the gym was shut because don't forget, the gym was my apartment too. I'd vacuum, dust, clean the mirrors and keep the toilets clean. I mean, I kept the toilets clean throughout the day actually. I still do the same at my own gym now. Freddie was at the gym until around 6pm then he'd leave and I would lock up at 8pm. I'd repeat the same tasks that night, go to sleep, wake up the next morning and enjoy another day in Paradise.

'When I think back now, I can remember the peace I used to feel in the empty gym once I'd cleaned up and I was on my own. It was warm, so I wouldn't lock the door to the gym. I'd just have the wire door that kept the insects out shut, a cool late-night breeze coming though the gym, and I'd watch tapes of boxing all night on the VCR.

'So in the first few weeks that I'm there, Freddie has to go away because he's training fighters outside of LA too. And he's gonna be away for a couple of weeks. So I say to him, "What do we do while you're gone?" And he kind of looks at me funny and says as if it's the most obvious response in the world, "Train the fighters. I'll call you every day, just train the fighters. You know what to do."

'I mean, half of me was thinking that was fine, I knew how to instruct and train fighters. But the other half of me was thinking that a few weeks ago I was in the Channel Islands, and now I'm coaching world champions. It was like somebody giving you a job in a store and then saying, "Oh, by the way, here's the keys for the stock and the safe. I need to be out of town for a while." It felt weird, but he must have trusted me. So I just got to work.

'When Freddie came back, we were in the gym office one day and the phone rang. So I picked up the phone and answered it the same way Freddie used to, and he just used to say the word "boxing". So I did. And this voice doesn't introduce itself at all and just sort of grunts, "Get me Freddie Roach."

'So I ask who's speaking and the voice says, "Don't motherfuckin' ask me who's speaking – just get Freddie Roach."

'I say, "Dude, you called me, just tell me who's speaking and I'll get Freddie Roach." So the voice gets more irate and says, "Motherfucker, just do as I say and get Freddie Roach!"

'So I hung up.

'I go back to the little office and Freddie asks me who it was and I say "I dunno so I hung up" and we leave it at that.

'Training continued for a little while and then the phone rang again and I answer like Freddie with "boxing". And straight away there's this barrage from the same voice that says, "Hey motherfucker, don't hang up the motherfuckin' phone on me again. Put Freddie Roach on!"

'I say, "Oh, it's you again. You must have called back because you're gonna tell me who you are this time. And by now he's like, apoplectic, and he's shouting down the phone like his veins are about to burst and his eyes pop out or something. He says, "I ain't gonna tell you who I am motherfucker. Just put Freddie Roach on the phone!"

'I say, "Dude, it's the second time you've called. Who are you? I'll pass you over. Give me your name. That's all you've got to do." And just as he starts up again with "You mother..." I hang up and go back to the little office. Freddie looks at me and goes, "That him again? The same dude?"

'I say, "Yeah, but he won't give me his name."

'Then the phone rang a third time. By now, Freddie's in his usual pose, resting his head in his hand and looking over his shoulder. He's got this half smile on his face as if he's saying "it's gonna be that dude again" and he's daring me to answer.

'So this time I answer the phone with a "hello". The voice immediately says, "Listen motherfucker, I'm gonna come up there and put a cap in your ass."

'And I say, really calm and deadpan, like as if I'm offended and confused at the same time, "You're gonna shoot me?" He repeats himself, so I say, "Look, you don't know who I am, same as I don't know who you are. So who are you gonna shoot?"

'That's when he says, "Motherfucker, I'm James Toney."

'And it didn't click with me for a few seconds, so I say, "Listen, I don't give a fuck whether you're James Toney or not."

'Suddenly I hear Freddie shouting, "No Paddy!" and he's getting all flappy with his arms and demanding that I give him the phone. So I do, and then all I can hear is Freddie saying, "Hey James, listen, it's OK. That's Paddy, he's cool."

And I could hear James ranting on the phone and Freddie keep saying "he's cool, he's with me" to try and calm James down. He keeps saying to James that I'm from Europe and that's how we are in Europe – we ask who's on the phone.

'Thing is, I had to learn quickly. Phone conversations are different in America. For example, no one says goodbye. When you're done with the conversation, you hang up. That's it. Sometimes, Freddie would catch me holding the phone and ask me why. I'd say, "I think he's gone, but I'm not sure." And Freddie would start laughing and tell me, "We don't say goodbye like you do over there. When we're finished talking, we're finished."

'I told him I thought that was weird and he said that the Americans thought that we were weird saying goodbye all the time.'

James Toney is one of my favourite fighters since I was introduced to him through Donald McRae's excellent book *Dark Trade*.

Toney can comfortably be described as an all-time great in boxing, and Paddy agrees. An exceptional defensive fighter, a master of the shoulder roll and a devastating counter puncher. Toney is one of boxing's few triple champions, fighters who have won world titles in at least three separate weight divisions. He had 92 professional bouts with a 77-10-3 record, including 47 KOs and the distinction of never having been stopped himself. Toney was twice voted *The*

Ring magazine fighter of the year and ranked in its top ten best middleweights of the past 50 years.

And if that is not enough to convince you, then consider this. Today, great fighters like Vasiliy Lomachenko and Oleksandr Usyk are considered to be doing well if they have two fights per year, and not always against the highest calibre of opposition. Year on year, Toney fought regularly after only six to eight weeks, not months, of recovery – and against excellent opposition.

Just look back to 10 May 1991, when Toney fought Michael Nunn for the IBF world middleweight title. Nunn was a great fighter and an eventual two-weight world title holder, with a record at the time of 36-0. Toney wins the title in a sensational fight and then on 29 June, only six weeks later, he defends it against the highly rated Reggie Johnson, himself an eventual two-division world champion with a record of 29-1-1. And Toney wins that fight too.

What's even more impressive is that this pattern of limited recuperation between fights continued year on year. His record reminds me of the greats of the 1920s, 30s and 40s. Fighters like the 'Manassa Mauler' Jack Dempsey (59-6-10); the 'Fighting Marine' Gene Tunney (79-1-4); the 'Brockton Blockbuster' Rocky Marciano (49-0); and the 'Bronx Bull' Jake La Motta (83-19-4) to name but a few.

But it's also true that Toney has a darker side, which is articulately described in McRae's *Dark Trade*. He has a reputation for having an incendiary temper when angered, for being unpredictable, volatile and full of trash-talking gangsta rap when speaking about his opponents.

I can't imagine speaking to a fighter of James Toney's fistic calibre, or a man so associated with danger in this way – and surviving fully intact.

It is also true, as it is with most human beings who are complex characters, that Paddy's experience of James Toney includes a different man.

Paddy told me, 'Listen, me and James, his wife at the time and Kerry, we'd go out to eat and to the movies. James was never disrespectful to anyone in those circumstances. Sure, he was a dude from the street, and he'd have his talk, but there was nothing crass.'

In the end, I think to myself, in order to protect a record of his quality, Toney must have developed a strategy to maintain the level of determination and intensity required to win so many titles and defeat such high-quality fighters as he did.

'It was the street in him too,' Paddy adds. 'You know, the idea that you can't let another man who is challenging you see any weakness from you. When you're on the street, and you give away any weaknesses you might have, as soon as your opponent sees the cracks, he feels more powerful. James couldn't allow that. His attitude was simple. There are *no* cracks in James Toney.'

It can be no surprise that part of this strategy was creating a character who would intimidate and dehumanise opponents, and was the polar opposite of other elements of his personality.

'That's right,' continues Paddy, 'because James had an act for differing situations. He could be sweet and as nice as pie. He was always a gentleman to Kerry. But he

would always stamp his authority on the gym as a fighter
– *always.*'

'Freddie knew that's what James needed. And James knew
that Freddie was the captain of the ship. But James wanted
everyone else to know that if they laced gloves on, they were
beneath him. Simple as that. That was James' attitude.'

When did you see James Toney next, I ask him?

'It must have been about a month later and I heard these
cars pull into the gym car park downstairs. I'm next to the
little office at the top of the stairs in the Wild Card gym, so
while I can hear someone's arrived in the car park, I don't
know who.

'I was stood at the top of the stairs, leaning against the
wall as he walks into the gym. Four or five black brothers
are behind him strutting up the stairs to the gym. The first
thing that I notice is that this dude's dressed like a champion.
He's got this eight ball topped walking cane and he's draped
in substantial gold chains, with gold sovereign rings and
diamond earrings. And he's walked in like he means business.

'At the time, I didn't click that it was James. He's put on a
bit of weight in between fights, which Toney had a propensity
to do, and he's wearing a beard – so he doesn't look exactly
like his fighting image.

'I'd trained myself not to take too much notice of the
stars at the gym because it was normal to see *anyone* at the
gym. If I was star-struck, I couldn't have worked effectively,
so I would purposely *not* see that there were stars around,
if you get my meaning? How would I inspire confidence if
I was like, "Oh my God, that's such and such! How will I

wrap his hands?" So my head wasn't into getting surprised by star names.

'So, I'm looking at this dude looking at me. He's standing with his legs apart, his hands on the top of his cane, which is positioned between his feet, and his homeboys are lining up behind him. He's just staring at me, so I say, "Hey, what's up?"

'He waits a few seconds and then says, "Are you that motherfucker on the phone?"

'I laugh, because I know who this is now *and* what could happen. I say, "Ahhhh, *you're* James Toney?"

'"Yeah," he says. "And you're the motherfucker on the phone."

'"Yeah, I'm the motherfucker on the phone," I say, still smiling and hoping that this isn't going to go too badly.

'Next thing, James calls me a crazy motherfucker and then says to Freddie, "Hey Roach, why you bringin' crazy motherfuckers to this gym?"

'Then, Freddie starts laughing and gives James a big hug before James says to me, "You're lucky Freddie says you're alright, otherwise, I would have put a cap in your ass!"

'And I just say, "Yeah, you're probably right." And from then on, me and James was cool.

'I remember one time, James was training in the gym and he was staying at Jerry Rosenberg's place, like I did when I first arrived in LA.

'I don't think at the time that James had organised anywhere to live while he was in training camp, because he wasn't from LA and so Jerry was putting him up for a while.

'Jerry would drive James to the gym in James' truck. James would change for training and would take off all his bling: his diamonds, his rings, his chains, and his watch. He'd put his belongings in a plastic bag and hand them to me, asking me to lock them in the office for him, and look after them.

'So on this day, I'd gone out for some reason, and when I came back in, I walked back into the office and I notice that one of James' Diamond earrings is missing and his car keys are gone too. I look out the window and I can see that James' truck has gone too. I went up to Freddie in the gym and I whisper quietly to Freddie and ask if someone was going to rob James, why wouldn't they take all of his jewellery, as well as his car?

'Freddie rubs his face and says quietly but with that sense that the answer is totally obvious, "Fucking Jerry."

'"I go, how do you know?"

'And Freddie's like, "Paddy, this is typical Jerry."

'"So what the hell's he doing," I say, 'because it was me that James entrusted his stuff to and so I'm feeling a bit responsible, you know – and I'm also considering the possible repercussions if there's a problem.'

'"He'll have just gone for a ride," Freddie says calmly. "Just don't tell James, or he'll go mad."

'I don't have a death wish, so I'm happy to comply with that instruction.

'I decide to wait it out as James still has a good bit of his workout to complete and after an hour, the truck comes back into the parking lot. But strapped to the top of world champion James Toney's brand new SUV are ten of those metal fence panels that you see erected around music festivals to keep people out.

'I thought that was pretty bad but next thing I see is four Mexicans jump out of the vehicle with Jerry. And next thing, Jerry is having a full-on argument with these Mexicans in the parking lot – and I can hear them asking Jerry for money, and he's refusing to pay them for whatever it is they say he promised he'd pay them for.

'When they close around him a little threateningly, I can hear Jerry say if they don't all leave, then he'll get the fighters down to bust their scrawny asses. And while these Mexicans were screaming abuse at Jerry, the threat of the fighters was enough because they were backing off as they did it, and eventually they left.

'Jerry then comes up the stairs and he's just purely bold about the whole situation, even though I'm feeling a bit stressed and I say, "Jerry, dude, you took James' truck?"

'And he says, "Yeah, so?"

'And I'm like, "But James doesn't know you've got his truck. That ain't right, man."

'Jerry just exhales really loud as if I'm nagging him about taking someone's coffee mug or something and I say, "Listen dude, just give me the car keys." Jerry tells me it's alright, no big deal, and doesn't give me the car keys. Then I point out to him that he's actually *wearing* James' diamond earring and he says, "Don't worry about it."

'*Don't worry about it?*

'When James finally comes into the office after training, I've thankfully got the keys to his truck back, and James never knew that Jerry had taken it. But the top of his truck was scratched, on account of Jerry having to take the metal fencing off himself without his Mexican helpers.'

What was he doing bringing metal fencing to the boxing gym, I ask?

'It turned out that Jerry wanted the fencing for his dogs. I said to him, "Where'd you get all the fencing?" and he says, "McDonalds."

'I'm confused so I say, "What, the restaurant?"

'And he's like, "Yeah, the one just down the road. They're doing some building work, and I liked the fencing, so I went into McDonald's and spoke to the manager. I just told him that we were going to take the fencing and replace it with some better fencing for him. I also saw some Mexicans on the corner and I say to them if they help me load and unload the fencing, I'd give them 50 bucks. But I was never gonna give them any money for bringing that fencing a few hundred yards up the road, was I?"

'I was on the Mexicans' side. I said to Jerry, "No wonder they were angry, you told them that you would pay them 50 bucks."

'He says to me like someone who is a bit shocked that I can't see the sense in what he's saying, "Of course I *told* them that. They wouldn't have helped me otherwise."

'I mean, even if I obviously don't agree with what he did, you've got to respect the balls of this dude and the way he thinks. He's like, "Here's some fencing. I like this fencing, but there are no tools in the truck that I have taken that does not belong to me that allow me to remove the fencing that I like. What do I do?"

'What he does is goes into the McDonald's and bold as brass asks the manager to let him borrow a tool to dismantle the fencing. Having secured the tool, he robs the fencing in the middle of the day, without the manager knowing what he is doing. Then he fraudulently contracts the Mexicans to help him carry the stolen fences and load the truck, and as their reward, he robs them at the other end.

'Following that, he strolls back into the gym and puts the keys to James Toney's truck back like it was nothing. He hadn't even broken a sweat. He couldn't have cared less.

'And James, he didn't realise it had even happened. He didn't even realise that one of his diamond earrings was gone, and Jerry could be seen wearing it in the gym for months afterwards.

'I've got a lot to thank James for, actually. In terms of confidence, other than Freddie, James gave me the confidence that I could coach and support world champions successfully.'

How did he do that, I ask?

'You have to remember that when we were working together, you know, around 1997, Google hadn't been invented. It wasn't invented until 1998. So, people didn't check the internet for information at the drop of a hat like we do now.

'So I'm sitting at ringside with James and I'm wrapping his hands, and we've been getting on great. I've been wrapping his hands now for around six months and I've been in the States for around eight months. So James has decided not to kill me and he's got a load of his dudes stood behind him while I wrap his hands. They used to come with him in his truck when he trained.

'Out of the blue, he goes to me, "Hey Patti Duke", which is what he used to call me. "Do you box?"

'Instantly, there was just a feeling in my mind of "shit, here we go."

So what did you say to him?

'"Yeah," I say. "I boxed." I didn't want to say "yes" because I wasn't sure where this was gonna go, but I did.

'James says, "Oh, you did? Amateur or pro?"

'Now I'm thinking I just want to say amateur, and talk about the good stuff. So I say amateur and I had a few pro. I thought it best to tell the truth but maybe if I don't make a big deal out of it, he'll forget the pro bit.

'He says, "Oh you did. What did you do as an amateur?"

'"I won a couple of Limerick titles and I was a silver medallist in the Munsters."

'"Munsters," he says, "What the fuck is that?"

'"Ireland's split in four," I tell him. "Munster was the part I was from and I won the silver medal in this part."

'"And you boxed pro?" he asks.

'I hoped he'd forget that, but I said "yeah, a little bit" and he asks me, "How did you do?"

'"No good."'

He says, "No good?" and I'm thinking, "Please stop prying, man. I was no good. Let's leave it at that."

'There was a split second when he first asked me the question when I wondered whether I should just lie about it. Nowadays, everything's on Google and can be checked out, so most people wouldn't think about lying about something like that. But back then? You could lie about what you wanted. There was no Google and things were hard to check. These days, we think it's normal to know something about everybody because most people have some kind of internet footprint – but not back then.

'But I thought, "No. I'm wrapping an all-time great's hands. I've been coaching him. I'll tell the truth."

'And this conversation with myself happened in my head in less than a second.

'But James kept prodding away, so I told him that I was like 0 and 5 in the pros. James just nods as I tell him, thinking about what I'm saying.

'The second I said it, though, one of his boys just says to me, "What the fuck are you doing wrapping James' hands then and coaching pros when you were no good?"

'It was just really derogatory and there was no build-up to it – just wham, here it is.

'And in a split second, without even thinking about his response, James goes, "Shut the fuck up, bitch. Two men wrap my hands in this gym: Freddie Roach and the other one is doing it right now. So why don't you just shut the fuck up and go and get my CDs out of the car? And get my boots too."

'And this guy is like, "James, I was only..."

'And James just cuts him off with, "Shut the fuck up, motherfucker, and go get my boots."

'I remember at the time thinking I was glad I had told the truth. It was done then and it had been bothering me. I mean, I was worried because I was eight months into a different life and I was worried that if I wasn't accepted, then I'd have to go back to where I was before, and I didn't want that because it was a dark old place.

'What James did was a really big deal for me. I don't know if he's aware of that. But having a world champion acknowledge me, in front of his homeboys who were with him all the time in the gym like that, was huge for my confidence and my credibility. I knew that James was responsive to me because we were doing mitts every day and I was working his corner in sparring too – three days a week. Freddie had also told me that James liked me too.

'But it was a huge big deal to me, to get that support, and the thing is, James never brought it up again.'

8

'Have a Lights Out Day, Baby!'

August 2019

IT'S AROUND midnight UK time during the English school summer holidays, on a Monday evening moving into Tuesday morning, when I receive an email from a guy called John with a simple message and his number in LA.

'Call me tomorrow and we can set up a time and date.'

This is a time and date to talk with triple champion James 'Lights Out' Toney.

I am delighted by this.

I decide that I will call the next day at around 6pm UK time, which should mean around 10am on the US west coast.

Not long after 6pm, I make sure that my daughter is upstairs preparing herself for bed. My wife is also upstairs sorting something out in our bedroom and chatting with my daughter. I sense a 10- or 15-minute window of opportunity and think that, assuming I get through to John, 15 minutes should be enough to set up the time and date of the interview with James Toney.

Previously, I have sent John a copy of the questions I am going to ask James. He hasn't returned comment on them, so I assume that they are OK.

With the sound of water from my daughter's bath running upstairs, I give John a call.

After a few rings, there is an answer.

'Hello, John?' I say. 'It's Lee Simpson from the UK.'

'Hey, Teach, how are you doin'?' returns a really broad American accent.

It seems that my nickname has gone Transatlantic, and I am ridiculously proud of this.

'I'm well,' I say, conscious of sounding really British for the first time in a long time. 'I'm well. I'm just calling to see if we can set a date and time to speak with James, please?'

'Yeah, Teach, can you hold a minute please?'

I hold.

And then I hear a slightly muffled conversation where John says, 'Hey, it's the guy from the UK gym. The one they call "The Teacher". You know, the book about the Irish guy.'

I hear another voice, deeper and more muffled, say, 'Yeah.'

Who is that voice, I think?

'He wants to talk with you, remember?' says John to the voice.

'I'll talk to him now,' says the other voice.

And then it dawns on me as John comes back on the phone, 'Hey, Teach, you good?'

'Yes,' I say, realising exactly what is about to happen, but too late.

'You're in luck. James is right next to me. I'll put him on the phone. This is James.'

They say that it is the punch that you don't see coming that knocks you out.

I'll vouch for that.

Because the next voice I hear is very different to John's and starts with, 'Teach, this is James Toney.'

I have a moment then.

It's a split second in which many thoughts go through my head all at once and I have to make a decision – a decision that could jeopardise the interview, reduce the quality of my story and insult a man who I definitely do not want to insult.

If I make the wrong decision.

I am not prepared.

My questions are on my computer, which I don't have time to access. I am speaking on my phone with a world champion, so I can't look at my emails on this device either.

All I have is a notepad on the dining room table.

Do I ask world champion James Toney if he wouldn't mind scheduling an interview with me and I'll call him back, knowing full well that the consequence of this may be that I piss a world champion off to the extent that he thinks I am an unprofessional time waster? Or do I go ahead and do the interview, relying on my memory, and my wits, to get me through it without making too much of an idiot of myself?

I make my choice and suddenly I feel panic – which I have to suppress.

'James?' I say tentatively, unsure of how I am supposed to address a member of what most people would consider boxing royalty.

'Yeah, hello sir,' comes the reply.

James Toney has just called me *sir*? I know this is an American form of politeness, but I am still thrown by it.

My heart is screaming, 'Shit! This is James Toney!' And my head is telling me to pull myself together and just ask him the damn questions because I can remember most of them.

And I might never get the chance again.

That's when I realise that I need to make sure I'm not interrupted as my child is expecting me to come upstairs and bathe her in a few minutes, not conduct an interview with a world champion.

That is also when things get a little surreal.

I am aware of how British I sound when I say, 'James, could you possibly excuse me for a moment while I make sure I have the quiet to really hear what you are going to say?'

Why am I talking like this? I never sound like this normally – like I'm some jumped-up butler in *Downton Abbey*.

'Sure,' says James, and I wonder what he is thinking of me.

I cover the part of my mobile which picks up my voice in order to muffle it.

I didn't dare put James Toney on hold.

I walk to the bottom of the stairs and shout to my wife. When she arrives at the top of the stairs I say, 'Could you do bedtime? I've got world champion James Toney on the phone and I need to talk to him now.'

She nods and says, '*The* James Toney?'

I nod back and go and sit down at my dining room table to begin the interview that I *thought* I was calling to organise.

But that's boxing, I suppose. One of the things we love about the sport is its unpredictability and that's what's happened here.

So I just jump straight in with feigned confidence.

'Thank you for speaking with me,' I say. 'I know that Paddy will appreciate it too.'

'No problem,' says James.

I am conscious that I don't want to come across as rude. So I ask James how he is and what he's doing now?

'I'm good, Teach. I'm in California with the weather and my kids and I'm loving it. I'm in the gym too. I love the gym, and being around the people in the gym, you know?'

James Toney has a very interesting accent. It is very US, a little like Marlon Brando as Kurtz in *Apocalypse Now*. Sometimes he is exceptionally clear. At other times, when he speaks more quickly, he can be hard to follow.

I have to tune in and really concentrate.

I know that the tag question at the end of his last sentence requires a response to show that I am in the conversation with him. And I do know what he means about the gym as in my own, admittedly very small, way I feel the same about Paddy's gym too.

But I'm still a little panicky, so instead of making small talk, I just stick to my script.

I ask him where he met Paddy?

'We met at the Wild Card gym when I was training with Freddie Roach. Paddy was a very cool guy – a delightful man.'

117

Paddy told me that you used to have a specific nickname for him at the gym. What was it?

'There were a lot,' he says. 'But I remember that I used to call him Patti Duke. It was from a TV show. I used to shout right across the gym at him, "Hey! Patti the Duke!"'

I say to James I have spoken to several fighters Paddy has coached or trained and they talk about how analytical and technical he was about boxing. What was your experience of Paddy as a trainer?

James tells me that he valued Paddy's honesty and integrity. 'He very much forces himself on you and makes you believe in what you do. I appreciate him 100 per cent, no 1,000 per cent. I loved having him in my corner.

'Teach, boxing is about camaraderie and relationships too, you know. I knew I could trust him. Paddy's a great dude, 100 per cent. A great trainer. He knows the ins and outs of the boxing game. He's very smart and knowledgeable – that's why I had him in my corner. He just loves boxing. Boxing is his obsession.'

I think for a split second about the comment 'that's why I had him in my corner'. It's what is *not* said here that matters. That there would have been no chance of working with a champion like James Toney if Paddy had not been up to scratch – period.

I'm feeling more comfortable in the interview now, and like a boxer adjusting his angle of attack, I change the angle of my questions and ask James, 'Did you know that Paddy felt that it was the confidence that working with you gave him that allowed him to go on and succeed in the way he has?'

'I appreciate that,' he says humbly. 'He would have succeeded with or without me, though. I truly believe that. He's good at what he does.'

I don't want to come across as only interested in Paddy, because I am not. James Toney is one of my favourite fighters. So I ask James if he knows that he fought a lot more than some of the all-time greats like Jack Dempsey and Rocky Marciano? I also ask him if he knows that his record, especially covering the period 1991–1994, actually resembles the records of those greats, fighting high-calibre opposition every six to eight weeks or so.

It's something you can't imagine modern fighters like Joshua, Fury, Wilder, Canelo, Lomachenko or Usyk doing. 'Thanks, I appreciate that,' is what he says, and keeps saying, throughout our conversation. I feel humbled by how humble his responses are.

I hadn't expected that. Exactly what had I expected? I'm not sure. I have read a lot about James Toney. And I've watched his fights and his interviews. I know what he can do and what he is capable of *saying*.

But that's in a fight context.

In our conversation, James Toney was engaging, honest, enthusiastic, friendly – and *very* easy to talk to. I am humbled and impressed by this from a man who has achieved so much.

I take the conversation back to Paddy and ask whether James can remember any funny stories from their time working together?

'There are so many,' he says. 'We used to play jokes on each other.'

I remember Paddy had told me that James had a sense of humour where he enjoyed practical-type jokes.

'As me and Paddy got close,' he continues, 'we played jokes on each other. We had water gun fights and threw raw eggs at each other in the gym.'

What? During training for really significant fights, I ask him?

'Hey Teach, you can't be a bull head in training all the time. You must relax too.'

I get that. I imagine that maintaining the intensity of the 'Lights Out' persona must take huge strength. Anyone would need a break from that.

'Oh, and Paddy has those hats too, man.' James bursts out laughing. 'He was obsessed with them!'

I take the opportunity to tell James that we are calling the book *Hats, Handwraps and Headaches* at this point.

'Good call. Good title.'

James Toney likes our title. I am pathetically proud again.

Though it seems like a lot less, I've already been talking to James for ten minutes and I've asked all of my questions.

Those I can remember, anyway.

'I'm delighted that someone is writing a book about Paddy,' James says without a prompt from me. 'His story needs to be told.'

I thank James for giving me his time and then tell him that at the main school where I work, I do boxing training with the students and that one of the main fighters I get them to study is James Toney.

'You do?' he says.

'Yes – as a defensive master and devastating counter puncher,' I tell him. 'The kids are always impressed because at first they are all like "Canelo and AJ and Fury", but when they watch James Toney they are like, wow, "Lights Out!"'

'I appreciate that,' he says. 'That's cool.'

The conversation ends with me thanking James again.

Then, full of enthusiasm and optimism, he says, 'Hey Teach, have a Lights Out day, baby!'

James 'Lights Out' Toney – an all-time great.

9

Froch v Groves I

IBF and WBA super
middleweight titles

Manchester Arena, November 2013

IT SOUNDED to me like everything was going smoothly in the preparations for George Groves' first fight with Carl Froch then? Surely nothing happens like that?

'No Teach,' Paddy says with a shake of his head, 'It doesn't.

'The night before the fight, I'm gonna go out for a bit so I call for the lift to take me down to the lobby area. When I get in the lift, George and "The Father" are in there already. That's not George's father, it's *The Father*, which is the nickname I gave to Barry O'Connell, George's conditioning coach, on account of the fact that I thought he looked like a priest. I even had Sky TV convinced that he used to be a priest in the Marines. So for the whole first camp, all the reporters thought that.

'I say, "What you up to boys?" pretty matter-of-factly and George tells me he just wants to have a little, "shake out" in the basement.

'"OK, I'll come too," I say and I said to The Father, "What's this about a shakedown?"

'And The Father says to me, "I don't know how to tell you this, Paddy."

'And I say, "Just tell me."

'I forget exactly what he said then, but it was something extreme, and it turned out that George was around six or seven kilos [15 lbs] overweight, with the weigh-in tomorrow.

'I was shocked and I'm like, "What the hell, Father?"

'"Sorry Paddy, he told me this morning. It's what George does."

'I couldn't really get mad at The Father. Me and George had agreed that he would manage his weight and let me know if there were any problems. There was nothing I could do, so I stayed with him, he worked out, and he got the weight off.'

Doesn't it normally affect a fighter's performance if he drops weight that quickly?

'Yeah, 100 per cent. But more worrying than that, you're dehydrated and you don't have enough fluid around the brain. More concerning than affecting the performance is compromising the safety of the fighter.

'But listen, if this is what George does, I had to accept that. I was head dude. I had chosen to allow George to manage this facet of his preparation because we only had nine weeks to prepare. I was ultimately responsible. Going forward, it was something that I would change. But right now, what could I do?

'The Father was exemplary as a conditioning coach in my experience, and he called me the next morning to let me know that George was OK and we would make the weight.'

Let's move on to the fight itself, Paddy. You've done what you do during the day to keep George relaxed and pass the time, and then you're in the changing room before the fight.

'Everything was good: settled, nice, balanced and composed – very professional. What I knew about George up until then, and definitely what I know about George now, is that if you pile the pressure on that man he just gets better. George knew there was a lot riding on the fight. He knew that his coach, that man who had led him to the position that he was in nine weeks before, the man who had helped him win his titles and gather the significant success he had experienced, Adam [Booth], wasn't with him any more. George knew the pressure was on *him*, but I felt good because I knew that George believed in our gameplan and that he trusted what I was telling him.

'I also know that it was Adam who guided him to a Commonwealth title in only his eighth fight and a British title in his tenth fight. Not many fighters get that kind of success in their whole careers. Adam helped George achieve that. So I knew that we were good to go technically, but more importantly for me, we had bonded too and everything was cool.'

Were you feeling the pressure before this world title fight?

'Well, George didn't have Adam with him any longer and George knew that all of the pressure was on him, really. There was no pressure on me because part of the gameplan was to act like I was simply hanging out with George, helping him in the gym.

'When we left the changing room and went for the ring walk, there was this long platform that we had to walk down. I said to him, "George, I'm not going to go on that platform. I'll make my way underneath to the end of the platform. You walk down on your own. I'll be at the end of the platform and as you walk, just lock eyes on me. We know where we are and what we have to do. We're cool. I'll walk with you to the ring from the end of the platform."

'It also fitted in with the narrative of the gameplan, suggesting that George was pretty much on his own in the fight. So George went to the top of the platform with the rest of the corner. I was at the bottom and when the ring announcer called his name, George paused at the top of the platform enacting a confident and dominant look that he made sure could be seen by everyone in that Manchester Arena. He came across really well to the audience, and remember, George had kind of been presented as the villain when compared to Carl in the media build-up to the fight. But this look he was giving, this look clearly told everyone there, "I've got this."

'Then we made eye contact. I smirked at him and nodded my head and he looked back and smiled. Everyone saw that smile and I knew we were good. We were in a great place.'

So, everything is going great and then George has an awesome first round that really stamps his authority on the fight and lets Carl know, if he didn't before, that he's not in for an easy night.

'Well, in some ways, yes. But, when the first round was over, I realised that possibly the worst thing that could have happened actually happened. Not only did the first round play itself out *exactly* as we had predicted to Carl – but George dropped him hard too. And if you look back through history, sometimes the worst thing that a fighter can do is drop a dude early on. Because the fighter who has put his opponent down suddenly thinks, "Wow, it worked! I know what gets him now. I landed that shot. I was right. It'll be there for me again and I can do that again."

'The guy that got dropped, though, he's thinking, "Shit, what the hell has just happened here?" So, fast forward two or three rounds. The guy that got dropped is still in there and he's thinking, "OK, this dude might be able to punch, but I'm still here so I can take his best shots." And the guy who was dropped starts to get a little bit more mentally composed now because he's getting through it. On the other hand, the guy that dropped him is now thinking, "Damn, he's still here. I haven't found that shot again." And the psychological battle can begin to tilt slightly in favour of the fighter dropped in round one. And sometimes in these situations, it tilts *really* badly.'

It didn't tilt really badly then for George, though, did it? Most, if not all, observers had George winning the fight against the two-belt world champion.

'No, that didn't happen to George. But what did happen was as soon as George dropped Carl, he started pulling other moves and shots out of the bag *too soon*. Things that we had planned for round four he started doing in rounds one and two. Things we had planned for rounds six and seven he was doing in rounds two and three. And I was like, "George, slow it down, man. You're getting away from yourself. These things, yeah, we've got them planned – but relax. They'll still be there in a few rounds. Don't pull them out now."

'You're right that George was dominating the fight, Teach, but he wasn't dominating *every* round. He was taking a lot of punishment to the body and taking other serious shots too. In some ways, George was trying to keep up with the success he'd had in the first round. He was chasing things a little bit – trying to finish the job in what he felt would be style. So my job at that stage was to try to get him to relax and slow the fight down, particularly in his own head.

'Truth be known, we didn't manage to calm the fight down as much as we should have. And the problem then is that by rounds six and seven, every trick we'd planned for the 12 rounds had already been pulled out and used. So then you've just got to keep repeating what you have already done. As a fight goes on, if you don't give a man something new to think about, and you just keep repeating what you've already done, then you give a pattern to your opponent. And if you give a pattern to your opponent, it makes you easier to read. And if you're easier to read, then you're easier to counter. Therefore, the opponent can make adjustments to manage you and what I would like any fighter to do in any fight is to control his gears to avoid patterns. Sometimes a fighter might start in a lower gear and build up, other times he might start in the top gear for a few rounds and then slow the fight down. Ultimately, from a coach's perspective, we don't want our opponent to predict our fighter.

'So when we hit round five, I'm thinking George is winning the rounds. He's working hard, and winning the rounds, but he is taking some shots. They're big shots too. And maybe they aren't being seen by the judges and spectators because of the shock of his success, because we need to remember that Carl was the favourite by a long way and according to the newspapers before the fight, George was going home between rounds one and three with that new Irish dude he was working with.

'Suddenly it's round six, we're still here, everyone's shocked at the pace and quality of the fight George is fighting, the level of control George is demonstrating, and people are thinking he's dominating and not getting touched by Carl. But let me tell you, he was taking some shots.'

Watching the fight, you notice at the beginning that the crowd are not on George's side. Cast as the upstart villain of the piece, cocky and unlikeable, childish yet quick-witted, and a Londoner too, which would have resonated negatively with a northern fight crowd, the press compared George with Carl's down-to-earth, calls a spade a spade, people's champion from the East Midlands type of presentation. The boos ringing around the arena that were aimed at George were palpable. The vast majority of the audience were there for one thing: to watch the upstart lose and head off back down south with his tail between his legs.

Did you get a sense that the crowd were changing their view of George at this point in the fight?

'The crowd were definitely changing, 100 per cent. Listen, facts are facts, and they could see what was happening. We had told Carl and the whole world what was going to happen in the first round. No one believed it, yet here it was, playing out exactly as we had predicted. So there were 20,000 people nudging each other and saying, "He said that would happen. He said that would happen!" And with that level of shock and excitement, with every piece of action, even if it was close, they're thinking, "Wow, look at Groves now." So their focus was on what George was doing to Carl, *not* what Carl was doing to him.'

It's at this point that I bring up the controversy of the stoppage in round nine. With George clearly on top in the fight, and to most observers' eyes holding a clear points advantage over Froch, he's hit with a series of good shots from Froch. Pushed against the ropes, George doesn't answer back, covers up, and appears to sway a little. It's clear that he's hurt. And at this point, the referee, the experienced Howard Foster, steps in and stops the fight.

I've watched this fight over and over again. And the things that have always stuck with me are firstly the look of pure anguish on George Groves' face as he pulls away from Howard Foster's arms. Yes, he's hurt. His cheeks are flushed and shock and disbelief are etched across his face at the realisation of what has just happened. But to my mind, he seems lucid. He seems aware. And he seems mightily pissed off with the decision.

And secondly, there is Paddy, hurtling towards Howard Foster and appearing to dispute the decision to stop the fight as forcefully as he possibly can.

10

Crashing Freddie's Car
– LA Style!

*'Hey Roach, that crazy Irish
motherfucker just wrote your car off!'*

WE'VE TALKED a lot in our interviews about George
Groves recently, so I bring the conversation back around to
the Wild Card gym.

So were the Jerry Rosenberg and James Toney incidents,
the Tooth Fight and sleeping in a boxing ring the maddest
experiences you had at the Wildcard?

Paddy laughs out loud. 'No, there were so many. Like I
said, the Wild Card gym was full of different faces, including
top sportsmen and women, actors and even business types
and lawyers.

'The place was so unique and crazy that you would have
a Hollywood lawyer like Robert Shapiro, who was famous
for working for celebrities and was lead counsel in O.J.

Simpson's legal team, sparring with a world champion like James Toney.'

What, I blurt out incredulously, for real? Wouldn't Toney have just destroyed him in seconds?

'Yeah, if he'd wanted to. I mean, I would just see James shoulder rolling, moving his head, catching shots on the gloves and kind of complimenting Shapiro, you know. Like, "hey, good shot man", while James just avoided everything that was being thrown at him with total ease.'

Why would he do that?

'Look Teach, this is Hollywood, right? I remember saying to James that Shapiro was probably going back to his office after a lunchtime workout and telling his colleagues that he'd just sparred with world champion James Toney, when obviously you couldn't *really* call what had happened a spar. I asked James why he bothered and I remember he just smiled and said, "You never know when I might need a good lawyer."'

Without warning, Paddy bursts out laughing then starts another story.

'And there was this time – it would have been not long after that incident with Jerry and James – that Freddie says to me did I want some lunch? He used this phrase "I buy – you fly" and I asked what it meant. It was simple enough. Freddie would buy the food if I went to get it.

He wanted me to go to California Chicken, a few miles down the road, and get a chicken caesar salad. I'm fine with that so I say, "How do I get there?" He says, "Just take my car. You can drive, can't you?" 'I was a bit concerned because I didn't know my way around at all. But Freddie says, "Listen, you're gonna love LA. Getting around here's easy. Everything's in straight lines. If I say go this amount of blocks this way and this amount of blocks that way, you'll get where you need to go. It's easy. You can't get lost in LA.'

'So, I'm driving down the road to the chicken place in Freddie Roach's Lincoln. Everything's great and I'm thinking about what a ride this whole experience is. And I'm thinking about Freddie's style. You know, Freddie pays a lot of attention to detail and we're similar that way about cleanliness and tidiness. I like to have the gym clean and organised. Freddie's like that too. He'd even have his remote controls lined up for the TV, and I'm the same. I have to have things tidy and lined up before I can go to sleep. So that was another reason that we got on.

'I get the food and I drive back to the gym. I'm just about to turn into the gym and I've got to cross three lanes of traffic to do this – so I'm waiting for the right moment. It's busy. It's lunchtime but the traffic lights are keeping everything organised and the traffic has stopped to allow those of us on the right to turn left, which was into the gym.

'So I make the turn and drive across and then bam! Out of the blue, I get side-swiped. I shit myself with the shock of being hit and when I stop spinning and come to a standstill, there's these two women in the car that hit me also in shock and staring into space.

'I'm like, "What the feckin' hell just happened?" These two old girls have come down the bus lane, which they shouldn't have been in, haven't read the road correctly and they've just wiped me out in Freddie's Lincoln. They're in the wrong. It should be OK.

'But then I'm thinking, "Lord save me" because what I do know is that I've only just arrived as Freddie's employee – and already this has happened.

'I pulled into the gym's parking lot and when I look up I can see the gym windows that overlook the car park. There's around ten heads pressed up against the window and the women who have hit me have also pulled into the car park behind me.

'When I look up at the window a second time, I see James Toney's head above the rest of them. And he's laughing, barely able to control himself, and he's shouting, "Hey Roach, that crazy Irish motherfucker just wrote your car off!"

'The windows to the gym are open to let air in, and I can sort of hear Freddie's muffled voice and then James shouting, "I ain't joking, man. He wrote your fucking car off!"

'And James is in tears now, laughing, and I'm just thinking, "What just happened here? The car's wiped out?" A world champion is leaning out of the window laughing his ass off at me – and that's gonna wind Freddie up. And then I see Freddie's head come to the window and he mouths, "Oh shit!"

'Freddie comes down to the parking lot just shaking his head. He didn't say much. He's a really calm character, Freddie. And as he's doing this, I go over and open the door to the car that hit me and ask if the women are alright. I say, "What were you doing coming down in the bus lane?" and they tell me that they don't know. I tell them, "You side-swiped me and totalled the car. Are you sure you're OK?"

'Next thing, Freddie comes up alongside me and taps me on the shoulder. The women are still facing forward, as if they were still driving, not really looking at me talking to them at the side door. They're obviously in shock. They're looking at their feet, the dashboard, the windscreen, anywhere really – they just can't seem to focus on the conversation.

'Freddie pulls at my sleeve. I look at him, and he's motioning for me to go. And I'm thinking, "What?" And Freddie gestures for me to go again before putting his hand on the top of the car, and saying to the ladies, "Are you women OK?"

'I don't know what to think at this point as I've only been here a month. I've been in a wipeout in my boss' car, James Toney is pissing himself at the window and Freddie's now having to sort out this whole mess.

'So I left the parking lot, walked around the block, came into the gym through a little side entrance, and then in one of the craziest moments of my life, I'm now stood next to James Toney looking out of the window at Freddie picking up my pieces and dealing with my problem,

'And the guys in the gym are telling me that Freddie's gonna be really pissed off with me. But I'm saying, "No, Freddie told me to get out of there. He's sorting everything out."

'After ten minutes or so, Freddie comes up the stairs and tells me the problem is sorted but if the police call, to let him know and he would speak to them.

'I was OK with that!

'So later on, I'm in the gym and the police come in and ask to see Freddie Roach. I ask them why, and they tell me it's regarding a car accident. "In that case officers," I say, "He's over there, in the office!"

Paddy bursts out laughing at his own story now, almost as loud as I imagine James Toney was laughing when he saw Paddy step out of Freddie's battered and crumpled Lincoln.

'In the end, I did Freddie a favour, man, because when he got rid of the Lincoln, he got this nice Chevy truck with remote-controlled access to the vehicle – and in 1997 that was pretty cool!'

11

Froch v Groves I

A loss turns to a victory

I'M STILL thinking about how Paddy rushes over to remonstrate with the referee Howard Foster when the fight is stopped. Based on my experience of the man, he is both measured in his approach to life and respectful, so as blatant a challenge to the referee's authority as this is out of character.

What was going through your head when Howard Foster made his decision?

'When the fight got stopped, George was hurt. And there was that split second where he fired off the ropes and then his torso dips down slightly. That's when Howard Foster jumped in, that split second. And in that split second, he had to make a decision. Was George out on his feet for that split second? Or had George realised Carl had tied him up again, so did he drop his shoulders to extricate himself before building an attack again? Yes, everything sort of slumped as George was hit, and that definitively showed us that he had been tagged by Carl and hurt.'

I decide that now is the time to bring up the 'controversy' surrounding the presentation of George as having a suspect chin and whether, in Paddy's view, this presentation somehow influenced the outcome of the fight.

'I was there when George got tagged by Carl. I was close enough to know that he was hurt, but this is boxing. I also still felt that George had been in control of the fight as a whole from the beginning. It was a world title fight. People get hurt at this level.

'I had brought up the thing in the press surrounding George's chin at the rules meeting the day of the weigh-in with the Board of Control. Neil Sibley, who was George's lawyer, was there to take notes and Carl's team were present too.

'I made a big deal of it, saying, "Please, I want to make sure that everyone understands this. For nine and a half weeks, it's been in all the papers that Carl has a cast iron chin and George has got a glass one. Carl *has* got an iron chin. He's proved it. But there is nothing out there to show that George has a *glass* chin. Number one, he's undefeated. Number two, he's only been on the canvas once, and then he got up and knocked the other guy out. So how does any of that prove he has a glass chin?"

'What was bothering me was that this had been in the papers non-stop for over two months, so I said to everyone present, "I'm asking you, please gentlemen, understand that this is a world title fight. This is not just a fight to get into a big fight. You cannot as professionals supervising this bout buy into the narrative that Carl has an iron chin and George has a glass chin. Please allow this fight to play out. These are two top men in a fight. So these men can both hurt each other. "Don't worry Paddy," is what they said to me. "Everyone is experienced here. We know what we are up to."

'I reinforced my point of view saying, "I'm asking you gentlemen, please be aware of this. It's gonna be on people's minds. How could it not be? It will *influence* people's judgement." And though I didn't explicitly say so, I was directing this to the people inside the room with me, as well as the public in general. "It's all we've heard for over nine weeks. Be aware. George Groves is undefeated. He deserves his shot. He's the mandatory challenger. He's worked hard for this." They nodded and told me they understood.

'So when the fight got stopped, I knew that George had been hurt, but I knew also that what I said could happen had happened too. George was in such a dominant position in the fight. It was a world title contest. Surely the referee should let it carry on that extra little bit? Give George the benefit of the doubt?

'But in the back of my mind, I couldn't get rid of the screaming siren that was shouting out, "I told you this could happen!" So that's what I jumped in the ring and said. I went up to Howard Foster and I said, "I told you in the meeting yesterday that this could happen."

'I don't think that Howard Foster thought to himself, "Right, I'm gonna stop this dude" in any malicious kind of way.

'I am absolutely not saying that. He's a referee. He wants to look out for fighters. He was in a pressurised situation. He tried to do what he thought was for the best.

'Remember too that the repeated messages about iron jaws and glass chins were in my head too, not just Howard Foster's, so I was acutely aware of how the message had permeated all of our conscious thoughts. So I admit that I was frustrated.'

What about if Howard Foster had allowed George to continue?

'Would George have survived? Who knows? But the fight got stopped, so we'll never know. George was gutted. George acted like a gentleman and I kept him calm, even though he was fuming. I kept saying, "George, be cool, just be cool." He was really struggling with anger and the disappointment and I said to him, "Just keep it cool and let this play out. It's done now. We need to be cool." They announced the winner and then we had to go and sit at ringside for the interviews.'

Did you hear the crowd, I ask Paddy, because they had clearly changed their view of George by now. They didn't seem to have wanted the fight to be stopped and appeared to be finding it difficult to accept their previous favourite, Froch, as the winner of the fight.

'100 per cent, definitely. The shift in attitude had started around round six, but it massively ramped up during the post-fight interviews and their boos transformed to cheers as George spoke. The TV people interviewed Carl first, because he had won. As they were interviewing Carl, I had my hands on George's shoulders, just trying to massage them and help him to keep calm. You can clearly see it on the footage. And while I'm doing that, I'm listening to the crowd, and even though Carl was right beside me, I couldn't really hear the words he was saying, but I could feel and hear the crowd getting more and more boisterous *against* Carl.

'I didn't initially understand why because all Carl had done was what he was supposed to do – act like a warrior and go out and win a fight. But it didn't matter. The crowd had turned on Carl.

'My instant reaction to that realisation was to whisper into George's ear, "Be humble. They've turned on him. They've turned against him so just be cool and they'll be on *your* side." He nodded and then when he did the interview, he was calm, measured and respectful.'

I've watched this interview many times, and the change in George is impressive.

In contrast to the arrogant, brash and confident presentation of himself in the press conferences and interviews before the fight, George manages to come across as composed and fair in the way he handles what at the very least must have been a massive disappointment, and at worst a huge miscarriage of justice to him.

It must have been so tempting for George to accuse the referee and Carl of robbing him of what he deserved. And yet, if he had done that, he would have seemed like a spoiled child crying about how life is not fair, playing up to the media stereotypes generated for and about him before the fight.

Instead, he is magnanimous in defeat, even finding the strength to compliment Froch.

I admit to being impressed with George's ability to read the situation and improvise such a well-constructed response to win the crowd over, while simultaneously expressing respect for the man he feels has unfairly beaten him.

'We did that interview there and then on the ring canvas,' says Paddy, 'and it was clear that at the very least the vast majority of the 20,000 spectators didn't feel that it was fair to stop the fight – and they surely didn't feel that Carl had won the fight.'

I agree and deep down I am not sure that Carl Froch thought he had won the fight convincingly either.

So surely, there would need to be a rematch?

12

Losing Freddie's Car – LA Style!

'Paddy, tell me you know where
you parked my car?'

HOW LONG were you out in LA with Freddie Roach then, I ask Paddy?

'Two years overall. The thing is, I was there way longer than I should have been because I went over on a visa waiver. I came back in 1997 to train Glen Catley for the British title. He was fighting Neville Brown. Glen had been a sparring partner for Steve Collins and so he called Freddie and asked Freddie to train him.

'Freddie thought highly of Glen but Glen couldn't come over to the States and Freddie couldn't leave the States with the commitments that he had – and so Freddie sent me over instead.'

A visa waiver – isn't that for a temporary stay, I ask Paddy? What was the situation with your right to work in the US?

Isn't it difficult to get residency permits for any significant length of time?

'I never had one, Teach. And I knew when I left that I had been in America too long because I only had a three-month waiver – and now it was way over that, so there was no way that I would get back in.'

What could you do, then? With the greatest respect, I wouldn't have thought that boxing trainer was on the most-desirable list of skilled workers in professions experiencing a shortage of staff in the US?

'You're not wrong. I had to think about how to get back in before I left, so I wrote to me Mam and asked her to get me some passport application forms and send them to me in America. And me Mam's the type that if she didn't think that there was something wrong, then she wouldn't ask questions, so she sent them.

'When they arrived, I filled them in and sent them back to her and asked her to send them to Dublin from our home near Limerick, so that the application forms came from an *Irish* address. So she sent them off and a couple of weeks later she calls me and tells me that a package has arrived for me. I was like, "Cool, I'll pick it up when I get home" because I knew that it was the new passport I had applied for as part of my plan to return to the US.

'When I went through customs in LA to come to England to train Glen, I got what I expected when the officials checked my passport. They told me I had overstayed my visa limit. So the official says to me that I'll be banned from entering the US for five years as a consequence of this contravention.

And he goes and stamps my passport with a mark that tells anyone who looks at it that I am to be refused entry if I try to return to the US in the next five years. But crucially, back then, it was just a stamp on the passport. They didn't enter my name and offence into any computerised database.

'So when I left, I just threw the passport in the bin because I knew that I had the new one waiting at home for me at my Mam's. And when I went back to the States, I came back in on the same visa waiver that I had used the last time, only with my new passport.

'Freddie told me that this was a similar trick to one the Mexicans would use when they crossed the border for a weekend after overstaying their US welcome and then came back in with a new clean passport with no stamps against their names. The US authorities got wise to that weekend land border trick quickly, but not to the same trick pulled by someone flying back to Europe. I imagine that it's all computerised now, though – so that'll have stopped it all.'

So, you worked with and studied Freddie Roach for two years. What do you think you learned from Freddie?

'Well, if I have to choose one thing from Freddie, it's the idea that direction is better than hype. I also learned from Freddie that how you talk with a fighter is as important as what you show him or her technically because each fighter is different – and you have to know how to work with the personality to get results.'

Angelo Dundee, Muhammad Ali's trainer, was a master at this – what he called applied psychology. He talked about how Ali had to think that an idea was his own for him to put it into practice. So Dundee became skilled at planting the seeds of the ideas that he wanted Ali to act upon in Ali's brain weeks in advance. Then, when Ali *would* ask Dundee what he thought about this new idea, Dundee would say, "Great idea, champ," and smile with satisfaction. What matters is how well a fighter performs. A coach's job is to make that performance the best it can be, in the most efficient way possible.

'I learned from others too. From Buddy McGirt, I learned that boxing is all about you, and not the other dude. From Roger Mayweather, the uncle of Floyd, it was to go to the body. And from Manny Steward, the famous trainer from Detroit City's Kronk Gym, it was the logic of using one punch to guide an opponent into another more damaging punch, because Manny liked his power punchers.

'It would be an insult to Freddie to say that that was all I learned in my time with him because he has such an amazing brain and I learned so much from him.

'I'm a good student, too. If I like something, I will study it – relentlessly. So every single thing that Freddie did in training when I was there, I recorded in my memory, and I have used since: from how he wrapped hands, to how and when he said certain things to fighters. Freddie loves analysis and gameplans for fights, so I would talk with him about strategy all the time.

'I remember at the time that the gym was full of coaches talking about how good Freddie was. That he was an amazing coach who achieved excellent performances from his fighters. And then they would do things completely different to him. I just didn't get it. So I watched. I learned. And I thought,

"I'm going to train my fighters using the exact same methods Freddie has used to get his results." I mean, why look at an amazing and successful example and then do it another way? Sure, even if you don't understand why Freddie was doing it the way he was, just look at the proof in the success of his fighters that shows his methods work. And if you use the methods, and achieve success with them, then gradually over time you will come to understand the methods. So I studied Freddie as a trainer as much, if not more, than his great fighters. 'Teach, working with Freddie was a great time for me, and I'm not overstating the point to say that he saved me. He *saved* me. He gave me an opportunity that definitely, definitely, *definitely* changed the course of my life – *100 per cent*. I will be forever grateful to him for that because I'm still doing the thing that I love.'

The gratitude that Paddy feels towards Freddie is palpable. I can hear it in his voice and how it has moved from the vivid, excitable, charm-laced tone he uses to tell story after story with what appears to be a practised ease to a lower, more sombre and thoughtful one when he reflects on how Freddie's offer changed his life for the better. I can see it in his eyes too – an expression that has moved from the glint of the Irish raconteur to something much more profound.

When he finishes the last sentence, his voice is barely above a whisper and he is looking down at the kitchen table, his head bowed almost as if he is paying his respects.

I decide to lighten the mood a little to finish our conversation because while Kerry, Paddy's wife, has never been anything other than welcoming to me in her home, I'm conscious that it has already gone past 11pm and we've been talking for hours.

So leave me with a final story from your time with Freddie, I say to Paddy – something that will make the reader smile.

'What, like another story about me messing up, you mean?'

I nod.

'Well, we had Japanese cruiserweight Yosuke Nishijima fighting on a Don Chargin show. Don's passed away now but he did most of his promoting events in north California, so Freddie says he's gonna go fly up a few days early with Nishi, get me to drop him at the airport and then leave me to run things at the gym for a couple more days, and then I take his car to the airport, park it up, fly up to join Freddie and we both return on the same flight and take Freddie's car back to the gym – simple job.

'So, following the plan, Freddie goes up with Nishi. Two days later, I park Freddie's car at LAX [Los Angeles International Airport] and join him – job done. It was a great experience.

'I think we were in Sacramento and everyone loved Freddie up there because he'd done a lot of fighting there when he was a pro – and they still remembered him. Remember that Freddie was known in boxing when he was a fighter, but as a trainer as well. Back then, he had already trained around 11 world champions too. So, wherever we went, someone was like, "Hey Freddie!"

'The fight itself was a pretty routine affair. Nishi won without too many difficulties and we got on the plane to come home soon after the bout.

'When we were leaving LAX, Freddie asks me what car park I had parked in and where? I was like, "Dude, don't worry about it. I parked near a bus stop, so the car would be easy to find."

'He says, "Yeah, OK, but *which* car park?"

'I'm like, "What do you mean *which* car park?"

'Then, Freddie's tone changes and he goes, "No, Paddy, what are *you* talking about?"

'And I say, "What do you mean, 'What are *you* talking about?'"

'He says, "Paddy, there are at least *three* car parks!"

'And that's when it hits me and I say, "You're joking, right?"

'Freddie's shaking his head then and he says, "Paddy, tell me that you know where you parked my car? Tell me that you know which car park you parked my car in?"

'I couldn't tell him that and he just put his head in his hands saying, "Ah shit Paddy, what have you done?"

'"I've parked your car's what I've done," I say. "I just don't know where I parked it."

'I remember that I thought he was joking, and he thought I was joking, and neither of us could quite believe how much of a pain in the ass this was gonna be until we actually started walking around these massive car parks looking for his car.

'So we had to get on the bus and go to all the car parks. And each time Freddie's saying to me, "Is it this one? Can you remember?"

'And I'm like, "I just don't know."

'Luckily, we found Freddie's car in the second car park, but it was no quick fix, I can tell you.

'And he still let me work for him – even after all that!'

13

Froch v Groves – Getting the Rematch

SO WITH such an unsatisfactory outcome to the fight for George and a very large proportion of the viewing public, a Froch v Groves rematch was pretty much certain to happen then?

'Not at all, Teach,' says Paddy, sitting up and with a very serious expression on his face. 'Not at all. That's not how the business of boxing works.'

OK, so why not and what did you do? It seems obvious to me that in order to settle the controversy and answer the unanswered questions raised by the outcome of the fight, a rematch was necessary?

'Of course, and a lot of people thought like that. But it wasn't as simple as that.

'When we got back to the hotel after the fight, I said to George that he needed to appeal the decision in order to get a rematch. And George wasn't sure because he just didn't know whether if he appealed, which might be seen as an aggressive move, that he would secure the rematch. Maybe an appeal would mean he *didn't* get the rematch?

'I said, "Dude, do you honestly think that they're going to give you the rematch if you don't appeal? Tonight you did to Carl Froch what no one else has done to him. Do you think Carl's team are gonna call you up and say, 'Hey, George, will you come and do that to Carl again?'

'"Are you joking me? You won't get the rematch. I'm telling you now that you've got to go for that appeal."

'He said to me, "I dunno. Let me have a think about it."

'And then, that was it. Soon enough it was the next day and we were on the train travelling back south. Everyone was putting their opinions forward and we're hearing accusations being flung around suggesting that people have been cheating in order to ensure that George lost the fight. I'm sat opposite George and his wife Sophie, and we have Neil Sibley, George's lawyer, with us and then someone says to us that Howard Foster even said on Facebook that he thought George would be stopped in the fight.

'My ears pricked up then, and I say, "Howard Foster did what?" And this bloke says that Howard Foster *liked* a comment on Facebook that George would be finished in the ninth round. And remember, this was *before* the fight.

'I said to George, "Howard Foster actually *liked* that comment? That means his brain *agreed* with the comment. I made it clear to George that I didn't think that Foster had consciously set out to do anything untoward, because George's emotions were still high after the fight and he was using language like "that was a set-up".

That fact was I didn't think that Howard Foster was in any way questionable or that he had done anything consciously untoward in my view.

'*But* he did make a mistake, a professional mistake he should not have made, on Facebook. Because he *liked* that comment *before* the fight, then it stands to reason that he *expected* the stoppage to happen in the ninth, or at the very least the later stages of the fight. And what can't be argued with is that Howard Foster made the conscious decision *to agree* with that comment – and we are accountable for our opinions.

'That wasn't professional of him and it certainly wasn't in the spirit of a fair sporting contest. Even if he thought Froch was the stronger man, he should never have liked a Facebook comment like this.

'Immediately then, I asked if the *like* was still there. It was, and we got on Facebook and took a photograph of it for our records.

'Not too far from London, I asked George whether he had thought about the appeal. He had already spoken with Neil, and Neil had told him that the appeal would cost around £20,000. He was unsure about the appeal from a financial perspective. £20,000 is a lot of money to risk losing. So I said, "George, it's true that you risk the possibility of losing this money if you appeal. But you can know for certain, if you don't appeal and try and force this rematch, they won't give you a rematch.

'That's definite. So if you decide that you want to take that risk, I'll pay half that appeal for you. That's the proof of how much I believe you can win this appeal. I will pay £10,000 for you.

'He looked at me then as if to say, *"Really?"* And I said I'll pay half, so he said that we'd appeal. "But what do we do?" George says to me.

'"Listen, the last thing that you want to do in an appeal is arrive and start shouting and crying about how you've been wronged. They won't be interested. We need to produce this like a court case. I want a psychologist who specialises in advertising's report, a psychiatrist's report, a DVD of the fight with everything that Howard Foster said because he gave Carl three or four last warnings, and I wanted the volume raised so that these could be heard and I also want the words that are spoken by the referee along the bottom of the screen so there can be no mistakes.

'I also wanted the opinion of someone from advertising regarding the Facebook *like* about the ninth round because if an idea could be placed in the mind of an influential person, and who knows about influencing us more than advertising professionals, then surely that could have affected Howard Foster's judgement, especially when he heard the bell sound for the ninth round?'

So you genuinely thought that in some way, Howard Foster's objectivity as a ref could have been compromised before the fight?

'I've always been interested in advertising – the idea that you can adjust a man's thinking to get him to do what you want. And I've always seen a connection with boxing too, because that's what a fighter needs to do with his opponent.

The facts are the facts here, Teach. Combine the constant iron chin versus glass jaw narrative in the media and Howard Foster's *like* on Facebook and it has to be admitted that there is at least a possibility that the man was *influenced*. We're all only human – and advertisers know that.

'I made the connection with advertising in relation to the Facebook comment because if I were looking to buy a product, and I *liked* an advertisement for a particular brand on a Facebook advertisement, when I went into town to buy the product, and I saw the brand, I would be considerably more likely to buy the brand that I had liked than another version of the same product. I would have been *influenced* by advertising. That's how advertising works.

'When the bell for round nine went, it's not that Howard Foster did anything underhanded, I explained to George, it just must have been somewhere in his head that this round was where everything *could* go wrong. So, when George did get hit, and it did seem to start going wrong, surely there must have been an element of, "I knew this would happen. I've got to stop this to keep him safe."

'Howard Foster wasn't being underhand, or nasty or vindictive. The opposite is true. He felt he was protecting George. He hadn't said himself that George would be stopped in the ninth. Arguably, he had just *agreed* that the fight would play out like that. And now it was. So he was stopping it on safety grounds. Referees are under pressure. We've lost two men, God bless them, only recently. We lose lives in this sport. They have to do their best for fighters, and that's what Foster was trying to do. I wasn't disputing his moral motivation. I was disputing his *objectivity* – because it seemed like he may have already decided what was going to happen in the fight, before it happened, whether he recognised that or not. Again, not because the fight was fixed, or anything like that. And not at all because he was dishonest. He was just unwise to like that comment, and you can't but wonder if somehow it played on his subconscious as the fight played out.

'George thought that my plan was all a bit detailed and I said, "Look, it's gonna cost us £30,000 when we factor in the reports probably. But I know one thing, if we don't do this then we won't get the rematch. If we do, then the £30,000 won't matter."

'George was set to do it and I insisted that we do it properly, like a court case. I asked Neil to organise everything that we needed and when the time came, we all dressed sharp and ready for business, which was important.'

So where was the appeal? Was it in the UK?

'No, it was the IBF who were the sanctioning body so we had to go to the States, New Jersey. I said to George, "Let's set up some meetings while we're out there with Golden Boy [Promotions] and Lou DiBella to see if anything might come of having a chat with them. You're a free agent. You can meet who you want to. They'll have all heard about the controversy of your fight with Carl, so this is a good time to get talking."

'I went out to New Jersey with George and Neil Sibley, the lawyer. We arrived a couple of days before the hearing, so myself and George went out for dinner with Lou DiBella and heard what he had to say because at that time, George didn't have a promoter and we thought that Lou would be potentially a good choice.

'Next day, we had the appeal meeting. We all arrived in our suits and sat down for the hearing. George said hardly anything because it would have been difficult for him, or anyone, with so much riding on the outcome to avoid becoming emotional – and this hearing was supposed to be about facts. I asked Neil to lead off as he was our legal representative. I would chime in if I thought it was necessary regarding the psychological reports or how advertising influences the brain. The DVD pretty much spoke for itself.

'George was really tense in the meeting, which was understandable, but we handled it all well. When we finished the meeting, I didn't know that we had succeeded in persuading the panel of our point of view, but I knew we had done well. I could read their body language and they were clearly taken aback by the detail in our appeal.

'It was 2014 then and I'd been 17 years as a pro coach. I'd been around. I had heard enough people tell me how they had gone to appeals and failed to persuade the panel, so I'd listened to what they had told appeals panels that didn't work. Failed appeals tended to be structured around telling the panel what you wanted them to do. Well, that ain't gonna work, is it? You *tell* a man aggressively what you want him to do and that he has to do it – well, that man is most of the time gonna look for a way *not* to do it just because you told him to do it.

'We decided to take our appeal from a different perspective, saying, "Guys, this is just about the facts. We're not coming in here saying someone was right and someone was wrong. We just want the right thing to be done. The facts tell us that a professional mistake has been made. An error has been made. All we want is to rectify a mistake. We're not looking for punishment or blame. What we are saying is that as an error has been made, the fight should not have been stopped, George deserves his round ten. We can't go back in time but we can schedule a rematch at least in order to rectify the mistake.

'We presented how a psychologist who operated in the highest courts in England had studied the fight's stoppage. How the psychologist had looked at the idea that Howard Foster had been at least influenced by the comments surrounding George that he had *liked* on Facebook. And crucially, that the psychologist had agreed that the influence of the comments and Howard Foster's own seeming agreement with the comments about George could have had a strong bearing on his decision to stop the fight for what he felt was George's safety. A decision that was, from our point of view, unfair – especially when Carl had been allowed to continue when he had been hurt but George had not been extended the same opportunity. So what was this difference if not the influence of the media?

'We reinforced the fact that Carl had been given more than one opportunity for the fight to continue when he was hurt. Yet George hadn't been given any. That wasn't fair. We drew attention to the notes Neil had made in the pre-fight meeting where I had asked that the idea of George's perceived weaker chin not be taken into account, and the fight not unfairly stopped on account of this idea. These were official minutes taken by a lawyer – so they had weight behind them. We made sure that the panel could see that I had brought up the concern that the fight could be stopped – and exactly for the reason that it was.

'So when we left, I felt pretty good about the meeting. The panel thanked us for our time and I could tell that they had bought what we were saying. Of course, you never know. They could have been thinking, "How do we get out of this one? But they knew that what we had said was articulate, concise, precise and based in evidence. It would be hard for them to pick holes in our reasoning, and that had been the main thing that I had wanted to achieve – a presentation where there was no room for argument.

'As we were leaving the building, George was ahead of me on the escalator to the hotel and I said to him, "How are you feeling, George?"

'He turned to me and I could see he was really emotional.

'I said to him, "George, be cool man. That was probably the best presentation that they've ever had. If there is ever an appeal that is going to be won, it's this one, for you."

'He wasn't in a talking mood right then so I suggested we have a drink and we decided to find an Irish bar and get some Guinness inside of us. Neil couldn't immediately join us because of some notes he needed to check but he reminded us to take it easy because we were flying out later that day to go and meet Golden Boy.

'Me and George find an Irish bar across the street and order Guinness, which they serve up to us, and it looks like pig slop – but that's New York Guinness. I get talking to the waitress, flirting a bit, asking what else she has and soon enough we're having the *craic* with the waitress, the barman, they're all drinking with us and we're getting well oiled as Neil gets to the bar and joins us. Before you know it, we're all drunk – and we had to catch a plane in two hours.

'When we got to the airport, by the time we got through and into the departure area, we hadn't had a drink for a while and that's the worst thing, isn't it? That's when you start to feel it. And then we see the announcement that our plane is delayed a couple of hours.

'At this point, the alcohol is starting to leave George's system and he's starting to get a bit hungover and he says, "Forget this, coach, I'm going back to the hotel."

'I say, "You can't do that, we're meeting Golden Boy in LA tomorrow. We have to go and listen to what they have to say."

'He wasn't having any of it and he was insisting that he was going to go back to the hotel in New York.'

'I'm like, "George, don't screw this up. We're here now."

'And so he stayed.

'A few weeks later, after we had returned to England, we were informed that we had won the appeal. George would get his rematch with Carl. George was elated. We were all elated.'

In the end, did George sign with Golden Boy or Lou DiBella?

'Well, in the time between returning from LA and hearing about the appeal results, George told me that he had signed with [promoters] the Sauerlands.

'I knew that George was talking to the Sauerlands but I had wanted him to talk with Eddie Hearn too.'

It's getting late again and as we finish talking, I remind myself that after successfully winning their appeal, Paddy and George would go on to contest the IBF and WBA super middleweight titles at that now-famous night in front of 80,000 people at London's Wembley Stadium.

Oh, and remember, Carl Froch was there too!

14

'Wartime' – Vatche Wartanian

I'M MEETING one of Paddy's fighters from his time working in LA and Las Vegas around the year 2000. Vatche 'Wartime' Wartanian is his name. He is a Swedish-Armenian super welterweight with a 10-4-3 professional record who was based in the States.

As I gather my notepad and voice recorder together, I'm thinking about the hyperbole of the fighting name 'Wartime'. I'm impressed by it. The name alone is enough to make anyone wonder about the explosive nature of his fighting style. But I imagine that it came with some pressure attached too. I mean, it's a lot to live up to, isn't it? If you were looking down a boxing card and you saw a fighter with *that* name, you're going to have high expectations, aren't you?

For Paddy, Vatche is *more* than a fighter he used to train. Vatche is Godfather to Paddy's oldest son D.J. and the more time I spend with them, the more I can see how close they are. The relationship between this fighter and his ex-coach is particularly strong, which is another reason why I wanted to talk to Vatche.

I wanted to know how what must have started as a business relationship metamorphosed into this friendship.

It's a Sunday afternoon. I've arranged to meet Paddy at his local pub round the corner from his boxing gym in the centre of town. When I walk into the pub, it is full of punters eating traditional Sunday roast.

Initially, I don't see Paddy. I hear him, though, laughing and talking in the slightly louder way that most of us do when we are lubricated by the drink.

When I locate Paddy, I notice that he has settled into a comfortable area of the pub that he has made his own and that one or two pints of Guinness have been consumed already.

'Hey Teach!' Paddy shouts as I walk over to the table he is sitting at. Paddy is dressed for the occasion. He is wearing a wide-brimmed hat, tipped at a slight angle, much larger than a fedora, I think, though I am no expert. He has on a velvet jacket over a waistcoat, very smart shoes and he is carrying an umbrella, which reminds me of the canes carried by gentlemen in the Victorian period.

Paddy has clearly made an effort. Maybe it's because it's a Sunday? Maybe it's because Vatche has come a long way to spend time with him? Paddy and Vatche are accompanied by two other men who smile at me genially.

Paddy points to where he wants me to sit, between Vatche, who it turns out has also been known as 'The Warrior', and a younger black man called Alex. Alex is exceptionally polite as he introduces himself to me. I shake his hand and notice that he is drinking a slimline tonic and carefully watching what he is eating, refusing the bar snacks that are on offer. At 22, it transpires that he is one of Uganda's current amateur champions and that he has been selected to represent his country at the Olympics, so I am not surprised that he is taking care of himself.

One of the other men, a coach Paddy has worked with before, generously offers to buy me a drink. We have never met but as Paddy has vouched for me, I can only assume that he already thinks that I'm OK.

Where I sit, Vatche is to my right. From the moment I meet him, he makes me feel welcome – and he can *really* talk.

Paddy had tipped me off about this fact, but nevertheless, I am impressed with his skill as a storyteller. He is clearly practised at holding an audience and later he tells me that he is an actor in Swedish movies, and that he considered a career in stand-up comedy for a while.

I can see why.

I have entered a conversation that had been developing for a while before I arrived. Vatche is explaining how Europeans living in the States sometimes found the insular attitude and limited awareness of the world around them of the average American really annoying.

'How do you mean?' Paddy asks Vatche.

'Look,' says Vatche, sitting upright and leaning into us all slightly as if he is letting us into a secret. 'I was training at Johnny Tocco's gym in Las Vegas and there's this really attractive woman watching me train. I don't take much notice and just continue with my workout. As I finish off and start my stretching routine, the girl comes over and asks, "Where are you from?"

'"Sweden," I tell her and she says, "Where's that?"

'So I say, "It's in Europe."

'"Oh, Europe," she says enthusiastically. "I've been to Europe."

'"Have you," I say, trying to be friendly. "Where did you go?"

'"Mexico," she says.

'I look at her a bit confused by what she has said, but it doesn't seem to put her off and she asks me, "Do you have, like, televisions in Sweden?"

'I don't remember what I said to her then. I think I just walked off. Americans, man!' says Vatche, rolling his eyes and sitting back as Paddy belly laughs while nodding his head in agreement.

As I begin to find out more about him, Vatche informs me that while he is Swedish, he is of Armenian descent – and that this is important to him. In fact, he hopes to relocate to Armenia in the near future having bought some land as a well-chosen investment of the money he made while boxing. It turns out that as well as being an actor and running a restaurant, Vatche intends to open a walnut farm and a shop specialising in the wine and cheeses of Armenia.

And as if this is not enough to give the casual man an inferiority complex, it turns out that Vatche is something of a polyglot.

As a teacher, I lived in Spain for a couple of years and learned to speak a passable form of Andalucian Spanish, which I've always been proud of. But Vatche tells me he can speak Swedish, English, Armenian and Spanish – *and* he is teaching himself Russian!

Oh, and just so that I remain anchored to the point of why I'm *actually* speaking to Vatche, he reminds me that he was also a successful fighter, winning Swedish titles and boxing out of three countries over his career.

In conversation with Vatche, I reflect on Gene Tunney's famous comment after one of Jack Dempsey's entourage before their world title fight – which Tunney won – questioned Tunney's sexuality because he saw the heavyweight challenger reading Shakespeare. When Tunney was informed that his masculinity had been questioned because he was reading, he is reputed to have responded, 'Why does the world heavyweight champion have to be illiterate?'

Clearly Vatche is intelligent, sophisticated and cultured. He is also a boxer.

I love the way that Vatche challenges the accepted stereotype often attached to a boxer's level of academic intelligence – namely, that they are limited in this area.

Vatche is right up my street. And if anyone is still labouring under the illusion that boxers simply think with their fists, then consider this. Mike Tyson, while incarcerated in prison, read literature that scans like the set texts on a Liberal Arts-type degree course: Niccolo Machiavelli's *The Prince*, Sun Tzu's *The Art of War*, Marcus Aurelius, Alexandre Dumas, Ernest Hemingway, Karl Marx, Leo Tolstoy and Voltaire to name a few.

I know that for every cerebral, intelligent, sophisticated boxer such as the Greatest, Muhammad Ali, or undisputed heavyweight champions Gene Tunney and Lennox Lewis, I could be offered an example of a savage beast of a man consumed by his primal desire to do battle.

But that dichotomy isn't exclusive to boxers, is it?

It is not hard to see that Vatche is still sparring and training. Even though Paddy makes the odd joke about his friend having put on a little weight from his super welterweight days, Vatche's physique is impressive. His skin tone is lightly olive in the way of southern Spain, or Greece, or the southern Balkans. His hair is shaved very close to his head.

Most impressive to me, though, are his eyes.

As he tells funny stories to us about his boxing experiences, they twinkle with mischief. And then, as soon as he starts to talk seriously about his old profession and the level of intensity needed in order to be a success, his expression shifts. There is now steel in those eyes that moments ago seemed full of humour and laughter. I can only imagine how he might have used them to intimidate an opponent in a staredown.

I drink a couple of pints while scribbling notes as I listen to Paddy and Vatche reminisce about their time together in America. Then, as Paddy realises we have been talking for a couple of hours and run out of the roast potatoes the landlord has been bringing over to us as snacks, I am invited back to Paddy's for a meal.

As we walk into Paddy's kitchen, his wife Kerry is putting the final touches to a roast – with a twist. Kerry is Jamaican and I can smell the distinctive blend of herbs and spices from the island permeating her kitchen.

Paddy tells us all where to sit around his kitchen table and as before I am positioned between Vatche and Alex, and opposite Paddy.

I have never eaten a roast like this. The seasoned chicken is amazing and the gravy for the roast potatoes is spicy, not just salty like a lot of English gravy.

In front of my plate, rather than a wine glass or a glass to receive water, there is a shot glass.

Smiling, Paddy pours out a transparent fluid that I have tasted in his company before. The spirit we are drinking with our meal is Irish moonshine, or *potcheen* in its anglicised form. The Irish spelling for this liquor is poitin and its name derives from the Irish word for a hangover – *poit*. Imagine a more powerful but better-tasting type of vodka and then you have potcheen. Some tasters consider potcheen a toxic drink, probably on account of its unpredictable strength. Those who brew it vary the strength of the product and it is regularly between 40 per cent and 90 per cent proof. It's difficult to tell the strength of the liquor before you drink it, though, as it is brewed by Irish people for Irish people and decanted into whatever glass bottle is to hand. So it's a bit of a gamble with your insides. To my palate, though, it's a good drink, though maybe not as an accompaniment to food!

After we have eaten, I manage to sit down with Vatche and ask him about his memories of how he got into professional boxing in the US as a Swede and how difficult this was.

'It was difficult, man. Back then in the late 1990s and early 2000s, it wasn't like it is now. Organisations like UFC and the way people use the internet to follow their favourite fighters has opened things up for fighters from lots of different countries who are based in the States now, but it wasn't like that back in my day. The American management companies and promoters only signed Yankees and a lot of Latinos. They liked the Latinos because it was good business. If they paid the Americans millions of dollars, then the Latinos for the same level of fight got hundreds of thousands instead. They would sign Mexicans, tell them they were fighting in a week's time, and pay them peanuts – and the Mexicans would do it.

'I didn't want that. I wanted things to be fair. It had to work for me. But it wasn't always like that. You learn this quickly in boxing. I remember one time I was called with one day's notice to fight Alex Hernandez – *one day*! But I fought him and I beat him. It's not a good way to work, though.'

So how did boxing start for you?

'I was 15. I was fighting a lot on the streets in Sweden, you know. Like anywhere else in the world, Sweden has its tough areas. Then my friend tells me that he's found a boxing gym and that we can go there and fight as much as we want. So I went and it was like a beginners' session. Most of the people who were there had gone for different reasons than me. I was there because I wanted to fight. Most of the kids there seemed to have been bullied at school and their dads had taken them to the gym saying, "Now you're gonna learn how to punch back properly son." Vatche deepens his voice to an exaggerated growl to sound like an angry father.

'I didn't go to the gym to box. I went there to fight. I remember the training. I didn't take to the discipline at first because it was like, "Number one, throw the jab. Then practise the jab. Number two, slip the jab." Then we would practise slipping the jab. But I was just like, bam!, hitting things hard straight away and following the technique instruction well and quicker than most.

'One of the coaches said to me, "You know what, you're talented. You have to move up to the competition group."

'So I did, and on my first night the coach says to me, "Vatch, what you've been doing for the last two weeks, you need to do to this guy over there." I was 15 and the guy in the opposite corner to me was 27. He wasn't a brilliant boxer but he was older and more developed than me.

'The first thing he did for me was hit me – bam! And he broke my nose. After that, I became really motivated because I thought to myself, "One day I'm going to kick his ass" and I started training really hard. [I was] learning and starting to really understand boxing. But in my fourth fight, I fought a former Swedish youth champion in the Swedish youth championships – and I beat him. After that, I started noticing that I was getting written about in the papers, so I realised I had ability.'

Who inspired you as fighters? Any Swedes?

'Of course, Sweden has had many champions. But in particular, Ingemar Johannson. He was a real legit champion from back in the day. And now, we have Badou Jack, a real legit champion too – a great fighter.'

How did you get the ring names 'The Warrior' and 'Wartime'?

'It was Paddy who gave me the "Warrior" name. I was "Wartime" before that. My last name is Wartanian, but it's pronounced *Vartanian*, and the Americans couldn't say that, so "Wartime" was something they could say easily. The idea of the name "Wartime" came when a boxing trainer from my gym heard me introduced in the ring as Vatche Wartanian. The next time I was at the gym, when I entered, he shouted at me, "Hey, Wartime! Wartime is in the gym."

'I kept the name in the States and then Paddy changed it to "The Warrior" when I relocated to Europe.'

Given the differences in political attitudes, and the tensions across Europe, this seems like a pretty astute decision, I say to Vatche.

'Yeah, it was. It also suited me because I was busy all the time. Not like Mexican busy, but I was always active in the ring and punching.'

How did you meet Paddy and start working with him as a coach?

'I was good friends with Justin "The Destroyer" Juuko, three times world title challenger, and he introduced me to Paddy. My first trainer in the States was Miguel Diaz. I had two fights with him but I wasn't comfortable with the relationship. We were just sparring for training and then he'd be like, "Do six rounds on the heavy bag, two on the speedball," and it didn't feel like I was being *directed*.

'So, I switched to a guy called Casey Higgins and did one fight with him. And then I said to Juuko, "The trainers these days suck, you know. I'd be better off training myself." Juuko says to me that he knows this guy and he took me down to the gym where Laila Ali was training. That's where I met Paddy.

'After what Juuko had told me about Paddy, I just thought that he was for me so I walked in, walked up to Paddy and said, "Justin has told me all about you. You're gonna train me." And we started from there.'

So you trusted Justin Juuko's judgement and started to work with Paddy. What made him a good coach for you?

'Variation – there was a lot of variation in his training. He reminded me of my amateur days. Paddy went into the relationship with his whole heart when he trained you. And he never talked about money with me. He just wanted to make me a champion. And that's how we got close to each other too. The relationship was about far more than business from the beginning. We always help each other too. We became friends. Paddy is the only coach I had where this happened apart from my friend in Sweden, who trained me for a while too, but we were friends before he trained me. Every coaching relationship I had, other than with Paddy, was just business.'

There is a pattern here. When I talk to Paddy's ex-pros and current pros, they almost all say the same thing about him. That the relationship was more than just a coach and athlete relationship. That Paddy genuinely and sincerely cared about them as people, not just as professional athletes. And it seems that this was a major factor in his success as a trainer – his credibility with his fighters and their knowledge that he believed in them, which meant, of course, that they believed in him too.

I tell Vatche that he is not the first person to describe Paddy like this.

'I saw it first hand. There were many people where Paddy said, "I don't need to train you – go."

'And people would be like, "Paddy, how can you let him go? He's gonna bring in a lot of money."

'"I don't care," Paddy would say. "A lot of money, but with headaches. I don't need that headache."

'A little less money, a better life, and no headache. That's Paddy's way. And I'm like that too.

'Paddy's training methods were better than what I had experienced before. Every day in the gym was something new. And we were always working on my weaknesses. He wasn't happy until I had got something right and I like that. I don't like to do something halfway and then go and do something else. And even though we were focusing on my weaknesses, there was variation around the training all the time. I never got bored. I never got burned out.'

Vatche smiles and laughs suddenly. 'Well, that's not entirely true. I remember I had fought Mariano Flores the week before I fought Chris McDonagh in 2002. I won both fights, but I felt burned out then. And that's one of Paddy's great strengths. He saw that and made me take some time off to rest – and that wasn't usual. In the States, you see, everyone was in it for the money, you understand? They don't care about you. They care about the money. If you fight, you make money for them. If you don't make money, you're nothing to them. Not Paddy.'

What are your best memories of working with Paddy?

'Wow, there are so many. I think the best memory is the Alex Francisco Velardez fight in Vegas 2003 and my fight with Chris McDonagh as both of them were undefeated at the time, and I beat both of them. The Velardez fight, man, I beat him with one day's notice! They called me on Friday and I fought him on Saturday.'

What do you think allowed that to happen, I ask him? Were you so exceptionally well conditioned and trained that you could compete at that level at such short notice?

'I always believed in myself and I remember Paddy asking me if I was sure I wanted to take the fight because from the opponent's team's point of view, they just wanted a win and probably thought I wouldn't be ready, so it would be an easier fight. Paddy was looking out for me. But I was always prepared. I was always training. And then Paddy says to me, "Vatch, I've seen him fight. He's a southpaw and you're gonna beat him."

'I'm not stupid, so I had some reservations about the fight. But Paddy convinced me I could do it. In the end, he said to me that I would have to take some chances if I wanted some success. I wasn't American, so things wouldn't come easy for me. I would have to get noticed and prove myself.'

Did you have a gameplan to take on a southpaw?

'I had 93 amateur fights, and I fought a lot of southpaws in the amateurs, so it never bothered me. I never watched my opponents. Paddy did. And Paddy designed our tactics. See, for me, if I watch a guy I'm gonna fight take on five different guys, none of them are me. I followed Paddy's gameplan during the fight. If I thought of something new during the fight, I would execute it, but mostly I would stick to the gameplan.

'I was really proud of winning the Velardez fight. I won it in style. We really thought we were going to go somewhere then. And I remember the promoter of the fight saying, "If you take this fight, it's a step up for you. And if you win, there will be people interested in you."

'After the fight, there was talk of promotional companies being interested in me, like, "Hey Vatch, Top Rank are interested, blah, blah, blah, you know." So, three months later, I fought and beat Marlon Cortez – but we never heard from any of the big promoters again.'

I can sense Vatche's frustration with the business side of boxing as we talk, and it's clear that he feels that if he had an anglicised American name and background, then he might have been a more attractive prospect to the money men who ran the sport.

'That's when I got bored of boxing and Paddy says to me, "Hey Vatch, I got an offer from Germany."

'So, I went with Paddy, fought two fights in Potsdam, and won them both. But I'd lost something by this point. I took two more fights after that, against pretty average fighters who I know I could have beaten. One I drew and one I lost. I just wasn't hungry any more. Mentally and physically, I was struggling because even if I won, what was going to happen? I wasn't going to hear from anyone, was I? And without that goal, it was hard to motivate myself.'

Do you think the business side of boxing took away your passion for the sport, because you fought 93 times for nothing as an amateur?

'Yeah, it took away a lot of my passion. Then three years ago, at 41 years old, I was re-born. I fought a combat against a 23-year-old guy and I outboxed him. I outboxed him *totally*. I was so hungry because if I beat him, they promised me a shot at the Swedish title.

'And then they did it again. I didn't get the shot. So I was like, "Fuck this."'

Do you think in boxing, though we might not want to admit it as fans, that those people who get the chances and opportunities are not always the best fighters?

'100 per cent,' Vatche says with steel in his eyes and total conviction. 'I beat that guy totally and still got nothing. It's like this. When we were in Las Vegas, I sparred a lot of champions. Some I was better than and some got the better of me. That means that if I could have fought the right champion on the right night, I could have been a champion. If I had been moved right by a promoter, I would have been a champion.

'There are several fighters who I got the better of who went on to have world title fights or become world champions – and they weren't better than me.'

How do you think they secured the chances that you didn't? It calls into question the idea of a fair sport with the best fighters taking on the best fighters, doesn't it?

'Boxing isn't fair. Perhaps no sport is fair. But the fight game isn't fair at all. Look at the UFC, for example. There's a guy called Gegard Mousasi, he's in Bellator now and he's won a belt. But he never got a shot in UFC. I remember in his last press conference he questioned why he hadn't been given a title shot. He asked if it was because of his colour, because he had beaten the top guys in the UFC.

'With me, in my time, I know that by and large the English signed English, Americans signed Americans and Latinos, the French signed the French and so on. It's not just me that struggled to get interest as an Armenian-Swede. I knew guys with similar backgrounds to me who had won bronze medals in the Olympics, which is what Deontay Wilder did for the US, and they weren't getting picked up either. Look at Justin Juuko – he didn't get the chances he deserved either.

'It's simple really. Unless you are a Lomachenko, who could sell anywhere because he is so spectacular and one of a kind, then it works like this for a promoter. If I am an English promoter and I have the choice of Jamie Cox, an English fighter, and Vatche Wartanian, and both are good at what they do, who do you choose?'

He doesn't wait for me to answer his rhetorical question.

'Same in America,' he says with a sense of concrete finality.

I want to lighten the mood as Vatche has become increasingly more pensive as we talk about his frustrations with the machinations of the boxing industry. I ask him about any times that he found particularly funny or ridiculous when he was with Paddy.

Vatche's expression changes and his eyes relax as he tells me, 'Paddy was a personal trainer with regular people as well as fighters at the time.'

I love how Vatche refers to those of us who are not fighters as *regular* people. I wonder if all fighters do that? Yesterday, I listened to an interview with Deontay Wilder in which he described all fighters as different kinds of human beings. He said that to be in the fight game, fighters must have a 'mental illness' of some kind – that fighters were 'crazy'.

He said it with laughter in his voice, but he meant it too. And I think he must be right, at least in a way, because to walk forward voluntarily into a life of pain in the hurt business must take a 'special', or at least 'different', type of person.

Someone who is not – *regular*.

'Paddy lent me his car once, a big jeep, and when I was driving it, I accidentally put it in reverse and I must have driven into something, though I didn't know it at the time.

'Later, when I have given him his car back, Paddy calls me and says, "Hey Vatch, did you smash my client's car?"

'I had no idea it wasn't his. And the car was like a tank so I had no idea that I had damaged it. I had to pay for the repairs, and they weren't cheap!

'The best memory I have is when Muhammad Ali came. Paddy was training his daughter Laila at the time too. Ali was doing magic tricks and entertaining everyone.

'Ali stayed with us for one and a half hours. It was amazing. I fought two days later and I must have been inspired by the great man because I won by a knockout! And even better, Ali was at ringside watching me. That was good.

'And then, on top of that, after my fight when I'm on the way to the showers, there's a knock on my door and it's Thomas "The Hitman" Hearns. And he says to me, "Great knockout, man!"

'I have the picture at home: me, Paddy, Juuko and "The Hitman".'

Are you still in boxing in some capacity, I ask Vatche?

'I train, all the time, and I still spar. I do good in sparring still against the young guys, but it doesn't really pay so I can't put much effort into it. I help the young guys and I am organising my business affairs so that I can move to Armenia and open my walnut farm and wine cellar/charcuterie. I intend to take out my own wine brand too. I'm looking at 120 acres of land – around 12 football fields – full of walnut trees.'

Did boxing look after you, I ask? Did you get enough out of the sport to be able to look after yourself?

'I didn't make no millions, but I always did business on the side. So my boxing money I would always send home to my accountant in Sweden and we looked after it wisely. Boxing did look after me a little financially, but it is the experiences of other countries that it gave me that I value the most. With the national team, Sweden, I saw America, England and Germany. As a pro, I added plenty more too. Boxing has given me life experience. I have friends all over the world. Even today, I can call Russia or Cuba or places like that – I have friends there.

'So I'm not complaining. I'm just a little bit regretful that I didn't get to the Olympics for Sweden. I was eliminated in the trials. And as a pro, I would have loved a title. I was going for a big title, like the WBC, but I would have been happy with a lesser title. It just never happened for me.

'I know I trained hard. I know I beat some great fighters. It frustrates me a bit that Alex Velardez became a WBC champion after I had beaten him, and I was his only loss. Top Rank called me after Alex had won and I was like, "Why are you calling me to talk to me about how another guy won? You told me that I would get my chance, and I didn't." They were straight with me and said, "'Yeah, but Vatch, you know, he's Mexican and he's easy to sell here in America, *blah, blah, blah*."

'That's when I decided, "I'm outta here."

'I don't think that sport today is about honour. It's about money. I think that it's much harder to be an Olympic champion than a pro champion. There is only one Olympic title, but you know how many there are in the pro game. You can secure just one of those titles and make millions.'

How do you manage this frustration psychologically, I ask Vatche. I don't want to annoy him, but he has been very clear about how he felt cheated by the sport as we've talked.

'That's what I find hardest. But then I think again and I say, "I'm healthy and I don't have any problems – and isn't that the name of the game?" I took a chance on boxing, and I got plenty out of it. I also took part in 110 fights and I've come out of the game unharmed. That's a lot to be thankful for.'

It's getting late, and I'm conscious that Vatche has been talking to me for a long time. Paddy has just arrived with a bottle of whisky too, so it looks like I might become less capable of interviewing as the evening wears on.

As Paddy walks over to us, Vatche shouts, 'I think I'm his closest fighter, you know. He's been involved in training 13 or 14 champions, but we are closest. Even if we didn't make no millions. I'm gonna tell you something, Teach. Even if I had millions, I wouldn't live in a mansion. I like to help people instead. I'm teaching my kids that too. To be content, and have what you need, that's happiness. I like to travel, that's where I spend my money. If I get extra money, I hope to be able to help people too. It makes me happiest to sit round my kitchen table with 20 friends who are not fake and have a good time. And then the next day, they say, "Vatch, you come over to my place." I don't need the fast cars and the material things – because they don't matter.

'But friendships do.'

Friendships like the one that Vatche has with his ex-coach and now lifelong friend Paddy.

15

Froch v Groves II

IBF and WBA super middleweight titles
Wembley Stadium, May 2014

SO HOW was George's preparation for Froch II? He must have been on it with how important the fight was to you all? How did training camp pan out? Did you do anything differently in the build-up to the rematch?

'Well, remembering the weight problem from the first fight, I said to George that this time he would not be in charge of it. It's now on The Father's shoulders. He's responsible. [I said to George], "You dropped too much weight before the first fight, and I don't like that. You performed great, absolutely, but everything can be improved, so we'll do it like this. There's no way it can be good for you to lose that much weight the night before a fight. So, if you don't have to put yourself under that pressure, surely you will be even better."

'It was down to The Father, and boy did he have George's conditioning on point. He was perfect.

'I returned to the psychological warfare really quickly in the preparations for the rematch and I told George that Carl would believe everything that he would say because what he told him he would do in the first fight, he did – and this would be on Carl's mind.

'So I said to George, "Here is what we're going to tell Carl. You're gonna tell him that you'll knock him out within three rounds. I'm gonna tell the reporters round five."

'That confused George a little and he said, "Why are you going to tell him differently to me?"

'"So we can get five rounds out of the psychological ploy. So we can have him wondering what's going on. Have him thinking about us for five rounds and not his own game. Round three will come and he will expect something big to happen. But if it doesn't happen, he can't think, "OK, I'm fine now" because his coach [Paddy] said round five, not round three. So we'll keep him anxious and mentally busy for five rounds. Not knowing when you're going to jump on him, but expecting it at the same time. If we can keep him thinking then he's either going to over-react or under-react to something that you do. Either way, you can use that to your advantage.'

So what about those press conferences between Carl and George? It seemed like they really did dislike each other, and that this had intensified from the first fight. What was the thing with the Rubik's cube, I ask?

George had brought the puzzle along with him to the press conferences and he would work on it while Carl was talking in a deliberate attempt to suggest that he was bored and would rather be somewhere else. Is that right?

'That was all George's idea, not mine.'

What was the idea behind it? Froch said that it really did get on his nerves.

'See, I think that actually got on Carl's *nerves* rather than on his *mind*. You know that saying, "Do something to me once, shame on you. Do something to me twice, shame on me." I think there was a bit of that. To me, the mind games needed to be based on the boxing. We didn't really need mind games. It was more *proof* games now. Because we had shown Carl that what we said, we would do. So all we had to do was make sure that he knew that. When you start with too much of the mind games, then the opponent thinks, "I've seen this before" and the effect is gone. I think there was a bit of that here.

'George was trying to expand on the "everything for a reason" thing we had used, but it didn't quite pay off. One thing we do know, though, is that George can complete a Rubik's cube pretty quickly!'

Paddy bursts out laughing at the memory.

'I remember in the press conference when George started playing with it, thinking that he wouldn't be able to complete it, but he did – so fair play.'

Do you think that Carl was more prepared mentally the second time around?

'Carl was more ready for the psychological games in the second fight, absolutely. He had employed a psychologist to help him. But he was still feeling the pressure. Look at his breathing in the second fight. I could hear it from early on in our corner, even though he was well conditioned.

'And that's stress.'

Paddy imitates the heavy breathing of Carl and it reminds me of what someone who is really out of shape sounds like doing circuits in his boxing gym. 'On reflection, you can perhaps play too many games with someone, though, can't you?' I think about this question that is hanging in the air for a moment before bringing the conversation around to the fight itself. 'Before the fight,' says Paddy, 'when we were still in the hotel room and ready to go to the arena, George asked to speak with me, just him and me. We went to a quiet room and he says to me, "Before we go out, I just want you to know that I trust you completely and I know that you've got me ready for this fight completely. I believe everything we've been doing." So I was feeling good.'

The second fight was at Wembley Stadium, London, in front of a post-war record crowd of over 80,000 spectators. It was a huge event. The fight was what the media call a 'mainstream crossover event' – a sporting occasion that attracts people who aren't necessarily big boxing fans but will pay big money for a one-off event.

What do you remember about that, I ask Paddy?

'I think that the event had crossover appeal. The public thought that there was a man, George, who had been hard done by. Here was a man many thought had been done out of an amazing victory and that was plain wrong.'

I suppose the underdog idea played well with the British public. George had been the underdog in the first fight, and yet in many people's eyes he was on his way to winning the fight. The British love an underdog – especially one who might win or who ends up cheated out of his right. The public wanted to be there now to see George proved right, or for Carl to stamp his mark conclusively this time around.

'It's amazing how fickle fight fans can be, Teach. Remember how after the fight was stopped the crowd who were earlier booing George were now doing that to Carl and celebrating George.

'But boxing crowds being boxing crowds, Howard Foster, the referee, wasn't going to be interviewed, and Carl was – so they booed him, even though 30 minutes ago they loved him. Probably, people didn't even plan to boo at all. But it only takes a couple of people to start and it sort of catches on, doesn't it? Especially when people are in a heightened emotional state.'

Obviously, the controversy and drama of the first fight, the sense that George may have been 'cheated' and that Carl was somehow 'lucky' and had a point to prove, promoted the fight already. But I'm sure that the rivalry between the fighters and the way George promoted the fight, and his continued rivalry with Carl, had a massive influence on the ticket sales.

Anyone who watches the press conferences or media stunts set up to advertise the fight can see that George did a brilliant job turning the fight into a drama between two diametrically opposed characters. And to me, without the character George presented himself as so knowingly contrasting so acutely with Carl's, the fight couldn't have sold in the same way to such a wide audience.

I ask Paddy if he sees it the same way.

'George sold the fight really. He was the only one doing the interviews. If you think of the recent build-up to Ruiz v Joshua [2019], AJ was nowhere to be seen really. He got his head down, did what he needed to do, kept things low-key and focused in his training camp. Carl did that in the second fight.'

This is something that Carl readily admits in his autobiography, admitting that he trained and focused for the second fight in a way he hadn't for the first because he knew how dangerous George really was.

'Carl didn't really do much promotion for the second fight,' Paddy continues, 'but George sold the ass off the fight.

'But what we do know is that if George had acted like Carl in the build-up to the rematch, there wouldn't have been 80,000 people there. What would there have been for the public to talk about? Where would the conflict that the average person who knows little about boxing could relate to be? What would the public have hung on?

'Look, George couldn't have sold the fight without Carl, but Carl couldn't have fought in front of 80,000 people without George. Eddie Hearn couldn't have sold this on his own either. In the end, George did really well out of this fight. He did well out of the first one, but he did *really* well out of this one. And he did it because 80,000 people showed up. And they showed up not just because of the controversial ending of the first fight, but because of how that result was sold over the next six months.

'It's also true that a big part of selling the fight was that the IBF had mandated that the fight *had* to happen. And that happened because we petitioned it, and we were successful. There was an element of excitement in the fact that the fight was happening not because Carl, the world champion, wanted it, but because *we* had petitioned it. The IBF had to make the decision, of course, but the fact that Carl now *had* to take a fight he most likely did not want to because it was mandated was even more intriguing for the audience.'

Only this time, it wasn't as simple as Carl the hero and George the villain.

Things were complicated by the stoppage in the first fight and the fact that many fans watching felt that George was unfairly treated. They felt that George was winning when the fight was stopped. Unlike the first time, there were now plenty of punters backing George to win.

There was also the fact that this time around, the fight was in the South, not the North, and in London, George's home town. That more comfortable home-crowd dynamic had changed for Carl too.

All, perhaps, in George's favour.

So, a huge fight, and yet I recall Paddy telling me that coaching George in front of over 80,000 spectators at the national stadium was one of his most peaceful experiences in boxing.

I bring up the idea that fighting at Wembley was a 'peaceful' experience with Paddy. This fight was massive, wasn't it? Four times bigger than the first fight at least. So how can you describe it as peaceful?

'The thing is Teach, as strange as it sounds, it's because it wasn't closed in. It was open air. It reminded me of when I was in Japan with Nishi [Yosuke Nishijima] when I was out there for the Pride Fighting [MMA]. We had over 50,000 in the audience over there, and yet you could hear a pin drop. I found Wembley that way. It was different to the enclosed environment in Manchester. With an open roof, and not closed in, it didn't have the acoustics of an inside venue. I found that very peaceful.' Because it was London and George had a lot of support in the venue, did that not affect you in terms of the noise?

'I didn't hear it. I was aware of the noise and the atmosphere, but it didn't feel intense. It didn't feel magnified. It didn't feel like 80,000 people – that's for certain. It felt calm and peaceful.'

You described the ring walk in detail for the first fight. How was the ring walk for the second fight planned? It was very different, wasn't it? A lot more extravagant?

'Not too many people are carried to the ring on a red London double-decker bus! George is a showman and we need that in the sport. It's one of the big things that I admire about him. He can be in the middle of something like that fight, with every distraction possible, and yet be focused on the things that he knows need to get done. He knew he wanted this ring walk, this statement, and even with all of these extra distractions, he absolutely made time for everything that he needed to. I liked that about him.'

But you felt there was a change in George?

'George went into Wembley with complete belief and knowing that he could beat Carl. Because of the first fight, George now *knew* he could beat Carl, and that was different.

'In the first fight, he *believed* he could and now he *knew*. Even though the first fight was stopped, for George it *only* got stopped because of Howard Foster. There was no way in his mind that George felt that he would have been knocked out by Carl if the fight had continued.

'George is bold and even though he was coming off a loss in the first fight, he presented himself as full of confidence – and he was.'

Did George find the experience as peaceful as you?

'George was focused – 100 per cent. He was presented with a great opportunity but an opportunity that had a huge amount of stress attached to it, and yet even with all of that extra stress, George came out and carried himself, and *fought*, with composure.

'The gameplan for the fight was clear for us. We had put out there about the third and fifth rounds. Any hesitancy from Carl for the first five rounds bought George more time to box and then by midway the plan was to turn the second part of the fight into the first fight they had.

'George was winning that second fight, far easier than the first fight. I was really comfortable with the first four rounds. We were winning the fight on George's excellent jab alone. He was cleaner and he was taking no punishment. When David Haye and Amir Khan [the TV commentary team] were interviewed between the rounds, they made it clear that they thought George was controlling the fight with his jab.

'George was dominating in those early rounds. We had planned to do what we did well in the first fight, but to do it in the second half or third segment of this fight. And when we did get to that point, we would really open up and throw it on Carl.

'The first five rounds we felt would be in the bag because we knew from the first fight that George had the better jab and the better footwork, so we would take control in that way. I knew that if we could keep Carl hesitant for the first five rounds and win all of them with George's jab, then that was five of 12 secure.

'The plan was working beautifully [from] rounds one to four and then for no reason that I could see, in round five George skirts along the ropes rather than hold the centre of the ring.

'In the lead-up preparation to the fight, I had formed a ring inside a ring in the gym. I used elastic ropes from one side of the ring to the other to form a smaller ring inside the actual ring. George had to spar like that so we could ensure that he didn't have his back against the ropes and could function successfully with almost two feet between him and the ropes. As soon as his back touched the inside ropes, he would move away.

'In the first four rounds, George went nowhere near the ropes. In the fifth, he's on the ropes and catching Carl's shots. Carl's shots were easily blocked on George's gloves or with his elbows. He wasn't scoring a lot of points because of George's defence. But that didn't matter, because for Carl as a fighter, the psychology of the situation was that if he was hitting something, then he feels he's in the fight. As far as Carl was concerned, if he could make contact with George, he could get to him eventually. Carl is a determined and resilient fighter. I didn't want us to allow him to think that he could get to George. When George had him missing and kept tagging Carl for his efforts with his jab, that's draining the man's confidence.

'So now Carl is having some success that he didn't have in the first four rounds. George had a long walk to the corner at the end of the fifth round because the action had stopped over near Carl's corner.

'I was in the ring before George and I can see him walking over to me with a smile on his face. But he must have seen my face changing, because the expression on his face changed too. He sits down and I say to him, "No good." He looks at me shocked and says, "What?" and I repeat, "No good. You lost that round."

'He gets confused and says, "How did I lose that round?"

'"We didn't train for six months to have you dominating the middle of the ring, for you then to decide to go skirting across the fuckin' ropes. Get back in the middle of the ring where you're supposed to be. Get back to what you should be doing."

'Round seven, George comes back and he's got his jab going nicely again, so I say to him that it's time to start nudging Carl back. "Don't walk into the fire yet, just start adding the right hand in and backing him up."

'Early round eight, Carl gets George over in our corner and shoots a left hook, right hand. George caught the hook but Carl landed his right hand before George could land his counter hook. George went down awkwardly and heavily in our own corner.

'And the ref waved it off.

'These are things that can happen to the best of men at any stage of their career, and in any fight. You've seen excellent champions dominating fights, then making a split-second mistake and not getting the chance to make that mistake again.

'These things happen, and it happened to George that night.'

16

Fighting Females

IT MIGHT come as a surprise to you but female boxing as a spectator sport stretches as far back as the early 18th century, when the self-proclaimed 'European Championess' Elizabeth Wilkinson fought both women – and men – in an era when the rules of the sport allowed for kicking and gouging, as well as other more traditional forms of fistic attack.

Later, during the 1920s, Professor Andrew Nelson formed a Women's Boxing Club of London and yet female boxing remained hugely controversial.

In fact, female boxing first appeared in the Olympic Games as a demonstration bout in 1904 and there was a revival of the sport spearheaded by the Swedish Amateur Boxing Association in 1988. This was followed by the British Amateur Boxing Association sanctioning its first boxing competition for women in 1997, even though the British Boxing Board of Control refused to issue licences to women until 1998.

But still Olympic recognition eluded female fighters.

'There simply *was* no Olympics for women,' Laila Ali, world super middleweight and light-heavyweight champion and daughter of the Greatest, Muhammad Ali, tells me when I interview her in between her filming schedule in Los Angeles. There is no mistaking the frustration in her voice, presumably born of the fact that while she too became a world champion in the professional ranks, she wasn't given the opportunity to win an Olympic gold medal like her father did as a young Cassius Clay. Finally, though, the world caught up and the sport of female boxing achieved the recognition it deserved.

It propelled fighters like Nicola Adams, Katie Taylor and Claressa Shields to world fame when female boxing finally became a sanctioned Olympic sport at London 2012.

Arguably, however, the boom time of female boxing came in the US in the 1990s with world champions such as Lucia Rijker, probably best known for playing the villain to Hilary Swank's heroine in the movie *Million Dollar Baby*, and Laila 'She Bee Stingin' Ali blazing their fistic trails. Both are ranked among the top five female fighters of all time and both trained by, among other great coaches, Paddy Fitzpatrick.

I ask Paddy to tell me a little bit about the female fighters he has worked with in his career. He chooses to start with Lucia Rijker, the once IBO world lightweight champion.

'In my opinion, Lucia is as close to the complete fighter as you can get. That doesn't mean for a female. It means as close to a complete fighter as you can get. Period. She can box. She can punch. She has great hand speed. She can fight inside and outside. She has very good ring generalship. She has fantastic composure because she has fought for so long and from such a young age.

'A fighter must be able to fight, of course. But you need to be able to be *in* a fight also. It's one thing to have great technique, hand speed and power and because of that you can really dish it out. But what will you do when someone dishes it back when you are in a *fight*? One of the first things that stood out to me about Lucia was that she could do both.

'I was watching Lucia sparring world-class dudes who could punch in Freddie's Wild Card gym one day and she was getting nailed with big right hands. She came back to the corner and Freddie said to her, "OK, he's just loving that right hand at the moment. Here's what you do. Drop your left hand. Offer up the opening for his right hand. Keep your left hand nice and low so it's just below your waist and just out of his eyesight. And then as soon as he shoots that right hand, twist your waist and drive that left hook into his body. As soon as you see the right hand coming, don't look to defend it. Commit and land your shot first. His shot will go over your left shoulder as you land the hook."

'So she goes out, totally composed, drops her left hand and moves slightly to her left. Her opponent throws the right hand like she knew he would and as he does so, she whips in that left hook to the body. She does it twice and the right hands stop because now there is a consequence when her opponent lets go. Now he is getting nailed and what's worse, he isn't landing the shot either.

'She was an amazing fighter. But even more than that, she was one of the witnesses at my wedding too.

'I worked with Kelsey Jeffries [International Female Boxers' Association world featherweight champion] too when I was with Buddy [McGirt]. She was a warrior, with a warrior's mentality. She had a beautiful defence. She wasn't a puncher by any means but people make mistakes about a fighter like Kelsey all the time. To beat a puncher, you only have to hit them more than they hit you, and have the resilience to absorb their shots when they get through. It's about how often you land compared to the puncher. Kelsey might not have been a puncher but she would commit to every single shot, so they had impact. They certainly were not taps. You could see that she was putting everything that she had into the shots; they just didn't have the puncher's impact when they landed.

'She reminded me a lot of James Toney because you could see they both felt more at peace in the ring than out of it.

'She was so good to train too. If what you said made sense to her, she would do *exactly* what you asked of her.'

I have talked with Paddy on several occasions about his respect for, and training female fighters. He has never made a distinction between males and females as fighters that I have ever heard, and this comes across loud and clear in his descriptions of the strengths of the fighters he worked with.

I wanted to test this theory, so I contacted Laila Ali, who agreed to let me interview her during a break in her recording schedule for a TV show in LA.

This time, I was prepared. I had learned my lesson from the interview with James Toney. I need not have worried. Laila was the epitome of professionalism.

When we finally talked, I had to take the advice Paddy gave himself when he worked around so many stars at the Wild Card gym. I was talking to 13-year-olds in an English secondary school about the Spanish conditional tense one day, and world champions like Laila, James Toney and Lamon Brewster the next.

If I allowed myself to get star-struck, then I wouldn't be able to do my job and write this book. So I called Laila and pretended, at least until the end of the interview, that this wasn't one of the most amazing things I had done.

'Hey Teach!' she answered as soon as I called, again making me feel very pleased with my transatlantic nickname.

We made a bit of small talk as I asked her how she was and then I began as professionally as I could.

Paddy told me you were an outstanding fighter and a great champion. How did you meet him?

'My ex-husband knew Paddy from the boxing business and he was a great strength and conditioning coach. He knew boxing and we thought he would be a good addition to our team. So he was the one who brought him on to my team.'

I'm doing alright, so I continue.

A lot of fighters that I talk to say that Paddy is very specific and very technical as a coach. What were your thoughts on him as a coach?

'Well, first of all, Paddy is very professional, which is important to me. He is going to take the time to get to know you as a person and what your strengths and weaknesses are. He would come up with a very specific plan, you know, tailored to you. I've seen trainers and boxing coaches in the past who do the same thing with everybody and that's not the case with Paddy. He would also focus on the mental side of it all.'

A lot of fighters said Paddy focuses on the mental side really well. Would you agree?

'He does. Not all fighters are the same, though. I'm not one of those fighters who need that much work when it comes to the mental side. My confidence doesn't need to be built up. You know, your confidence comes from preparation. That's what I always say. Essentially, my confidence comes from preparation. So I prepared myself by surrounding myself with the best team that I could. People who were going to be honest with me. People who would find out what my weaknesses and strengths are and make sure that I am always living up to my best potential.

'And that was Paddy.'

Laila talks with such ease, conviction and confidence. I am interviewing her about her life as a fighter, so I don't want to bring up her dad, but when I listen to the tone of her voice, her laughter and the confidence with which she talks, I just can't help but think of him.

I snap myself back into the moment.

What are your best memories of working with Paddy?

'Paddy was a friend more than anything. He's somebody that I felt like I could trust because things go on in your life outside of the ring that affect your performance. So when you feel like you can share something and say "OK, this is why maybe I didn't have the energy to do it as well as I would have liked to today in the gym, here's what's going on in the background", that's a good thing.

'At the same time, you have to find that balance – pushing a fighter but not pushing too hard. Another thing about Paddy is that he knows when a fighter should take a rest, and that's really important. Sometimes fighters are overworked and they don't give their bodies the time to build up, and that's something that I see a lot in boxing.

'For example, like this whole myth that you shouldn't drink water while training: the idea that you work harder without the water. That's not intelligent. It alters your thinking. It alters everything. You need to be hydrated as an athlete. It's not smart. Paddy didn't subscribe to this theory. He educates himself. He educates himself to know how to help effectively, like with my supplements or my training. Paddy didn't depend on what he *thought* he knew. He made sure that he went and got the information that he needed.'

I express shock at the idea that fighters are trained not to hydrate themselves.

'Yeah well,' Laila explains to me, 'there's some old-school trainers who will say just keep sparring. They think they're doing you an effective mental job. You're thirsty, yeah, but keep working hard – keep pushing. They think that they're teaching you how to fight your way out of difficult situations but it actually does more harm than good.'

Laila laughs really engagingly, which makes it clear what she thinks of the water deprivation theory in boxing.

If you were in a training camp, or a fight, and it was challenging, how would Paddy approach you, or adjust you, to keep you focused and get you back on track if things weren't going quite right?

'I never really needed anybody to give me focus. I'm self-motivated and one trainer can't do that for a fighter – it takes a team. It's definitely important to have the right team around you.'

Paddy tells me, 'Lali [the name he called Laila] never had a training camp that didn't have stress attached. I've never been with any fighter ever who went through so many camps with so much bullshit going on. None of this was down to Lali, but inevitably it would be there. But no matter what was going on, she would always deal with it. Come fight night, even if training camp hadn't gone as well as we might have liked, we didn't need to worry. Lali always showed up and performed.

'And there are dudes I've known who became world champions who couldn't have coped as well as Lali with all of the bullshit and emotional pressure she was under. That's a fact.

'That really stood out about her. There's a difference between the classy lady that Lali absolutely is, and Lali the fighter. Fight night, Lali always showed up.'

What impressed you about Laila, I ask Paddy.

'She did everything really well. She had good hand speed. She could really punch. And I don't mean in that patronising for-a-female kind of way. She hurt dudes who fought for the light-heavyweight championship of the world. She broke ribs.

She could genuinely punch without a doubt. And she could really work inside because Roger Mayweather had taught her a lot about going to the body. Lali brought immense pressure to bear on her opponents that would emotionally cause her opponents problems. If a girl didn't give way to her power, then they gave way to Lali's intensity. Look at her record of 24 wins, with 21 coming by way of knockout – that says it all.'

So if you were taking Laila on, you had better be serious, then?

'Yeah, you bet you did. There was this time when we were training in my gym in Vegas. I called it the "Mindset Boxing Gym". One of my contacts was bringing some guys down to spar with Vatche and he says, "Hey Laila, I've got a girl who really wants some sparring with you."

'And Lali says, "Bring her ass down then," in a kind of "that's OK by me" way.

'And this guy says, "Yeah, but my girl says she's gonna do such and such."

'Lali's like, "Oh yeah, well bring her ass down then." But this time, her tone had changed.

'The next day, the guy says the same thing and Lali says, "Listen, I done told you already. If she wants work she can have it. But I'm telling you now, she better be able to fight the way she's been talking."

'So this girl arrives in the gym and my gym had roller shutter doors with my ring next to the doors so they could be lifted and let the fresh air in. The girl walks through the door. Lali is normally friendly, while at the same time expressing that she's top dog in the gym, when new people arrive. But when this girl arrived, Lali was just stand-offish. There was no friendliness at all.

'The girl starts to get ready and she's trying to put on her head gear, which won't even buckle up. It was comic. We had to duct-tape the head gear on and she looked like *Beetlejuice* from the film.

'She gets in the ring with Lali and the first round starts and Lali comes out and just starts putting it on this girl. Quickly, the round turned into two minutes of hell for this girl. And she's trying to find a door in the ring to get the hell out of there because Lali is simply beating on her.

'The bell hadn't even rung before the girl slipped through the ropes, out of the gym and started running down the street with her head gear and gloves on.

'I remember Lali sticking her head through the ropes and looking down the street after the girl shouting, "Get your ass back here! Don't expect to talk shit and come in here like we're cool!"

'But the girl didn't come back. And this shows the difference between the ever so class lady and the fighter. Lali separates the two.'

Did everything go smoothly when you worked with Laila?

'Lali was fighting Gwendolyn O'Neil in Atlanta for the vacant International Women's Boxing Federation world light-heavyweight title. I had told Lali that Gwendolyn couldn't box so well but that she would apply a lot of pressure and that she was game as a fighter. I told Lali not to let Gwendolyn build her momentum and to make sure that she got her jab going. I also made it clear that if her opponent started letting shots go, Lali should make sure she broke her rhythm – to stop the momentum. "Yeah, I got it. I got it, I got it," she says.

'"OK, just make sure you listen to me," I say to her.

'"I got it, man, shut up!" is what I get back.

'So, in the first round, Lali went out and did *completely* the opposite of everything that I told her *completely*. Hands held high. Letting the other girl tee off on her.

'I got her back at the end of the round and I say, "Are you finished now? Are you gonna listen to me?"

'She turns away from me, and I say something to her along the lines of, "Are you gonna take your head out of your ass? Are you gonna listen to what I'm telling you?"

'And then she says, "Yeah man, what?"

'"Do as I told you," I say simply. And then she goes straight back out in the second round and did exactly what she was supposed to do in the first and she won the bout by knockout in the third round.

'Lali is someone who would not give herself up completely to anyone. She knew her strengths. She'd follow a gameplan. But she could veer off just enough to let you know, "Ain't no one my boss."

'Sometimes you had to put your foot in her ass just to get her attention during a fight. She was a bit different like that.'

I decide to pursue a different thread in her relationship with Paddy.

How much does loyalty and trust mean to you in your team? Was Paddy someone that you felt you could rely on?

'Definitely – Paddy is one of the most loyal people I know. If you tell him something, and it's a secret, he's going to the grave with it. Any time you need him, he's gonna be there. He's gonna sacrifice his own livelihood, just to get something done for you. He goes a little overboard with it, if you ask me.'

Laila bursts out laughing before finishing with, 'Paddy's very giving. He's a giver – for sure.'

'Lali is one of the people that I feel closest to in life,' Paddy tells me. 'Even though we don't see each other as much as we might like, we're still close. I might not talk with her for a couple of months because of schedules, and then I'll talk with her non-stop for a couple of weeks. There are few people who I am able to separate the friendship from the training and being coach, and Lali is one of those people.'

Are there any funny stories from your time working with Paddy, I say to Laila?

'OK, so, the hardest thing for me was being disciplined when it came to eating. I love sweets, right, and of course you've gotta make weight so you have to make sacrifices and know that you did everything that you needed to do. I would be one who'd be sneaking stuff. It wasn't a physical thing. I never had a weight problem. It was more mental with me. I was an elite athlete. I knew sugar affected my performance and I knew what I had to do but every once in a while I would want to sneak something.

'I remember I had a party at my house this time. Paddy was at my house and I went out to the store to get something and I picked up a box of Krispy Kreme doughnuts for everybody else. And then I ate one in the car.

'When I got back, Paddy was like, "You ate a doughnut."

'And I was like, "No I didn't." And I just sat there and said to him firmly, "*No I didn't.*"

'I was doing my best lying possible,' says Laila, changing the tone of her voice from friendly to stern. "*No I did not.*"

'Paddy then says to me, "Yes you did because you have a crumb on your mouth."

'I was like "no I don't", like I thought he was joking and trying to make me think that I had a crumb on my mouth. I mean, it got to the point where I got mad with him. I really tried to win the argument. And even though he was telling me there were crumbs on my mouth, I wouldn't admit it because I still didn't believe him.

'But I actually did have crumbs all around my mouth and someone else had to say to me, "Hey Laila, you really do have crumbs all around your mouth!"'

She laughs loudly at the story.

'And then I'm thinking, "Man, I've pretty much showed him how well I can lie now" because I was being so convincing and I thought, "I'm never going to get away with this again" – because that was near the beginning of our relationship. He must have been thinking, "OK, I've gotta watch this girl."'

She laughs again.

'Afterwards, I was super embarrassed about it. There were lots of great times we had together. Paddy and I just always had a good time together and I was friends with his wife Kerry. I remember going and having training camp when I was training with Buddy McGirt. Paddy came and his wife Kerry came. And bringing Kerry along was great because she could do some of that Jamaican cooking.'

I decide to bring our conversation into the present.

Several of your opponents have said that your participation in women's boxing helped propel the sport to where it is now and that without your involvement, the likes of Katie Taylor and Claressa Shields wouldn't have the audiences, the opportunities or the respect that they have. What's your view on where women's boxing is at right now?

'I think women's boxing has made big strides but it still has a long way to go. Obviously because I have a famous last name, that brought a lot of attention to the sport. But then, of course, I lived up to the hype. Having the last name wouldn't have helped if I hadn't been a great fighter.'

I love how Laila tells me this so matter-of-factly, like it is so fundamentally correct that it is impossible for me to contradict her.

Paddy is not surprised about this.

'Lali fully believes that having the DNA of her father plays a part in her success. She understands that she is not her father, but she has a deep conviction that by having his DNA, his blood running through her veins, that while she might not physically fight like him, she has his mental strength.'

It must have been hard to live up to the name, though, I say to Laila?

'No, it wasn't hard for me. I knew who I was and what I was bringing to the table. But I would say what really took things to the next level was women's boxing being at the Olympics, so the sport got even more exposure on a worldwide level. This legitimised women's boxing as a sport as it was considered worthy of being in the Olympics. It also inspired more women to get involved because they felt that they could now fight for their country and go on from there, like Katie Taylor with her amateur background.

'Katie is an amazing fighter and I would say that she'd have given me problems if she had been in my weight class in terms of her skill and speed. I know that if she *were* in my weight class, she might not have been quite so fast. But she's the type of fighter I would have loved to have had the opportunity to trade with. It would have been nice.

'I think women's boxing still has a long way to go. It's nice to see the ladies do their thing but of course there's still a lot more to do. You can't just have one or two top names in the sport. There's not going to be any depth in the sport. There need to be more people with name value. People who fans can know, so they know their styles and study them. That's what makes boxing exciting. Knowing what one fighter is going to bring to the table when compared with another, so that you can imagine what the fight's gonna be like. Fans knowing only one fighter isn't going to make the sport exciting. And that's a problem that I had a lot of the time. Nobody knew who my opponent was really and I sometimes ended up having to fight girls who I knew weren't really going to be competition. There was nothing I could do. There just weren't enough girls available – especially in my weight class.'

At Paddy's gym, there is no distinction between males and females – they're both fighters.

You were quite a significant figurehead for women's boxing, I say to Laila. What advice would you give young female fighters?

'I'm not an advocate for people to become a boxer as such. I wouldn't say, "Oh, you should become a fighter." But I will say that I want everyone to do whatever their heart desires. If boxing is what you want to do, then you definitely want to go and find someone who is going to take you seriously as a female and train you up and get you ready.

'But you also have to know that you better love it because you may not make it. And this goes for any fighter. You may not make a lot of money. You might have to do a second job just to get by. Me personally, if I didn't think I could have become successful, and I mean financially successful, I wouldn't have become a boxer. There are so many other things that I have talent and passion for that I would do because I am also a business person. But I understand that if boxing is all a person has and all they want to do, well then you better be ready to go 100 per cent, 120 per cent even.'

Our time is up. It's flown by. So before I thank her for her time, I ask for any final thoughts Laila has regarding Paddy?

'Everyone has their own story and their own point of view. We all see things in different ways. I am glad I was able to work with Paddy. He's a great trainer, an excellent friend and I will always wish him every success.'

Laila 'She Bee Stingin' Ali – world champion and pure class.

This book is about Paddy and the fighters he has worked with. But I can't help but ask him about Muhammad Ali. I know that the memories of meeting Ali are precious to him, so I ask him, 'If you were training Laila, you must have spent some time with her father?'

'When I first met Muhammad Ali, it was the grand opening of Laila's own gym. There were queues of people right down the road because they had advertised that he would be there. We were doing a press conference for Lali's world title fight against Suzette Taylor too.

'We did the press conference and then, of course, there were lines of people who wanted to meet Muhammad and this thing went on for hours. Once the event had finished there was only me, Muhammad, Lali and a few others.

'I was sweeping up the gym and Muhammad beckons me over. I say, "How are you doing Big Man?"

'He says, "Sit down."

'I sit down and he beckons me to come closer before he leans into me and he says, "Are you a pimp?"

'I'm like, "No, I'm not a pimp. Sure, what did you ask me that for? I train your daughter."

'He just starts laughing at me then and we chat for a few more minutes before I thank him and then get back on with the cleaning.

'Later on that evening, I'm out driving my car and I get a phone call from Lali's sister Hannah. She says, "Paddy, where are you?"

'I told her I was driving up the Strip and she says, "My dad wants to see you."

'I ask her what for and she tells me she doesn't know. Then she gives me the hotel that they're staying at and what name they have their reservation under.

'I arrive at their hotel room door a little later and I go inside. Muhammad's in there with Lonnie, his wife. Howard Bingham, who did most of his photography, is there and Hannah is there too.

'When I go in, Muhammad calls me over and I sit down next to him and we start chatting. Then he says he's hungry, so we go to the bar because he's got this suite in the hotel, rather than a room. We're sitting together at the bar in the kitchen eating ice cream and Lali comes to the door.

'She walks in and she's like, "Daddy, what's *he* doing here?"

'And Muhammad just says, "I wanna talk to him."

'Lali is a couple of feet from us and she says, "Hey Daddy, you know Paddy likes black girls, right? His wife is Jamaican."

'Muhammad looks at me and he says, "You like black girls?"

'And I say, "You know that chocolate looks better with vanilla on top, right?"

'And Muhammad is really laughing at this.

'Next thing Lali says, "Oh my God, you two together is not good!"

'When he'd finished his ice cream, he said that he wanted to talk to me some more. So Lali, Hannah and Howard left and Lonnie says she has to go into another room and make some phone calls – so it's just Muhammad Ali and me.

'We sat together for two and a half hours. We talked about women first, then boxing and then religion. When we started talking about religion, he got out a Bible, opened it up and he said to me, "Read there."

'So I read the section out loud to him.

'Then he goes, "OK, now read this."

'He has all these notes with him and then he says, "Now go to here and read this bit."

'So I read the sections and he goes, "You see?"

'I say, "See what?"

'"Contradiction," he says.

'One of the examples he showed me was where a woman was called a "wife" in one section and then the same woman was described as a "concubine" in the next, which is like a mistress. It's a clear contradiction.

'Ali kept showing me contradictions in the Bible and then he says, "How are you supposed to believe that? It keeps contradicting itself. How are you supposed to live by that?"

'And then, before I know it, Lonnie comes out of her room, Howard Bingham returns and two and a half hours has passed. Lonnie says, "Hey, it's getting late, Muhammad. It's time to wrap it up."

'I took that as my cue to leave, so I stood up and he was sat in the chair and I said to him, "Muhammad, it's been an honour."

'As he was standing up, he says to me, "Why? I'm just another..."

'And I interrupt him, "No, you've got it all wrong, Muhammad. It hasn't been an honour for me. It's been an honour for *you*. I don't do house calls usually."

'He bursts out laughing then and falls back into his chair. He keeps laughing so much that Howard Bingham says to me, "Take it easy on him, man."

'I think he liked that I was as cheeky as he was and remember I had only just met the man at that point!'

There's another time that stands out to you too, isn't there?

'Yeah, there was this one time when I was staying at Lali's house and she says to me, "Daddy's in town today. Do you want to go and see him and we'll get some lunch?"

'I wanted to so we got in the car and went down to Beverly Hills because Muhammad was in one of the hotels there.

'We arrive at the hotel and go up into the conference room and as we walk in, Muhammad's at a table with three or four lawyers and he's got his back to the door. They were discussing postage stamps and how they were going to put Muhammad's face on postage stamps.

'The lawyers are all discussing this but Muhammad's paying no attention to them. He's got this napkin and he's drawing on it. When I get close enough to look at it, it's a matchstick picture of him fighting Joe Frazier. There's a crowd made up of dots around a boxing ring, Frazier is on the canvas and Muhammad is stood over him with a speech bubble coming out of his mouth saying, "I am the Greatest!"

'Ali looks up at me and he goes, "Do you like it?"

'I say, "Yeah man." So he signs it, "Mr Muhammad Ali" and goes, "Here, keep it."

'It was on a very expensive embroidered napkin with the name of the hotel on it too.

'I don't have the napkin now. I gave it to my buddy Deano, who has it framed on his wall because he's a huge fan of boxing.

'Anyway, after that Muhammad says he's hungry and he wants to get some food in his hotel room. So we go up. We ordered some food and we ate it while we chatted.

'Once we had finished, Muhammad says, "I wanna go for a walk."

'So we go in the elevator down as far as the first floor. The plan was to get out there and more discreetly make our way out of the hotel. You wouldn't want to get down to the lobby and the doors of the elevator open to reception to show Muhammad Ali, would you?

'So instead we walked down the stairs and kept walking a couple of steps ahead of Muhammad. Every now and then, Lali would turn around and say, "You alright, Daddy?" and then we would keep going.

'We got to the bottom of the steps and turned left to go out a quieter entrance of the hotel and as we turned left, we both realised at the same time that Muhammad ain't behind us.

'We turn around and by this stage he's making headway in the opposite direction towards the front entrance of the hotel. He's looking over his shoulder and starting to walk quicker and quicker too.

'There was this crowd of people in a circle that he was heading towards and they were all chatting to each other. Ali reaches them and sticks his head in between the crowd. He starts looking and listening and then this woman notices him and says, "It's Muhammad Ali!"

'And Ali looks back at her and he says, "Where?"

'The next thing is we get there and it's too late for Lali to say to him that we needed to get out of there because they're all talking to him.

'Then he starts getting out tissues and doing magic tricks for the crowd until Lali persuades him that we need to move.

'Thing is, by that time a crowd has built up to such an extent that instead of our walk, we have to get back into the elevator and go to the hotel room!

'I'm sure Muhammad didn't really want a walk anyway. He just wanted some human interaction after spending so long with so many suits in that conference room.

'You know, Teach, Muhammad Ali never made me feel like he was famous. That says a lot about him. That was an art in itself. The most famous man in the world and he can do that? He can seem like a normal dude? That's something.'

I enjoyed that. What boxing aficionado doesn't like a story about Muhammad Ali? But we are discussing the fact that Paddy successfully trained female, as well as male fighters. It's clear that Laila felt Paddy was a great trainer. But how about other females he worked with?

'There was this perception in the 1990s,' Lisa Van Ahn, one of Paddy's fighters from his time in Las Vegas with Laila and Vatche, says to me with total conviction in her voice and a steel behind piercing eyes that leave me in no doubt about how firmly she holds this opinion.

'There was this perception that female fighters just weren't as good as men. You know, the idea that they couldn't fight, couldn't punch straight and would just sort of slap at each other.' Lisa flaps her hands in front of her body in a parody of the stereotypical way some ignorant people might judge how female fighters attack each other. 'Paddy was just never like that. He saw a fighter and a human being – not a woman.'

I interview Lisa just as schools, pubs and gyms have been forced to close, including Paddy's, as the coronavirus pandemic sweeps the world. We video call just as the state government in Minneapolis, where Lisa lives, have enforced self-isolation on the entire community.

How are you managing over there, I ask her? 'Well, our city is pretty much on lockdown. Everything non-essential is closed from order of the governor and most people are working remotely. It's quarantine.'

Lisa is a successful kick-boxer and boxer who trained with Paddy, Laila and Vatche in Las Vegas after Paddy had moved on from Freddie's gym. Her wide, welcoming smile and open personality make me feel at ease to ask her my questions.

I have studied her biography as a fighter and notice how fit and conditioned she still seems years after she worked with Paddy. Now, Lisa has created the 'I AM' initiative, a dynamic and adventurous curriculum designed to empower and strengthen young women. She seems a pretty strong role model to me.

I tell Lisa that I am recording our conversation and I ask her if that's OK.

'Yeah,' she says. 'I'm gonna swear. Is that OK?'

I laugh then. I hadn't expected that question as a response.

'Paddy doesn't swear any more,' she says. 'He used to swear all the time, but he tells me he doesn't any more. I can shut it off if it offends you?'

It's fine, I say. I would rather hear you tell your story naturally.

How did you meet Paddy, I ask Lisa?

'I had moved to Las Vegas to box professionally. Previously, I was a kick-boxer in Minneapolis. I had met someone who had offered me a contract to box professionally, so I went with him and started my pro career. But after a little while, it started to seem a little shady. So I said goodbye to this guy. I trust my gut and if something feels off, then I peace out.

'So I decided to stay in Vegas and I started looking for a coach. I went into Laila's gym, which was her husband Ya-Ya's really, and Paddy was there. I did some rounds. He saw me box and we chatted. I told him I was looking for a coach. He asked me about my background and then he insulted me a few times. Then he told me to come back tomorrow.

'It might seem unusual, because if someone insulted you then normally you'd say, "I'm not fucking going back." But I actually liked it. In fact, I thrive off critical feedback because I want to grow. If someone tells me how awesome I am, then I'm not growing. I want you to tell me what sucks, so that I can improve on that. I don't take anything personally. And if you're gonna work with Paddy, that's a good philosophy to have.

'So I went back the next day. We trained and he insulted me again. Then he said maybe he could help me and I was sold on him. I liked his no-nonsense way of doing things. I liked his style.

'After three weeks of training with him every day, I called him on the phone and told him that I was having a day and that I wasn't going to make it into the gym. I wasn't feeling that great and I just needed a day off. I said, "Hey Paddy, this is Lisa, I won't make it into the gym today." And he was like, "OK, whatever."

'From the beginning of training at the gym, he called me "Blondie" on account of my hair – always Blondie.

'Next day, I go into the gym and I walk in and he looks at me and he says, "Fooking hell, Blondie. Where were you yesterday? Why the fook didn't you come into the gym?" Lisa laughs as she drops into her best impression of a working-class southern Irishman.

'He was beside himself angry with me. I look at him and I'm just like, "What are you *talking* about?"

'And he says, "Well, if you're not fooking coming into the gym, you've gotta fooking call me. I expect you to show up!"

'I know my accent is really bad but it makes things so much better when you do a "Paddy" accent.

'I look at him and I say "I did call you" and he's looking at me strange so I say, "Lisa – *Li-sa?*"

'And he says, "Fooking hell, Blondie! I don't fooking know your name," like this is totally normal.

'But you said, "OK", I say to him.

'"I didn't know who the fook you were!" he says to me.

'He just totally cracked me up.

'The thing is, Paddy gives you a nickname but if he gives you a nickname he loves you – and then, of course, he doesn't ever really know your real name.'

Lisa laughs and I tell her he doesn't know *my* name, even after we've been friends for over three years and I spend time with him most weeks.

'I'm amazed he doesn't swear any more,' she tells me. 'He used to be like, "Fooking hell! Bloody hell! Fook! Fook! Fook!" all the time.'

I ask Paddy what his memories are of Lisa.

'Blondie is funny because she was a world-class kickboxer but never had done boxing. Kickboxers don't work on the inside a lot, like boxers. The majority of their work is done at a longer range because they can kick. So the range is different.

'In the beginning, when Blondie would work inside, she would have panic attacks. When she freaked out, I would want to help her re-focus. She had this big freak-out one day and went into a panic attack in the corner. I had to catch her by the head gear and give her a slap to get her back focused. It worked because after the initial shock subsided, she was like, "OK, what do I do?"

'We were really close. In Vegas, I got really close to my fighters. I had Vatche with me then too.

'Lisa was strong. She didn't care about who she fought. She'd fight anyone, home or away. She gave everything that she had. And it was hard back then. There wasn't a great deal of interest in a women's fight. I brought her over to the UK and she bust up some of my boys. Three of them got bloody noses. She tore them up.

'You know, Blondie reminds me of Connelly [*Lady Luck* Bec Connelly, one of Paddy's current fighters]. They're both really into nutrition and healthy eating. Both individuals who have to manage a lot outside of boxing. And both warriors.

What did you like about Paddy's training methods, I ask Lisa?

'I'm a strategic fighter and Paddy was very focused on technique and strategies. I really liked his approach, which was based on clarity. I follow direction well so if someone says to me, "Do this and then this," I can follow that and get results.

'He was also tuned in enough emotionally, which is interesting and that's probably why he gets results out of the youth. I know he worked with a lot of top male boxers, but working with women he was clued in in a particular kind of way. He got it when I was like, "Don't push anymore." He would get that in a way other coaches didn't. And that would make me pissed [off] and when I'm pissed [off] then I don't listen. And when I don't listen, I don't get results.

'I have to be able to respect a coach and want to listen to him. I'm not going to listen to you if you ignore when I'm having an emotional breakdown. He would just get that.

'On the other hand, he would see when I was just like, "I don't really feel it" and he would be like, "Fooking buck up!" and that would motivate me too.'

Do you think that Paddy was a little bit ahead of the curve when it came to training female fighters?

'From the beginning, Paddy knew that women *could* fight. There were still a lot of people out there who didn't see it like this. But Paddy knew that women often bring a lot more heart into fighting and you can teach women proper technique, how to respond effectively and use strategy.'

The unspoken implication in this, of course, is that men are harder to teach because they don't listen. Do you agree, I ask Paddy?

'At the beginning of the coaching process, at the very least, females take instruction better. Unlike males, they don't come to a boxing gym with this preconceived idea that they are supposed to know how to fight. That wasn't the case with Lucia and Kelsey because they were already accomplished fighters when I worked with them. But when I started with Lali, she'd had around ten fights but without the amateur experience. So you could say she was at an early stage.

'If you get a dude walks through the door, though, and you say have you boxed before, almost everyone will say that he did a bit before when he was young. Very few men will say, "I know nothing, take me from scratch." It's a macho thing, isn't it? "I'm a dude. Of course I can look after myself."

'A female is much more honest. She'll say that she hasn't got a clue what's going on and if you tell her what to do, then she'll do it. So the girls don't get in their own way, like men often do.'

'It looks fucking good in the ring when women get it right,' continues Lisa. 'It doesn't look like a catfight or whatever people back then might have called it. Check out me and Laila. We're two skilled fighters who looked good in the ring. We weren't crazy, wide-punching and just running in at our opponents. Paddy understood that if you give women the same time and attention as men, then they can fight just as well – if not better.'

So you felt that Paddy treated you as an equal as a fighter?

'Yeah, he would put me in the ring with Kevin Kelley.'

Kevin Kelley once held the WBC world featherweight title and fought against other champions such as Marco Antonio Barrera, Erik Morales and Prince Naseem Hamed.

'I was like, "What the fuck are you doing?" I'd be like, "You want me to spar with Kevin Kelley?" Kevin would move his head when I tried to hit him and I'd keep missing and get frustrated. Paddy would help me not to get frustrated and explain that what Kevin had experienced in the ring meant he was better than me at that point. He had been fighting longer and this was an opportunity for me to learn and grow. We were similar weights, so it was appropriate to my development. He believed in me.

'He also put me in the ring with Vatche, who was training at the gym too. The first couple of times I sparred with Vatche, he was like, "No, Paddy, no, come on, Paddy, no."

'Paddy just said, "Shut the fuck up and just get in there and spar with her."

'Vatche would be like, "I'm not going to hit you so hard," to me and Paddy would correct him and say, "Get over yourself and just hit her in the fucking face and teach her to keep her hands up."

'Vatche would reluctantly spar with me.

'I appreciated that because it showed that Paddy saw me as an equal.

'You know, I love Vatche with all my heart, but at the time he was like, "Women shouldn't be fighting. Why aren't you cooking? Why don't you have a husband?"

'That kind of thing.

'He'd also say to me, "You're so pretty. Why do you box?"

'And I'd be like, "What the fuck? Me being pretty has nothing to do with anything!"

'Paddy simply wouldn't have it from Vatche because we were around the same weight, 135lbs. He didn't put me in with someone because they were male or female; it was about my weight class. That's why I never sparred with Laila. The weight differential in our classes was too great. It didn't make sense. Paddy wouldn't do that.

'Kevin and Vatche weren't the only men I sparred with either.

'The idea that he treats women as equals runs through Paddy. I noticed it in every encounter I had with him. Everybody was human. He doesn't see gender, religion, race or economic status. He sees people and gives them an opportunity as a person.

'If you fucked up and you were a shitty person, he would tell you. But that had nothing to do with anything other than you were just shitty. If you're a great person, you're a great person.'

I ask Paddy about treating female fighters the same as males, without discrimination.

'I just don't have time for that. Freddie Roach wouldn't have allowed that. He would say, "If you want to be a fighter, be a fighter. But act like a fighter. If you get your ass whupped, take your ass-whupping like a fighter.' Same way that Freddie treated James Toney, he would have treated Lucia Rijker. The same standards and expectations.

'You can't treat a person one way and expect them to act another. So I treated everyone like a fighter because that's what they were.'

Do you think Paddy's personality and understanding of you helped him to be a better coach, I ask Lisa?

'In the fighter/coach relationship, you spend so much fucking time with each other that you have to like the person. I spent hours with Paddy. If you didn't like the person, it would suck, right? It helped that I liked him – a lot. It also helped that we had mutual respect for each other.

'He was fucking hilarious too. He made me laugh all the time. I got his sense of humour. You know, during the time that I was fighting with Paddy, he would describe me as either "fat" or "skinny". I fought really light, around 119lbs. But I walk around normally at 132lbs. I was a lean fighter. Paddy wanted me to stay around 126lbs and then get down to 119lbs when I was nearing a fight. But I would still walk around at 132lbs because if I wasn't fighting I'd be like, "I want to eat some cake or have some cocktails."

'So in training, I would be in the ring sparring with some girl and he would be shouting at my opponent, "Punch some of the fooking fat off her!" And then, when I actually got down to the fighting weight, he'd be like, "You're too skinny now. There's nothing on you!"

'He just cracked me up. Some people might take it personally or get offended by it, but it made me laugh. Truthfully, I wanted to find this sweet spot where he'd be like, "You look good!" But I never found it. I was always "fat" or "skinny".'

I tell Lisa that all the fighters I have spoken to have told me independently about how Paddy is a really technical and strategic coach, but how the compassion and humanity he showed them ensured the relationship became one that was more than business – more than fighter and coach.

'It's a demonstration of the man that he is, right? When you get that level of consistency of response, then you know it's real. You've spoken individually with each of them and the same things have shown up. That's real. It's a part of who he is. It's at the heart of who he is. I had a great time with Paddy. He's a great coach.'

I finish the conversation with Lisa by asking her if she has any pictures of her time with Paddy that we might want to consider for our book?

She does, she tells me, and they are on the wall in her home. Images she looks at every day, which says everything to me about how important her relationship with Paddy must have been.

17

Building back to the top: A visit to GGG

The aftermath and a visit to Triple G

SO WHAT happened after George lost the second fight with Carl so conclusively? You both must have been pretty down. 'The next day, I called George and asked him how he was feeling.'

"'The truth, coach?" he said. "I was dominating that fight. I know I screwed up. But I feel good. There's not a mark on me."

'I asked him if he was open to me visiting and he liked the idea. I went round and asked him if he had seen the fight. He told me he had watched it that morning. I asked if he minded watching it again? I showed him how when we were following the gameplan, we were winning. And then, in round eight, I asked him why he thought Carl had landed the right hand.

'I showed him that he was the wrong side of the line to counter with his hook and that's why Carl's shot got home first. I played the finish again so he could see what I meant. As I was doing it, I was watching him out of the corner of my eye. I replayed it around eight times and then asked him if it made sense.

'He said simply, "Yes, I won't shoot a hook off the line again."'

It's clear that George was disappointed with himself and his performance in the second fight. I imagine that this would affect the confidence of a fighter. So I ask Paddy, how did he bring George back from this defeat? How did he restore George's confidence in himself?

'If George had needed his confidence building up, he didn't show it. He was very good and that was partly the reason why I went round to see him the very next morning after the fight. When I had got George to watch the knockout over and again, I wanted him to see that he had made a simple mistake and been punished for it. This wasn't a big emotional collapse. It wasn't that George had gassed. It wasn't like he was losing the fight either. It was as simple as, "There's your mistake and there's how you got paid for it. We can't do this again."

'A loss like that will affect any fighter, but how it affected him didn't show up for a while. He hides any questions he might have about himself very well. George is a confident man and a confident fighter. But I did have to help him answer the questions he might have. But that wasn't a lack of confidence.'

So what did you decide to do then to help George answer his questions? Is this when you decided to go to Big Bear for some serious sparring with serious opposition?

'The situation now was this. Regardless of why, we had lost two fights on the bounce. Regardless of why, George was undefeated two fights ago. A fighter is going to have questions. Questions are fine, so long as you have the answers, or someone can give them to you. We discussed the answers to George's questions, of course. In the first fight with Carl, George simply put the loss down to Howard Foster stopping the fight. He had dealt with this loss and compartmentalised it successfully. The second fight, we knew why we had lost.

'In order to help George, I needed to organise something that George could use to say to himself that he now had more proof of his ability to support answering his questions. The issue was, "How could I do this in between fights?" So what could we do in the gym so George could have confirmation that he still deserved to be competing at world level?

'The only way you can do that is through sparring. So I'm thinking, "If I get the very best guys in Britain, or even Europe, George will say, 'Yeah, but they're just from Europe – I already know I'm better than them,'" because that's how George thought.

'So the obvious answer was to take him to the States. But who to go to? I wanted sparring in and around George's weight division, so straight away Gennady Golovkin stood out. Golovkin was a weight division below George, but at that time, he was like the Tyson of his era. At that time he was a beast, and totally dominant.

'I knew Golovkin's promoter, Tom Loeffler, because he used to work with James Toney and Lucia Rijker from the time I was with Freddie. I called him and said I wanted to get George out for some sparring with Gennady and did that sound OK to him? He liked the idea. So I arranged it. 'For me, if I could get George some good sparring with a champion like Golovkin, then George should be re-affirming to himself his status as a fighter worthy of competing at world level because this is the man who everyone is talking about in boxing right now and George would be thinking, "I did well against him."

During that time, it was Abel Sanchez who trained Golovkin, wasn't it? How did it go?

'Yeah, it was Abel. George handled the experience very well. He'd lost two fights on the bounce and understandably, George was a little depressed. We all turn to different things under those circumstances and George turns to food, so he wasn't in shape really. He was a bit heavy. It wasn't a big deal, though.

'We had the fight with the European champion Christopher Rebrasse coming up. In the shape George was in, I knew we wouldn't get his best work but it wasn't about that. It was about getting enough quality work so that George could say he did well, and know that when he fought Rebrasse, he could be excellent again.

'I told George my reasons for the sparring. I wanted him to know for sure how good he was, so he was up against the best. George was really keen to do it and it was the way he said that he wanted to do it that made me love him even more as a fighter because there was no hint of him looking for an easier option. He was totally enthusiastic.

'In fact, the reason why we were fighting Rebrasse was because he wanted to continue with a *real* fight. When we were planning who to challenge, George came to me with three names he wanted to fight. He asked me to look at them and said he would be happy to fight any of them. He didn't want an easy fight. That was typical of George.

'When we got to Big Bear, there was no waiting around. We sparred the first day – six rounds. When we got there, the night before we went to the gym, I said to George, "When the bell goes I want you to walk straight out, without even using a jab, hands held high, and go straight inside and sit on Golovkin's chest.

'George gave me the same look he did the time I told him to tell Carl our gameplan in the first fight. "Why would I do that?" he said with a bit of shock attached to his question.

'I said, "Here's the thing. If you move behind your jab and try to keep him outside, he'll end up inside anyway at some stage and on his terms. I want you to go inside when you're fresh and on your terms because you have decided to, not him.

'"Because Golovkin is such a patient fighter, if we walked straight up to him, rather than let him hunt us down on his terms then that's going to have him asking questions about our motivation. That means he's thinking about us. So while he's thinking about us and touching you to work you out, you're buying time to allow you to get used to him and his strength."

'Golovkin was fighting in two weeks' time, so he wouldn't want to get into a war with George because he knows George is a bigger man and doesn't know what George can fully bring. Clearly, Golovkin wouldn't want to risk any damage in his last sparring.

'George boxed really well in the first session. But by the end of the sixth round, I could see Golovkin slip and have a look, pop this way and have a look, but he wasn't taking advantage of everything that he was seeing. He wasn't necessarily doing anything, but he would keep checking how George would react by moving to the same positions to see what he would do.

'At the end of the first day, George came out and I could tell that he was pleased with himself. In his mind, he was overweight and out of shape and Golovkin was two weeks from a fight – so he's thinking that he did well, and rightly so.

'Next morning, I wanted George to enjoy the confirmation that he had from the first day's sparring, knowing that we would be sparring again later that day. We didn't take much heat the first day, so George was OK to spar again.

'Over breakfast, I ask George how he's feeling, and I can see that there's a spring in his step and a little swagger as he tells me he feels good. So I say, "Listen, the spar will be different today." "'How do you mean?" he says.

'"There was a lot that you did very well yesterday, that's fact. But Golovkin hadn't sparred you before and he has his fight in two weeks' time. There was no way he was going to come out and get reckless against you. You're willing to get reckless because you're not fighting in two weeks' time. He's not, because he is. So what I'm saying is that there are a lot of reasons why yesterday was not as intense as it could have been.

'"That'll be different today," I say to George. "Because I saw a lot of slips and moves that he made yesterday and I could see that he saw some shots, but he didn't take the shots. But he was doing his homework, so be aware of that today."

'George nodded in acknowledgement.

'Later that day, when we were in the gym and getting ready, Abel is gloving up Golovkin from the other side of the ring. I'm gloving up George and Abel shouts, "Hey, Paddy, do you want to wear a body protector?"

'Looking up, I noticed three of them on the wall.

'"I usually get Gennady to wear one," he says. "Just for protection. I don't want anything going wrong in the last couple of weeks."

'I asked George and he says, "I don't want that."

'"Are you sure?" I say to George. "They didn't ask us if we wanted to wear it yesterday."

'"I ain't wearing that," says George.

'You make a split-second process of that kind of information and I'm thinking, "I'm not going to get into this with George here because we don't have a fight date around the corner. If something happens, it happens. But if it does happen then it's clear George made the choice. So I just said, "No problem."

'So I say "no thanks" to Abel and he's like "OK" but the way he said "OK" got me thinking, "*Oh shit!*"

'When the spar starts, George gets inside, walks straight up to Golovkin and starts beautifully. George is touching him and Gennady touches him back. Gennady whips in a little shot and George whips one in back.

'In the second round, George made a little bit of space, dropped some longer shots and then slid back in again.

'At the end of the third round, I see a couple of shots come in from Golovkin and then George slightly adjusts his position. Nothing drastic that someone could see, unless they knew him well.

'Then, the second the bell has sounded, George marches straight across the ring and out through the ropes and as he passes me he says simply, "My rib's broke."

'Golovkin's corner knew that something was up and I just waved at them and said we were cool and that was enough for us. And I could see Abel looking at me thinking, "I told you. I offered you the protector."

'He didn't actually *say* it, but I could tell he was thinking it.

'I look back at Abel then as if to say "I know", and George is looking at me as if to say, "Don't bother saying I told you so."

'And, of course, that was it. George's rib was broken. George wasn't able to spar again but he told me that he had gotten what he needed from the experience, so we were good.'

And so George headed back to England, ready to fight at the first opportunity for a major title against a quality fighter in the French European champion Christopher Rebrasse.

'I don't want an easy fight,' is what George had told Paddy. And what George did next impressed everyone – even his bitter rival Carl Froch. To add to the pressure on George, his conqueror was sitting at ringside scrutinising his performance.

18

'I don't want an easy fight'

*George Groves on Christopher Rebrasse
and the battle for the European title*

September 2014

I TRY to imagine being George Groves, twice a defeated world title contender, going into this fight for the European title against the well-respected Christopher Rebrasse in front of another home crowd in London. More than once, Paddy has told me how in all his time in boxing he has not met a fighter who performs under pressure better than George. But even so, I think to myself, George must have been feeling what most us would have considered a crushing pressure in the preparation leading up to this fight.

Christopher 'L'iceberg' Rebrasse, the French European champion, was a good-quality fighter with a 22-2-3 record who would later take both Callum Smith and Rocky Fielding to decisions. He arguably beat Fielding and pushed Smith hard, so he knew his way around a boxing ring and deserved to be fighting at this level. This was someone who wasn't just going to give his European title away. Add to that the fact that the winner would be mandated for a WBC world title shot, and you can see that this was no easy fight for George.

George must have known too that if he didn't win this fight in front of a hometown crowd at Wembley Arena in London, then his stock as a top-level fighter would diminish. After his two failed attempts to capture a world title, if George lost this fight it was going to be difficult, even for someone as articulate and persuasive as George had proven himself to be, to argue that he deserved to be taken seriously as a competitor at world level.

Oh, and just for the record, commentating at ringside for Sky TV was none other than George's nemesis, 'The Cobra', Carl Froch.

That's the pressure George was under, wasn't it, I ask Paddy?

Paddy nods in agreement, 'You know my views on George and dealing with pressure, Teach. He was the best.'

It's Christmas as I write this and me and Paddy have been to his local for a few beers because while he has the chance, he's closed the gym to spend a bit of time with his family. We plan to watch George's fight with Rebrasse together so that I can get his perspective on the event and how George managed what must have been a really challenging situation. But first, as one pint becomes two and then two becomes three, I just sit and talk boxing with Paddy.

He tells me stories about James Toney and Roberto Duran

training at the Wild Card gym in LA. We talk about the similarities between Roberto Duran and Mike Tyson and whether a boxer who comes from the streets and knows nothing *but* fighting, rather than a Muhammad Ali or a Sugar Ray Leonard, men from more stable backgrounds who were athletes and *chose* boxing, have more compelling stories?

I fall on the side of the former. I'm more attracted to the idea that boxing *chose* the likes of Sonny Liston, Duran and Tyson because regardless of how much of a cliché this is, without the saviour of boxing – what would these men have become? Ali and Leonard could have chosen another sport and been successful. It's hard to imagine Liston, Duran or Tyson being anything other than warriors, though, isn't it?

We could keep talking for a while yet. There are too many stories and not enough space in the book, but after a couple more pints, we head back to Paddy's to watch the fight.

There is this narrative that has developed around George Groves that suggests he became a fighter capable of working successfully on the inside *later* in his career after he won his world title against the Russian Fedor Chudinov. The implication was that it wasn't until *after* he had stopped working with both Adam Booth and Paddy that George started to really develop this area of his skillset.

I'm not convinced that this is the case. I had watched the Rebrasse fight before and I knew that George purposely attacked Rebrasse's body time and again, so I bring up this theory with Paddy before we start watching the fight.

Paddy looks away from me and into the air thoughtfully. 'There's some truth in the idea,' he says. 'Look at George's fights before he meets Carl and you won't necessarily see George choosing to work on his opponent inside because that wasn't George's modus operandi. He was more effective on the outside. And you won't see much work on the inside from George in the first Froch fight because we only had nine weeks to work together – so I kept things simple and played to George's strengths in that one. We didn't have time to work on anything new.'

We're watching the fight together for a lot of reasons. But one clear reason is I want to know if Paddy had planned for George to attack Rebrasse to the body so frequently, because before this fight George definitely was *not* associated with calculated and premeditated attacks to the body.

He does it here, though – again and again – and exceptionally well.

We start watching the fight and I draw attention to George's facial expression. He doesn't look like someone with career-defining pressure on his shoulders, and yet that is the situation.

'Dude, my favourite ring walk of George's is the one he did to this fight. It matters to me how a fighter carries himself.

'There's a picture of Muhammad Ali later in his career where he is captured with his hands low, his shoulders slightly hunched, and he looks fatigued. I made sure in this fight that George was aware that he sometimes naturally shaped his body in the same way and dropped his shoulders.

'So, at the ends of the rounds, I wanted George to return to the corner with his chest out and shoulders back, so he gave a bold presentation of confidence through his posture.

There's also the advantage that if a judge is wondering about who won the round, or the final exchange of the round, if you walk back looking like the boss then that will influence the judge. I also told George to take a deep breath as he made his way over to the corner, and hold it for five seconds before releasing it, because that would help to slow his heart rate down. It's about composure.'

George looks in excellent condition for the fight, I remark.

'He's around 12st 8lb there, but he was bang on the 12 stone weight limit at the weigh-in. In saying that, three weeks before the fight he was badly out of shape and well over the limit. The Father, one of my team, came to me and said that George had been going out and getting chocolate in the middle of the night, which was one of George's mechanisms to cope with the pressure.

'In fairness, The Father came with a problem but he offered a solution too. He had a nutritionist who could help and she did a very good job. George knew it was important, focused, and made the weight.'

Mentally, as the final announcements are made in the ring before the fight, George looks in total control. Wembley Arena looks full.

'I had so many times with George that I really enjoyed, and this was one of them. Winning the appeal with [the] IBF was another.'

Who chose for the fight to be held in London after what had happened against Carl Froch?

'That was George. George is a bold individual. He wanted to return to the scene of his loss to Carl, but the fight clearly wasn't big enough for Wembley Stadium, so he chose the arena. George was making a statement that he wasn't afraid to return to where he had faced his biggest challenge.'

There's a band playing in the crowd, creating a slightly fevered, patriotic atmosphere for 'the fighting pride of Hammersmith' in the capital city. They are loud and they really influence the crowd as the fight goes on.

So what about Rebrasse as a fighter, I ask Paddy as we settle down to watch the fight?

'Rebrasse was not the biggest puncher in the world but if you allowed him to get momentum, then he was going to cause you problems. It's easier to stop someone from getting going in the first place than it is to curb momentum when the fighter has built it up.

'When I told George that I wanted him to go out and meet Rebrasse over in Rebrasse's corner, he didn't look convinced because George's normal plan would be to move around the outside. But if George did what was normal for him, then Rebrasse would do what was normal for him too, and I didn't want that. I wanted George to come forward to stop Rebrasse getting momentum. So in round one, that's what George does. Rebrasse tries to come forward but George doesn't give ground and uses his jab effectively, moving laterally rather than backwards.'

At the end of the first round, what is George saying to you?

'He's saying he's tired. And this is the end of round one, mind. I'm saying to him, "You ain't tired. It's in your head. It's stress."'

I can clearly hear George say it as he sits down.

'When we were preparing for this fight people were saying to us that Rebrasse couldn't punch, so George would knock him out. That didn't make any sense to me. How did that mean George would knock him out? A lack of power in the punch means that a fighter lacks power, OK. But, it has no bearing on the chin. The view was that Rebrasse couldn't keep George off him, so he was bound to get knocked out. But that seems to ignore the fact that several fighters have had very limited punch power and yet they have possessed a chin of granite, which they used to their advantage.

'The Irish fighter Wayne McCullough had limited punch power but once he got up his momentum, you had to put up with a hailstorm of punches and deal with that constant pressure. He would overwhelm his opponent with pressure. No matter how much you came at him, he would still be there and firing back at you. He would break an opponent's will and break his heart.'

Like the late world champion Johnny Tapia, I say to Paddy. Not much of a punch but a very high workrate and a chin of granite that could absorb so much punishment that other fighters struggled to put him away?

Paddy smiles in agreement.

In round two, as we watch, George clearly starts to go to Rebrasse's body.

'Up until this fight, nobody would have described George as a body puncher. George would throw shots to the body, yes, but he wasn't what could be described as a stable inside fighter – and yet look at him in this fight. This is the first fight that George went to the body a lot, with intent, and not just because he finds himself in range. We're in round two right now but when we get to round four, you will really see George sustain his body attack.'

I refocus our attention on Rebrasse and comment on his really high guard and limited punch output.

'Well,' says Paddy, 'because George is commanding the centre of the ring, Rebrasse is finding it hard to get any momentum with his feet, so he can't build up any with his hands. Remember, the feet deliver the shot. And because Rebrasse can't build up momentum, he's not comfortable and he's starting to overthink his hands a little, which is to George's advantage.'

As we watch, the commentator for Sky TV is talking about the sparring with Gennady Golovkin and what impact this must have had on George's confidence.

'I think this is one of, if not *the*, best performance in George's career,' Paddy reflects. 'With all the pressure he was under to perform, and his career in the balance, to box like this, with such skill and composure – that's impressive. Look at George's punch output too. He keeps his workrate high and we had planned that because it's a great way to take away someone's momentum. We planned to go to the body in this fight, which you can see clearly from round four, because we knew that by George taking away Rebrasse's momentum, George would find himself in close in fixed positions against his opponent. He would be stepping around Rebrasse, rather than moving away. Rebrasse wasn't going to pull away from George because that wasn't his style, so the opportunity to go to the body would present itself frequently.'

The gameplan was working because at the end of the fourth round, George had clearly won them all, and he looked comfortable attacking the body.

'I had mentally prepared George, so he knew what type of fight he was going into. Physically, George was in shape but mentally he was exceptionally strong for this fight – and that's important. Your brain requires energy and a lot of energy too. So if you are anxious or nervous, that's draining – the most exhausting type of draining.

'It's like when I told you about James Toney sparring when he was out of shape. He'd be facing guys who, based on their physical condition, should have been able to beat James. But they couldn't. Because they were sparring *James Toney*. And mentally, they weren't prepared for that, whereas James was just like, "OK."'

At this point, Paddy turns to me and asks me directly, 'What do you see George doing?'

'Targeting the body – regularly and with clear intention as he holds the centre ground and moves laterally around Rebrasse,' I say, as we watch the fifth round unfolding.

In round six, the commentator makes the point that George has taken the effect of Rebrasse's jab away by using his own so well. Was that something that you planned, I ask?

'George has always had an excellent jab and he had that long before working with me. That will definitely have been worked on with Adam [Booth] and probably goes all the way back to George's Dale Youth days. George has a world-class, varied and spiteful jab.'

As we reach the halfway point in the fight, the Sky commentator states that George is sharper than Rebrasse and so far he feels that the bout is a shut-out for Groves – and Paddy agrees.

What advice were you giving George at this stage?

'I didn't really need to say much to George in the corner. He was winning every round and he was comfortable. It's just about staying composed. Sometimes, being dominant and getting success can switch a fighter off. Look at the second fight with Froch. Before the knockout punch, I thought George was winning it easier than the first one. And then George switched off and we know what happened.

'I couldn't allow George to switch off in this one because we were stopping the opponent gaining momentum – and that's constant work because you are always in a position that you are trading with your man. George was trading to the body well, so I kept reminding him of that. Everything had to come off the jab, and to step around Rebrasse rather than pull away so there was no space for his opponent to build momentum.'

As the fight enters its final stages, Paddy is clear that George has won all of the first eight rounds. While watching the ninth, Paddy asks me about George's punch selection.

'What are you seeing from George, Teach?'

'Jabs to slow momentum and a range of body shots,' I reply.

'Yeah, and we're in the final stages of the fight. I'd been worried about George maintaining the level of concentration required to do the job as well as this. After all, Rebrasse keeps on coming but you can see for yourself how George was managing the fight.

'Later on, some people said that George started using his jab and going to the body more successfully *after* the Badou Jack fight. But you can see for yourself what's happening in this fight – anyone can. And this is *before* we faced Badou Jack.'

As we watch the end of round nine, I can hear Paddy focusing on the mental element of George's performance. I imagine that George is feeling tired at this point, but Paddy is telling him not to let his mind dictate to his body that he is tired. To keep behind his jab. And then, Paddy notices George's focus slip. He notices George look over his shoulder and Paddy snaps, 'What are you looking at? Pay attention to me.'

What was George looking at, I ask?

'Rebrasse, because don't forget, even though George is performing brilliantly here, there is bound to be one fact playing on his mind. In his last fight with Carl, he was knocked out in the eighth round. In his previous fight with Carl, it was stopped in the ninth. Now, he's going into the tenth round. He's thinking, "This is when it happens to me. This is when it goes wrong." And that's a dangerous time for George. He needs to focus. So I say to him, "We've got three rounds left – nine minutes. We've worked for three hours a day for this. You think you're tired but you're not. Keep behind your jab. We don't need a knockout. You've been measured and controlled. We don't need anything wild. Keep to the plan."

'I could see George was drifting and as coach I had to act decisively. A fighter is more likely to drift when things are going well. When things are going badly, a fighter knows it. But when things are going well, complacency can slip in – and then you get mistakes.'

Did you feel George was risking complacency at that point?

'No, not at all. I just felt that George was thinking, "Why is Rebrasse still here? Is this where it goes wrong for me?" I needed to address that.

'Even in the last few rounds, I needed George to make sure his lead foot was near Rebrasse so we could continue to neutralise his momentum. Rebrasse delivered his shots with his feet so without them, with us in close, he would struggle to achieve anything significant. I just had to remind George what to do.

'When I worked with James Toney, it was the same. That dude had more talent under the dirt of his fingernail than I had in my body. So, I didn't *teach* James anything. I just reminded him what he was good at, so that he was making the most of everything that he did.'

As we near the final round of the fight, I ask Paddy if he planned for the fight to go the distance.

'I never plan for a fight to finish early unless I see something that convinces me that this will happen. George is a world-class puncher with his right hand and he has a world-class jab. But it was the same as when he fought Carl. I said to him, "Do not try to knock the dude out. He has never been stopped. Don't waste 12 rounds trying to prove something that no other man could. Just win 12 separate rounds and then bank them."

'I never expected Rebrasse not to be there at the end. If he wasn't, that would have been a great bonus. But this was about 12 three-minute fights, and we needed to win as many of them as possible.'

In the corner at the end of the 11th round, I hear Paddy firmly addressing George, explaining that he needs to see the fight out professionally. That they don't need a knockout. He reminds George that they have made a mistake before, and that they do not repeat mistakes. 'Forget about knocking this dude out,' he says. 'He has to come out and chase you.'

How dangerous was this time for George? It was the last round and a major title was almost in the bag. Did you tell him to play it safe?

'It was a very dangerous time. I didn't want George to change what he was doing. It's like Freddie used to say. If you have a fighter who has been going forward successfully for the last 11 rounds, the worst thing you can do is advise him to start moving around differently for the final round. Don't advise him to keep himself safe because he's won every round. You're changing what he was doing to be successful. All of a sudden, he starts moving differently and he lets his opponent in and you're in a shitload of trouble. If you are winning the fight going forward, stay moving forward. Do the thing that you have been doing well. And that's what I was saying to George. "Keep doing what you've been doing well." I didn't want George to try to knock him out because then I would be doing what Freddie taught me *not* to do.'

What are your final thoughts on the fight?

'Just that George did exactly what I asked in that final round. And that man was under so much pressure and he dealt with it so professionally. It's a shame. Ours was one of those relationships in life where I think, "What a shame, man." He did so well. What a shame it ended like it did.'

Paddy has genuine regret in his voice when he talks about his relationship with George, how it eventually changed and then came to an end.

And so, I reflect as I begin packing my laptop and notes away after another late night with Paddy, George saw out this tricky fight professionally; he earned a mandated ranking for another world title shot; and the 'George Groves for world champion show' looked to be firmly back on the road after an excellent performance that ended with a European title around his waist.

But that wasn't how this drama was going to unfold.

And while by rights this should have been another beginning, another chance to win a world title, and another chance for the Groves/Fitzpatrick partnership to achieve everything that they had planned for, in reality the cracks in their relationship were beginning to show.

Rather than a new beginning as European champion, with George and his coach riding on the crest of a wave towards world title glory, this was now the beginning of the end.

19

Vegas Baby!

The world heavyweight title and a near miss with a bear in the woods, 2004

RISING TO almost 9,000 feet, Big Bear Mountain range looks down on the rest of California. It is not the first thing you think of when you consider the topography of the Sunshine State. And yet, Big Bear's alpine environment, clad in pine and oak forests that flourish on the slopes of the peaks that form this mountain range, is as much a part of California as Venice Beach, the Hollywood Hills and the city of Los Angeles.

There are three major peaks in the mountain range: Silver Mountain, Goldmine Mountain and the largest of Southern California's peaks, Bear Mountain, which rises to 8,505 feet above sea level. During the summer, this area of outstanding natural beauty is frequented by nature lovers, hikers and boat fanatics taking advantage of Big Bear Lake. In the winter months, there is on average 100 inches of snowfall, catering for the most extreme tastes in alpine sports. Big Bear in California gets its name from the large population of grizzly bears that once roamed the area and outnumbered the human inhabitants. Nowadays, wildlife is abundant, with mountain lions, coyotes and bobcats frequenting the area. Unfortunately, or perhaps fortunately depending on your perspective, the Californian grizzly bear was hunted to extinction in the early 1900s. But bears are certainly not gone from Big Bear and there is currently a very healthy population of the American black bear roaming wild around the parkland's woods and mountains.

Though the elevation and physical geography of the Big Bear area is very different from the rest of California, it is only 100 miles from Los Angeles and just over 200 miles from Las Vegas. It is this ease of access from these bustling centres of opportunity that perhaps explains some of the attraction of the area for a boxing trainer and fighters who train for bouts held in these cities.

Big Bear is situated at a significant, though not extreme, altitude when compared to other high-elevation areas. To get there, you have to negotiate winding, dangerous roads that twist and turn through the natural beauty until they reach their remote destination, which is inhabited by around 21,000 people.

The area has been selected as a training camp for several notable fighters, including world champions like Oscar De La Hoya, Tyson Fury and Gennady Golovkin. Fighters and trainers cite the thinner air as advantageous to their training regimes. In addition to this, trainers reference the benefits of the natural solitude and lack of distractions as a way to improve their fighters' focus and refine the single-minded determination needed to overcome an opponent.

It is February 2004.

With the wintry weather still holding Big Bear in its grip, Paddy finds himself driving from the temperate climate of Las Vegas, where Laila Ali, Vatche and his other fighters are not currently training in earnest, to meet the soon-to-be heavyweight champion of the world – 'Relentless' Lamon Brewster.

'I remember thinking I knew where Big Bear was but not quite how to get there,' says Paddy. 'That's why we were meeting at the bottom of the hill.'

Lamon is driving from his LA base and they have agreed to meet at the foot of the treacherous road that will lead to Big Bear because, unlike Lamon, Paddy doesn't know the way to Big Bear. While Lamon led Paddy up the precarious stretch of road that would eventually bring them to their high-altitude destination, Paddy would help lead Lamon through a training camp that would transform him. Even though at this point neither man knew it, it would lead to the changing of a fighter from one who had suffered the trauma of losing a much-loved trainer to one who felt like he simply couldn't be beaten.

And all of this compressed into only six weeks. Let's go back a bit, I say. How did you meet Lamon?

'When I first arrived in LA, there was a poster on the wall that I saw that looked like a huge fight advertisement to me, but to the LA people was just a local show and it had Lamon and "Sugar" Shane Mosley on it. That was my first introduction to him. A couple of the guys I knew at the time were like, "Hey, that's my boy Lamon", so he was known in the gym. He was undefeated at the time, with most of his wins coming by way of knockout.

'It was one Saturday morning that I remember Lamon rolled up at the Wild Card and on this Saturday, Freddie wasn't in. I recognised his face but I couldn't put his name to his face because I hadn't been in LA that long and like I said, so many famous people would come in the gym to train it was a little bit overwhelming.

'So he asks me if Freddie is in, and when I tell him he isn't we get chatting and I work out that this is Lamon. He tells me he's just looking to do a bit of training and so I tell him "no problem" and he asks me if I'll wrap his hands.

'So I wrapped his hands and "T" [the initial represents Brewster's middle name Tajuan] was happy with my work. He got straight into some shadow boxing quietly and I was watching him for a while before I asked him if he wanted to do some mitts work. So we got in the ring, did some mitts, and then I watched him on the bags. We chatted a bit too and we connected that way. At the time, Lamon was training with Bill Slayton and he was managed by Sam Simons, one of the creators of *The Simpsons* who used to train at the Wild Card for fitness.

'We just sort of clicked with each other and from then on we were cool. I mean, anyone who met Lamon and didn't like him, well, there would definitely be something wrong with them. There are only a few people who stand out to me as pure class because they will never speak badly about someone, ever – and Lamon is one of those men.'

'It was 2003 and I'd been living in Las Vegas for a couple of years training Laila and Vatche. Me and "T" hadn't been in contact so much because of our differing schedules but he got hold of me and said, "Listen, I'm fighting [Wladimir] Klitschko in April in Vegas. I'm going into camp and I want you to come in and do my diet, nutrition and look out for me. Bill [Slayton, Lamon's trainer] has passed away. I'm going up to Big Bear around February and I want to know if you'd be on board."

'Bill had died in October and Shadeed Suluki, Slayton's assistant coach, was taking over the reins. I had a chat with Laila, Vatche and my other fighters and their schedules would allow for me to work with Lamon. I also had to take into consideration that Kerry was pregnant with D.J. at the time too. There's something funny about Big Bear, you know, because when I went there to train with George for the Badou Jack fight, Kerry was pregnant then too!'

Keen to catch up with him myself, not long after Christmas I called Lamon and spoke with him for well over an hour via video link at his home on the US east coast. As soon as I asked him if I could interview him about his time with Paddy, he was as keen to be a part of the book as I was to talk with him.

When I called him, he was wearing a longer beard than on the videos I had watched of his work as a pro, but he still looked like the fighter I was used to. He was smiling and enthusiastic throughout our interview and spoke articulately and thoughtfully about a range of subjects, from boxing to the existence of God. He said my mother, who had recently died, was always with me. It was a profound conversation and while boxing was the reason I called Lamon, it was not the reason I continued talking with him. Lamon is a very spiritual and intelligent man, and I was simply enjoying what he had to say – far more than I thought I would.

I asked him about how he came to invite Paddy to be part of his preparations to challenge the world heavyweight champion and he immediately started remembering his days at the Wild Card gym.

'I met Paddy because he worked at the Wild Card gym with Freddie Roach. And over the years, as you see somebody every day, I took a liking to Paddy. He's a very likeable person, a great guy. I'd see Paddy training other guys in the gym and I would watch his patterns with them. You know, I'm a big guy on *feel* and I could just *feel* that he would be good to have around me and be part of my camp. So I asked him if he would help me get ready for taking on the world heavyweight champion Wladimir Kitschko, and he agreed.'

Were you driving your car from the Vegas climate up to Big Bear in winter time, I ask Paddy?

'Yeah, I followed "T" up the hill and we arrived in the snow. I parked my car, and there was a period of four weeks in the six and a half weeks we were there that I didn't even see my car because it was simply covered in snow. It was also a two-wheel drive, so we weren't going to use that to get around in those conditions. We had two four-wheel drive trucks to use.'

It was a winter camp, so the area was even more isolated and remote, which added to the solitude. Lamon had been keen to train at altitude, as well as to avoid the distractions of LA and Vegas.

When did you leave Big Bear, I ask Paddy? Were you there for the entire camp?

'Well, while it's almost 9,000 feet up, in a few hours you can be back down to sea level and it doesn't take too long to acclimatise to the change in altitude when the altitude isn't extreme. That means that if you return to sea level too soon before the fight, well, you lose the benefit of the altitude training. So we stayed in Big Bear until a few days before the fight.'

What are the benefits of higher altitude training?

'There are plenty of educated men who argue about the relative merits of this type of training, so I'm not going to be definitive. There are lots of reasons to train at altitude. When you do train at altitude, the air is thinner, so it makes you work harder and you find that the first day you get out there and start running. The lungs burn as they try to operate. How long after you come down from the altitude the benefits of the training stay with you is up for debate. I think the benefits that Lamon had would have remained with him because we came down on the Wednesday and fought on the Saturday.

'He stayed with me in my house in Vegas. Kerry was away with an aunt in New York at the time. I didn't want Lamon staying in the hotel where he was fighting just in case he didn't sleep well with the hotel noise. I was only living five minutes from the Strip anyway, so it made sense.'

What did you employ Paddy to do, I ask Lamon in our interview, so that I can understand how he planned his training camp?

'Basically, he was like my babysitter,' Lamon laughs. 'I was away from home in camp, so Paddy helped me a lot. He cooked for me. He did my strength and conditioning training and we did a lot of meditation. He also focused on psychology. He really helped me to, I guess the phrase is, "tune up my motor" so that I could get my mind in the right place to face the calibre of opposition that I was going to come up against. He did so much in that camp. To categorise him in a single role just wouldn't be right.'

Who was with you in camp, I ask Paddy?

'With me and "T" were his new trainer Shadeed, his dad, his brother and one of his best friends. It was all cool. A man can have whoever he wants in his camp but every now and again you might question who is involved. I could understand why I was there. I could understand Shadeed's role – he was head coach. But then you start looking at other guys and when things aren't going so well you think, "Why the feck is he here?"

'For example, I come into the kitchen one day to check some white rice I've got boiling on the stove for "T" and I see his dad with his back to me and his shoulders all hunched up over the stove. I think to myself, "What's this dude doing?" When I look around his body I notice he has one of those kilo bags of sugar and he's emptying this sugar into the rice.

'I say, "Dude, what the fuck are you doing?"

'And he says, "I'm putting in sugar. My boy likes sugar in his rice!"

'I'm like, "Woah, the dude's too fat, man. He needs to *lose* weight."

'"My boy needs sugar in his rice!" he keeps shouting, and I have to be really careful and watch him because his dad is trying to keep "T" emotionally happy with food, which is understandable, I suppose, given the circumstances with Bill. But it's no way to run a training camp. It's definitely not the diet of champions!'

Was Lamon in a good place when you began the training camp?

'Most of "T's" time in camp was heartbreaking as he was mourning the loss of his lifelong trainer Bill Slayton. They were close and Lamon was hurting emotionally and mentally. On the table next to his bed, Lamon had a picture of his wife and family – *and Bill*. And that shows how close they were.

'Most nights, I would go to his room and we would sit and talk, just me and him, while the other boys were downstairs playing computer games and his dad was out walking. We could talk for an hour, or for several hours. We wouldn't plan what we were talking about. I couldn't because I didn't know what Lamon I would be getting from one night to the next. Sometimes we would meditate, rather than talk. Sometimes, he might break down a little bit. It was really hard for him and he didn't know the right way to get through what he needed to.

'It was maybe made even harder because Shadeed was having a tough time of it too. His mentor was gone and he was experiencing the emotions associated with that loss, so that couldn't have been easy.'

On top of this, Lamon was unfancied by the public, and many people within boxing, who thought he had little chance of beating Klitschko. A lot of the talk around the fight was of the punishing defeat the Ukrainian champion was going to hand out to Brewster – and why there was little that Lamon could do about it.

Lamon reinforces Paddy's view of his mental state at that time when I ask him how he was at the beginning of the camp.

'It was very difficult,' he says quietly as his tone of voice lowers respectfully. 'There was a lot of pressure on me, for sure, but losing my trainer and feeling something like a puppy that's just lost its owner was really hard. Paddy helped me psychologically to keep it all together.'

How was Lamon physically and in terms of his level of boxing at this point? Was he sparring effectively?

'We had a lot of good fighters in the camp to help him,' says Paddy, 'but in sparring, the men that were brought in to help were all *handing* it to "T" and he was not having a good time.'

So while Lamon was preparing to fight the heavyweight champion of the world, he was struggling in sparring?

'Yeah, and he was getting frustrated too, which wasn't helping the situation. His coach Shadeed was keep on telling "T" to "scoot up".

'Logically, I'm sure that "T" knew what that phrase referred to. After all, they had known each other a long time. It ain't like they just met two weeks ago. But with everything else that was going on in his head, I suppose he was just drawing a blank and thinking, "What the hell does 'scoot up' mean? So he would get frustrated and that wasn't helping his focus at all.

'Every now and again we would have a good day, but it wouldn't be on a *sparring* day.

'So there was this day when this martial artist, one of "T's" friends, came up to Big Bear to see him from LA, which is a big deal because that's nearly a three-hour drive each way, so you can imagine "T" appreciated the effort.

'It was a Sunday, which was "T's" day off, and the snow had eased recently and melted pretty quickly, so there wasn't much of it left on this day. So me, "T" and his friend went for a walk in the woods and we walked to this clearing right on the top of the mountain.

'When we got to the top, we sat down and "T's" friend asks him if he wants to do some tai-chi. Now, I didn't know what tai-chi was but they were doing it, so I watched and joined in. I just sort of copied whatever they did. "T" felt better from it and the relaxation he experienced, and his friend's effort to see him, resonated with "T" and he had a good day that day. He felt good.

'We went back into camp then and we had around two and a half weeks left. "T" started to get rough. Things still weren't right. He was saying he was feeling sick, that he had stomach pains, and I thought it must be a cold or something. He couldn't train, he said, and we were struggling – badly.

'Around that time, we sometimes had these team meetings which were called when Lamon or another member of the team felt that something was going wrong. I just couldn't be bothered with the meetings. There were a lot of voices – Lamon, Shadeed, Lamon's dad, his brother – and I just felt that Shadeed was the boss and he should have just said to the

'*Where it all began and still my favourite gym,*' with Paddy's son DJ to his right as you look at it, after sparring some St Francis' amateurs – St Francis gym, Limerick.

'*Blessed to be among the greats,*' Freddie Roach, James 'Lights Out' Toney and 'Manos de Piedra' Roberto Duran – Wild Card gym 1997.

Paddy with Freddie Roach and world ranked cruiserweight Yosuke Nishijima before a training session – 1998 at the Wild Card gym.

'Me and James laughing after a face-off. Neither of us broke the stare until I blew him a kiss. Thankfully, he saw the humour in it and didn't whup my ass.'

James 'Lights Out' Toney, 4 weight world champion (pictured with his WBA and IBA heavyweight belts) whose seal of approval meant a huge amount to Paddy as he worked as Freddie Roach's assistant coach at the Wild Card gym.

New coach is a big hit with Glen

by POST REPORTER

GLENN Cattey has plucked an Irishman from the heart of America to help him become a British boxing champion in Bristol.

Stapleton-based middleweight Cattey might not need the luck of the Irish to beat domestic 11st champ Neville Brown at Whitchurch on November 15, but he is taking no chances.

Paddy Fitzpatrick has been recruited from Freddie Roche's famous Los Angeles gym to steer Cattey to the very top of his Stapleton profession.

The 34-year-old Metabolism explained: "I felt I needed more specialised help and spoke to Paddy Roche. He invited me to cross out to the States and work with folks.

"But he already has Michael Moorer and James Toney on his books and I knew I would have to come behind them.

So imagine Cattey's surprise when Roche offered him the next best thing – his very own personal trainer in Bristol."

Paddy has been in Bristol for six weeks now and he's turned the inside out.

"He's altered my diet, sleep patterns and training routines, worked out a whole new road running schedule and improved my strength and stamina no end.

"There are still three-and-a-half weeks to go before the fight and I really three pounds outside my fighting weight. I feel absolutely great," added Cattey.

Fitzpatrick, no better than on average amateur boxer in Ireland, has certainly made an impact as a coach.

He said: "Good boxers don't make good coaches and good coaches don't make good boxers. I'm much better at one than the other.

"I've worked with some great fighters in America and I think Glenn Cattey could be right up there with them.

"I know my immediate job is to help Glenn beat Neville Brown, but I'm looking beyond that. I reckon Glenn will go on to box for a world title."

Despite his new partnership with Fitzpatrick, Cattey remains very much a part of Chris Sanigar's Bristol Boys crew.

He said: "I still train at Chris' gym in Kingswood and spar with the other fighters. I want to win a Lonsdale Belt for all of them."

Paddy with his cruiserweight Luke 'The Duke' Watkins (Irish and Commonwealth title holder) and four-weight world champion James 'Lights Out' Toney catching up during one of James' recent UK promotional tours.

Training camp for middleweight Glen Cattey v Neville Brown, September 1997. Paddy returned from the States for six weeks to work with Glen.

'I got him first.' Paddy doing the rabbit ears behind Ali in Paddy's gym, Henderson, Las Vegas 2003 before Ali got him back in Germany. Also pictured with Paddy are world ranked lightweight Almazbak Raiymkulov, Vatche 'Wartime' Wartanian and Bagrat Ohanyan.

Vatche 'Wartime' Wartanian being joined by Thomas 'The Hitman' Hearns after Vatche's win over future world champion Alex Velardez.

Last-minute shake-out for Laila Ali ahead of her successful challenge to become a world champion in two weight divisions.

August 2002 – Laila Ali vs Suzi Taylor for the IBA world female super middleweight title with Muhammad Ali in attendance at the Aladdin hotel, Las Vegas.

Taking a break from training camp with Laila Ali in Cape Town, South Africa, 2006.

'The Road Warrior' Kelci Jeffries, winning her IBA females' world featherweight title, California, July 2007.

Paddy's friend Deano with the napkin that Ali signed in 2005 at a Beverly Hills hotel. How many autographs did Ali give where he signed it, 'Mr Muhammad Ali'?

Taking a break from an Adidas commercial shoot – Paddy and Laila decide to do a take-off of her Dad's famous pose, *'I shook up the world!'*

2006 Berlin, Germany, DJ gets a kiss from Ali the night before the Laila Ali vs Asa Sandell fight.

'Got you back!' Berlin 2006, Ali gets his revenge for the rabbit ears joke in Vegas.

others that he was in charge of the boxing in the gym, that I was in charge of my responsibilities and that their jobs were to help out as and when required.

'I couldn't see the sense in involving the fighter in these meetings either. It was extra stress when our job was supposed to be to try to take the heat off "T", not involve him.

'I felt for Shadeed and Lamon. They were both suffering. Bill was more than a trainer and a boxing coach. He was a life coach and Lamon had known him since he was 16. Everyone in camp was trying to do their thing, wanted to do their best, but no one was really sorting anything out. No one really had the answer to the deep-seated turmoil that Lamon was experiencing.'

It's important at this point that I remind you that there are American black bears, among other predators, roaming wild in the dark places around Big Bear of an evening. In fact, Paddy recalled having seen bear prints in the snow and the mud as they ran or drove around the area, so they were clear that there was at least the risk of coming across a bear if a person wasn't careful. As a precaution, Lamon was equipped with a pistol, in case he felt the need for protection.

What's the story behind 'the bear in the woods', I ask Paddy, as I have read differing versions of the tale, some even saying that Paddy came face to face with a bear?

'There was this place near the apex of the mountain that was densely wooded and we could see it from the top of the road where we were staying. One day, I say to whoever I'm driving with, "Look how feckin' black that is in there." You couldn't see anything. It was pitch black. It was just forest

– no light at all. The only light you could see was from way down the mountain, which was the cabins we were staying in. And they'd all be cracking the jokes and saying, "That ain't no place for no black man in there. I ain't gonna walk my ass into that," and these type of conversations. But I was kind of drawn to the place.

'I'd been up around there before because I had gone with "T" and his friend to a clearing during the day to do tai-chi. Then, on a night when Lamon wasn't feeling too good, I just decided I was going to go for a walk up there – myself.

'As I was deciding this, I knew that there was danger. After all, I'd seen bear prints. But it was one of those things in my life that I have done which doesn't seem to make sense while I'm doing it. In fact, I'm scared to *actually* do it, but I'm thinking to myself that I have to do it and I can't hide from myself at that moment.

'So it's around midnight and I walked silently up the road to where the forest began and all I can see is a black wall. I turned around and looked down and it's dark that way too, but at least there are the lights from the houses to reassure me.

'I turn around and look in again at what seems like an impenetrable wall of darkness and I'm thinking, "What the feck am I doing?" But I start walking, nice and slow, going around 20 paces and then stopping and listening to the noises of the forest. Then I'd go another 20 or 50 paces, and I can still hear noises that are concerning me, but I keep walking. I'm shitting my pants but I keep walking.

'Eventually, I end up in the same clearing where I'd done the tai-chi with Lamon and his friend. And because this is a clearing, there's an opening and the skies are really huge in Big Bear. It was a clear night, so some light was filtering in. I find a place to rest and I sit down.

'I'm still scared stiff, mind you, but I sit down and I listen to *everything* because there isn't even the gentle rustle of my feet moving any more. I started to find peace, is the best way to describe what happened. And I got really into it in that clearing because I could hear everything going on around me, but now the sounds were OK with me, not frightening any more.

'I spent about 20 minutes or so up there on my own, in that peace, and I think to myself that I have to go and get "T".

'So I walked down the hill and went to his room and said, "'T', come for a walk with me." And he's like, "What?" So I say, "Come for a walk with me and don't bring your pistol. Let's go up to the top of the road."

'He's like, "Come on, you big dummy, it's the middle of the night," but I tell him to trust me and walk with me.'

I ask Lamon to take up the story when I interview him and he begins by saying, 'You know sleeping at night is something that has always been very hard for me. As long as I remember, even as a child, no matter how hard I would play during the day, come night time I wake up. Going to bed early for me is going to bed around 2am. I normally don't close my eyes until around 5am. And this fight was really challenging. If it wasn't for Paddy helping me to wrestle with my mind, I don't know how I would have managed that situation.'

So do you remember that night when Paddy came to you around midnight and asked you to walk with him in the woods, without your pistol?

Lamon smiles and laughs really loudly, 'Well now, see, I'm from the ghetto, right, and Paddy came to me and he was like, "Man, we gotta go and meditate. We gotta go and do this thing right, man. This is the biggest fight of your life. You gotta put that energy you're feeling out there."

'He was saying a lot of deep things that from one warrior to the next, I definitely comprehended. So he was like, "Let's mediate out there in the woods." And I'm like, "Fool, I ain't going into the woods in the middle of the night. I ain't gonna be the first black man to get *eaten* in those woods at night. Are you crazy?"

'And he's like, "Come on, brother. The spirits are with us and you've just got to believe that you're protected. You say that you believe in God, so let's do it."

'I allowed that dude to take me out. I thought we was just gonna walk to this little clearing because the house I was staying in was the nearest one to the woods. I thought we might walk around 25 yards or so. Instead, this dude took me so far back up into the woods I thought there ain't no way anyone's gonna find us again!

'The thing is, in Big Bear, every night you hear these noises. I don't know if it's coyotes or wolves and there are bears up there too, you know. And I'm thinking, "We're gonna get murdered so bad they ain't even gonna find our bones!"

'Eventually, though, we got to the spot Paddy wanted and he says, "This is the spot right here – I can feel it."

'He was talking to me the whole way up, which helped to make me comfortable and we meditated, man – we *meditated*.

'But seriously, in doing that man, he was right because the thing about success, *true* success, is about being able to conquer your fears. If you have a fear of failing, you will never be successful.

'That night to me was one of the most memorable and spiritual things in my life because we're like 7,500 feet up in the air in Big Bear. It's night time. It's as dark as I've ever known it and we're walking through the forest. We know there are bears around. We've seen the footprints and yet we went on to meditate. It was one of those things that really affected me.'

Paddy continues the story. 'So we walked up with me talking to "T" about this and that all the way. When we got to the forest, and we could see the darkness, we went quiet and then we continued into the woods, stopping every 20 feet or so to chat, and then going in a bit further. "T" is really quiet because he's experiencing this for the first time and I'm quiet because I am reconfirming to myself that this is OK because I've already been in.

'When we got to the opening, we sat down. We didn't really talk as such, we just sat down, and after a while I said to him, "Do you want to do some tai-chi?" Now remember, I haven't got a clue how to spell tai-chi, never mind lead a session. I've sort of done it once with his friend, but that's it.

'Lamon agrees, though, so the two of us stood up and without talking to each other, we start doing tai-chi. Mine would have been an interpretation of what I did with his friend and his would have *actually* been tai-chi, so I must have looked like a lunatic. I just did what I felt was right at that moment.'

I try to imagine the scene. It is gone midnight. It is pitch black in the middle of a dense forest on the top of a mountain known to have a large bear population, and a skinny white Irishman and the future heavyweight champion of the world are embracing a spiritual meditation session – without the protection of a pistol.

It seems crazy.

'I'm not sure how long we did it for,' says Paddy, 'but it was long enough and then we walked back.

'On the journey back, we didn't talk at all and when we got to the house, I just wished him goodnight and that was it. There was no reflection at all, from either of us.'

But whatever Paddy did that night had a significant impact.

Lamon told me, 'If you asked me to describe what I felt then with everything that we were working on in my camp, man, I'd just have to say that Paddy's my angel, dude.

'Even to this day Paddy is my angel because, if God came to me and said, "I'm going to put you into a battle and I'm going to let you choose five people that you believe in, and who believe in you," Paddy would be one of those five, man.

'If you're on that battlefield, in a life-or-death situation, Paddy's the dude you need. You don't need to look over your shoulder and think, "Will he be fighting or running?" You know Paddy will be by your side. You might even have to hold *him* back.

'Because the thing about Paddy is that he's a *real* dude. He don't never act fake. He's always Paddy. Every day, for better or worse, he's Paddy. And that helped to boost my confidence to help me know I could win this fight. I could *trust* Paddy. As I'd lost my trainer, I needed love and someone to love on me too. I'm no good without love and love gives me the confidence to do what I do.

'That's what Paddy represents for me.

'Me and Paddy's got a bond, and that's what made it so special about us being in those woods. Everything that I went through in that camp, he was always there for me. He was always about the mission. And he made sure our mission was done. I just couldn't have a better person by my side than Paddy. When you've got someone that solid, it makes a big difference in a person's psyche. Especially someone like me. I'm a mental fool. I'm a mental type because I can do anything if I *believe* I can do it. I needed someone to guide, reinforce and nurture me. I'm like an artist. Artists are temperamental and it takes special people to deal with that – men like Paddy. I was able to express myself all through training camp because this dude Paddy stayed *with* me.'

Did you talk about the night in the woods again, I ask Paddy?

'There was no need to talk about the experience again because a couple of days later, Lamon left his bedroom and came down the hall shouting, "The champ is here!" then he'd drum on the walls like this [Paddy drums with his hands heavily on his kitchen table]. "The champ is here!"

'He was a new and refreshed man, a new dude. There was a sparkle and a glow to him. It was like he had been somehow unburdened and he had found energy from something.'

Maybe it was the tai-chi, I say?

'Well, when he went back to sparring, wow did those boys get a shock because this was a *new dude* they were sparring.'

Tell me about the shield that you made Lamon. The one that he would hang on the corner of the ring during sparring and that he hung on his bed every night. The shield you made that he hung in the changing room on the night of his fight with Klitschko.

'Me and "T" would talk all of the time. I would describe Lamon as spiritual and religious. He's a Christian. I remember him telling me that he would see gold around us when we had a meditation session. Not like money, but more like protection. He would say, "It's protecting me."

'That stuck with me. And he would also talk with me about the "I Am" from the Bible, you know, the word of God.

'He was also under huge pressure because in his mind, he had spent so long saying to himself that he had to fight for his wife and children. "I ain't got nothin'" is what Lamon used to say to me.

'He could remember that when he was a kid growing up in the ghetto, he was crouching down behind a car in the street with gunshots going off and thinking, "I don't want this."

'But he didn't have the type of education to get a good job with a good wage to allow him to get his family out of the situation they were in and this was really breaking him too.

'I thought that he was putting too much pressure on himself. So my point of view with him was, "OK, as a husband, you want to provide for your wife. As a father, you want to provide for your children. But you really have to do this thing for *you*. Your opinion of a good man is somebody who provides for his wife and children. And that's OK. But if you're really going to do this well, stop trying to do it for Bill. Stop trying to do it for your wife and kids. Do it for *you*. And if you do if for you, and you win, well, what benefits you will benefit all the people that you care about.

'Little things like that seemed to help and that was part of the "I Am" on his shield too.

'So because the gold, the religion and the need for him to focus on his performance all came up at that time, I remember thinking, "I'm gonna make him a shield." So I got an old cereal box and shaped it. Then I bought some gold material and found this tiny little sewing shop and when I brought them my gold covered shield, I asked them to embroider the words "I Am" on to it.

'Lamon seemed to really appreciate it and it came everywhere with him. He had it on his bed and around the ring when he was sparring, so that he could see it.

'We even walked it to the ring on the night of the fight.'

I ask Lamon about the shield and whether he felt that it helped him to be successful in his world title fight.

'Oh man, absolutely,' he says. 'You know, man, that was definitely the highlight of the training camp for me because that "I Am", it goes back to the word of God. And God has always been to me, everything.

'In my life, God has always been present. He has visited me in dreams. Even as I was growing up and seeing the way my life turned out, the doors that he opened for me and all the doors that he closed for me, I know he has been with me. And so, getting ready for this fight, I knew that I needed to have this relationship with God because I had prayed to him my whole life for this moment.

'I can't believe Paddy even mentioned the shield.'

Lamon is genuinely moved and surprised that I have brought the shield up. His tone of voice and demeanour change when he talks about it. It is almost reverential.

'That is deep, man. This is the first time I have ever talked about this in life, *ever.* So in the Bible, God says to put on the helmet of salvation and the shield of faith. And it is by faith that we are delivered. That's what the Bible says. God says, "I Am that I Am" and the word of God is alive. The words that God speaks are alive. Things might not be what we want them to be, but they are what they are according to God's purpose for our lives.

'All I ever wanted to do with my life was be the best me that I could be in servitude to God. So, that "I Am" on that shield, that's reminding me that God is with me. And that's what I thought whenever I saw it. God is my protector. So I put on the armour of God. And if God is for you, what can be against you? So that shield represented all of that. And to be able to share that with my brother Paddy, even though there were so many other people around, we just became as one.

'When I held that shield, *I* wasn't just holding that shield because *He* was holding it with me. And when I was fighting,

I wasn't just fighting because *He* was fighting with me. And that's only the surface of what I can try to express to you about what that shield meant to me. It's hard to give you an answer because the effect of the shield was something that is embedded within me – and it's greater than words.

'I really appreciate you asking me that question, because I have never had this conversation before.'

Lamon's humility and integrity have come across hugely as we have talked and so I decide to lighten the mood a little. I ask him if he has any funny stories from working with Paddy.

'Well, the thing is man, it was always funny for me. I don't know where to begin or end when you talk about comedy because Paddy's attitude in life is so beautiful, man. He'd always be doing crazy things like this little Irish *Riverdance* and being Irish, he can speak the language like they did in that film *Snatch* with Brad Pitt, and he just cracked us up.

'When you're in a training camp, and you isolate yourself from the world, and all you're gonna hear are these 12 dudes every day, day in day out for months – then you have to find humour. And being a fighter with a mind that is preparing to murder somebody, I had to have some form of escape. So when I wasn't training, it was always about who was the funniest and what can we joke about.

'Paddy was hilarious, man. I remember the first time I asked Paddy to cook for me. I asked him to make me a turkey burger. He had never made one and I guess he thought that the meat would fall apart. So this fool, he wraps the turkey in a raw egg and tries to cook it in a skillet.

Oh my God, man! When he served it up to me, I was like, "What is this?"

'"This is what you asked for," he tells me.

'I say, "Paddy, I want a turkey burger, not a chicken egg turkey burger." I'm looking at him thinking, "What planet are you from? I want a turkey burger and you don't have to dip it in no chicken egg to cook it in a skillet!" It was hilarious. I had never tasted turkey and chicken at the same time.

'There are just a multitude of times where I was laughing so much it hurt.'

I tell Paddy about Lamon's views on his cooking skills, which really tickle him, and so I ask the same question about the times that made him laugh while working at Big Bear.

'We used to have to run, no matter the weather, as part of Lamon's conditioning. And when it was snowing badly up there, Lamon would be the slowest runner. His brother and the other sparring partners would come running with us, but I was the strongest runner in the group, so I'd run up front.

'Lamon had two pistols with him, so I would take one of them at the front of the group in my waistband and he'd have the other pistol near the back. We didn't have a clue what we would come across, and who knows, the locals might have laughed at us thinking we were over-reacting. But it's like Lamon says. He's from the hood. He ain't from the mountains. And he ain't no Grizzly Adams. So we had the pistols to be safe.

'When we had finished our run and we were back in the truck, I said to "T" that we needed to go to the local store and buy some things. When me and Lamon were in there buying some bits, I reached up to a top shelf to grab something, and Lamon goes, "What are you doing, you big dummy?"

'I'm like, "What's the problem?"

'He says, "You've got my pistol in your waistband!"

'God knows what a store assistant might have thought if they saw me reaching up with a pistol hanging out of my pocket.'

I ask Lamon if he can remember the running sessions too.

'I'm still mad at Paddy because every time that we would run he'd be shouting, "Come on, 'T!' Come on brother! Come on!" And when we finished, he'd only have one bead of sweat on his whole body, and he wouldn't be breathing at all heavily. But I would look like someone had just chased me with a Gatorade bucket from the Superbowl and just dumped that whole bucket of water all over me. It didn't matter how many miles we did, he'd never be sweating and I'm like, "Dude, are you even from this planet?"

'But Paddy inspired me to try harder and harder and harder. I could never beat this dude and that helped me keep on working to be the best I could be.'

It seems to me, I say to Lamon, that your experience of working with Paddy was more than what happens in the average training camp? Was it more than just work?

'To answer you in all honesty it was a spiritual journey, more so than work. Work was just a part of the spiritual journey that I feel God had ordained for my life. And the people that he brought into my life were supposed to be there. It was meant for me and Paddy to come together because we both were able to grow with each other, to learn from each other, to motivate one another and to hold on to each other.

'I tell people that I didn't win the heavyweight title, *we* won the heavyweight title. My success is based upon the people who can influence me. Look at the space shuttle. The shuttle can't get into space on its own. It needs so many different parts to propel it out of the atmosphere. That's like Paddy. He was like one of my rocket boosters, man. In fact, Paddy was so important he was like the paint even that covers *everything*.

'That's what Paddy was for me, and still *is* for me. When I look at the night sky and see it in terms of people, Paddy is one of the stars that I see there and he helps keep things light. I know that any time in this world, if I feel low, I can pick up the phone and call this dude. That's what I mean when I say he's a *real* dude.'

As I digest my conversation with Lamon, I can't help but think that the shield was clearly a major influence on him psychologically and then physically in his performance against Klitschko. I ask Paddy whether he realised at the time he was making the shield that it could have the kind of impact that Lamon described.

'I knew that it could have or I wouldn't have had it done. Everything that I do is for a reason. But you can only do something because you *believe* it will work. You can never do something because you *know* it will work because every circumstance is different. What you do for one fighter that works may not have the same effect on another fighter – because it is a different fighter.

'For example, a shield like this would not work for Lali. She wouldn't connect with that. It would mean nothing to her. But she isn't Lamon with his deep-seated religious conviction. And it connected with Lamon. Lamon believed in the shield and the protection and guidance that it provided him.

'And that made it true for him. Belief is essential for a fighter. Lamon now believed he could win and that made all the difference to his performance.'

So things were better then?

'When we left that mountain, I phoned a friend of mine who was one of the only two men in Vegas who set the gambling odds. The odds on Lamon winning the fight were 18-1. My friend would call me about the odds for most fights but on this occasion I called him and I said, "Hey, do you want to put a bet on for me on Lamon?"

'And he says to me, "How's Lamon getting on? I didn't think things were going that good."

'So I say to him, "God coming out of the sky is the only way this man is going to lose to Klitschko."

'And he says, "Paddy, that's not what I've been hearing. So why are you saying that?"

'I said, "OK, it's hard to explain. Something has changed and Lamon's flipped things. I'm telling you that God is the only thing that's gonna beat Lamon so can you put some money on for me at 18-1?"

'He put a decent bet on for me and then the very next day, presumably based on our conversation, the odds on Lamon dropped to 11-1!'

Let's talk about the fight then, Paddy. How did that pan out?

'Me and "T" went to my place but the rest of the team stayed at the hotel in Vegas. We had the final press conference to do and I remember at the press conference six weeks before this, Lamon had broken down and started crying. He went into a corner and I remember Klitschko looking and thinking, "What's wrong with this dude?" The fact was the passing of his mentor Bill had got too much for Lamon.

'But when we got to Vegas this time, Lamon was different.

'On fight night, the team decided that I would go and check Wladimir Klitschko's hand wraps. I had the rules on wrapping hands in my pocket and I had circled the clause where it explicitly states that a fighter cannot have tape directly attached to his skin.

'So I went to the changing room and Manny Steward is sat in front of Wladimir, who is taping his own hand. Klitschko was *applying tape* to his hand first.

'It ain't the biggest deal in the world, of course, and I am absolutely *not* saying that Klitschko was wrapping his hands illegally to cause damage. It was single strips of tape across the hand. He wasn't doubling and trebling up the tape to make some kind of solid cast which could be detrimental to the other man. This was probably just to protect his own hands so that he felt more secure.

'So it was a psychological thing for himself really. But I didn't give a shit about that. If I'm in your corner, I don't care what I've got to do, or how foolish I might seem doing it, I will do whatever I can to benefit our side as long as it is inside the rules. Some people might think me an asshole. I don't care. It is what it is.

'I remember watching them thinking, "This is good." And I'm positioned really close to both Wladimir and Manny.

'Now, I've been in training camp with Manny with Lucia Rijker when Lennox Lewis was getting ready for the rematch with [Hasim] Rahman. In fact, it was Manny who called me to come up and train Lucia in that camp. So I had spent three weeks with Manny talking with him every night over dinner about his philosophies and I would listen intently to everything that he had to say.

'And now, here we are a couple of years later, and he's looking at me like I'm the enemy and I'm looking at him in the same way thinking, "I'm gonna screw you in around three minutes."

'So I watch Manny finish wrapping Wladimir's hand and I say nothing. Then I watch Wladimir taping up the other hand, which he then puts out for Manny to wrap, and I say nothing. I know that I am eating into time here and I'm thinking the longer that I leave what I am about to do, the worse it will be for them.

'Then, as Manny is halfway through wrapping Klitschko's second hand, I say, "Manny, what are you doing? Why are you wrapping his full hand?"

'He says, "What the fuck are you talking about, man? I'm just wrapping his hand."

'I say, "Manny, you've done that one wrong."

'"What the fuck are you talking about?" he says.

'"Relax man," I say – but he's got tape on his skin.

'"You can't do that."

'"Motherfucker," he says to me, "I've been taping hands in this town for 25 years." He turns round to the official from the Nevada State boxing commission and he says, "Tell this motherfucker he can't tell me what to do."

'I say to Manny, "Hey dude, we're on the same level in here so I don't give a fuck how long you've been wrapping hands. You're wrapping them wrong. You can't put tape on the skin."

'Manny is really angry and the official comes over to me and mentions the TV schedule and that time is tight.

'"Listen," I say, pulling out my rules sheet and showing him the rule that says no tape on the skin. "That's your rules," I say to him. "The WBO rules. I don't give a fuck about the TV schedule. None of that is any of my business. He ain't going out there with his hands wrapped like that. He's got to start them again.

'Manny looks at me and then the official and the official starts off with, "Manny, look..." and I know that I've got him.

'So by this stage, both Manny and Wladimir are pissed off and Manny starts having to cut off the wraps.

'Now, it takes around 15 minutes to wrap a hand properly and wrapping hands to most coaches who do the wrapping, that's the last point where you really tune into each other. Often you're quiet, but every now and again you drop in a word or piece of advice from camp to help focus your fighter.

'And now I've ripped up this sacred time between them I'm thinking "good" because I've upset them. I don't want my fighter's opponent to be composed, do I? And don't forget,

Klitschko was coming off being badly knocked out by Corrie Sanders a few fights ago where he struggled. Since then, he'd only fought two taxi drivers – and I know that "T" ain't no taxi driver. He's got a chin like granite and he can punch like a mule. And the "T" I saw the last two weeks of camp is a beast.

'So they start the wrapping again. They wrap up one hand and then start on the next one and Manny realises then that he has missed a thumb, which I point out to him. I say, "Hey, Manny, you forgot the thumb."

'He shouts "motherfucker" and grabs some tape to put around the thumb and attach the gauze to.

'I say, "Manny, what are you doing? You're putting tape on his thumb.

'He's like, "It's the fucking thumb!"

'Calmly I say, "You can't put tape on the skin, Manny, sorry."

'At this stage, I know that I'm just poking a stick in a beehive and some people might say that's not sportsmanlike. But I disagree. That's bullshit. It's not like I was banging on his door all night before a fight. And while the tape in his hand might not have massively benefitted Klitschko's performance, making him take the tape off was a benefit to us because it would upset him. You don't want to be upset when you're going to war. You want to be composed. So it was good for us.

'All hell kicks off when I won't let Manny put tape directly on to the thumb and there's this moment when they both grab a roll of tape and they both want it. They're pulling it back and forth like the Chuckle Brothers, 'to me, to you', and inside I'm thinking this little bit of conflict is perfect.

'On the outside, though, I'm thinking I'm in here alone and this is dangerous. To make matters worse, I turn to the door and Wladimir's brother, Vitali, who is also a heavyweight champion, comes in. Someone must have sent for him.

'Vitali is like, "What's going on?" And right now I'm not feeling completely at ease! Vitali speaks to Wladimir in Ukrainian and then turns to me, puts his hand on the back of my neck and says, "An attorney are you?"

'While he's touching the back of my neck, I'm thinking what he really wants to do is wring my neck like a scrawny chicken. And remember, Vitali is a heavyweight champion in his own right.

'"No sir," I say in reply to his question. "I ain't no attorney."

'In the end, they finished the wrapping of the hands but it had taken *way* too long. They were all disgruntled. Manny was upset and this was his actual first fight with Wladimir. Wladimir isn't happy and I had seen them bicker a little too. For them, it was certainly not ideal.

'I went back to "T" and I said confidently, "Well, they ain't happy."

'When he asked me why, I just told him that I had made them take the hand wraps off and do it again. Shadeed was pleased because he knew that would have pissed them off.

'I didn't give "T" the whole story because I didn't want to upset his preparation. He just asked if everything was cool and I reassured him.'

Klitschko is known for his composure so you must have really disrupted him under those circumstances.

'Every little bit helps and the thing is I've never known a man make measured decisions when he's lost his temper. You can do it when you're angry, yes, but when you've lost control, you've lost control.'

And then it was time to fight.

'I remember when we walked to the ring, security wouldn't let me come to the corner because I didn't have my credentials with me. It was fight time, so I wasn't going to cause an argument and anyway, I wasn't the coach in the corner. That was Shadeed and it was his time to go to work. So I went and I sat just outside of the ringside position.

'As the fight progressed between rounds one and four, I remember thinking that "T" wasn't doing so good. He wasn't winning any rounds. Klitschko's jab was dominating and he was really putting it on "T".

'*But*,' Paddy says, leaving the conjunction hanging in the air as he looks at me confidently, 'I also thought that while Klitschko had thrown a lot of shots, it was not because he was seeing openings to punish Lamon. Emotionally, he was throwing those shots to get "T" *off* him. He wasn't laying traps and trying to bring "T" on to them.'

How do you mean, I say?

'Take David Haye. When Haye is prowling around the outside of the ring, he's eying up every mistake you're making as you walk towards him, measuring you as you come, and deciding which shot he's going to choose in order to ice you. Klitschko wasn't punching and moving like David.

'He was just getting busier and busier to keep "T" off him.

'So Klitschko was concerned that Lamon would overwhelm him, which, incidentally, is what happened. "T" was losing the rounds clearly but he was in full control of himself whereas Klitschko wasn't. He wasn't composed, measured or tactical with his movement or his shot choice. So at the end of round four, I'm thinking that there's another eight rounds left and how can Klitschko continue with this volume of workrate, just to keep "T" off him?

'He couldn't. So I wasn't thinking that "T" needed to change his strategy, even though he was losing the rounds. I thought that he'd be OK. And then in round five, "T" started to land a few decent shots and that changed things. Klitschko went down heavily twice and it was a powerful hook from "T" that finished him.'

Lamon despatched Klitschko with a barrage of brutal hooks, which detonated against his body and chin. After each exchange, Lamon jumped all over Klitschko with another shot and then another until the Ukrainian champion simply couldn't take any more and the fight was stopped.

'I respect Wladimir Klitschko as an exceptionally dominant fighter who will go down in the history books as a great,' says Paddy. 'But every single champion, no matter how dominant you are, will have weak moments in life. And make no mistake, this was one of the greatest upsets in heavyweight boxing history.

'In the end, to me, "T" is a special human being. This is a world heavyweight champion. He doesn't have to walk around and be nice to people. He's a fighter and he's the champ. But you don't get a nicer man. That's just the type of person "T" is. I never heard him say a bad word about anybody – *never.*'

Now, Lamon Tajuan Brewster, originally from Indianapolis, is retired as a professional and living back in his home town with an impressive 35-6-0 record.

So, the last question from me, then, I say to Paddy, is something that's been bothering me since we started talking about Big Bear.

He smiles at me and I pause a little in a pantomime gesture-type attempt to increase the tension.

Then I ask him.

Did you actually see or face a bear, like some of the stories of this event say that you did?

He smiles again, without saying anything, before telling me he did not.

I wonder, though, if the confused bears saw a pale-skinned Irishman doing a passable demonstration of tai-chi at midnight on top of a mountain in the middle of winter.

I'd like to think that they did.

I decide to leave the last words on the subject of Big Bear and winning the world heavyweight title to the champion himself. More than 15 years later, I ask Lamon, 'How would you describe your relationship with Paddy?'

'To sum up Paddy, he was the greatest babysitter a heavyweight champion could ever have!' Lamon says.

'But man, my relationship with Paddy goes beyond business, beyond friendship even. It's a vibration of understanding. The vibrations inside of me, and the vibrations inside of Paddy, they resonate through the universe, and we have a universal connection. This has nothing to do with us speaking the same language, being men, being rich or poor – it's on a level of energy. Like I told Paddy, your children are my nieces and nephews. We're family. I love that dude sincerely. I'm just like Paddy. This world ain't a Hollywood film. All I have in this world is my integrity and my word. And if I tell you I love you, I mean that from the bottom of my heart. And I love Paddy.'

Paddy and I wrap up another session of talking late into the night.

I can see that Paddy has enjoyed remembering this happy and fulfilling time with Lamon. I'm pleased about that too because what we are about to discuss is something altogether different.

Altogether different and altogether a lot more *painful* as Paddy reaches the end of his time with 'Saint' George Groves.

20

Time To Go – Leaving George

August 2015

This should have been the best of times.

When I think of a fighter-and-coach relationship, the best of times is how I imagine preparing for a world title fight should be.

The phrase keeps playing over and over in my mind as I think about how I am going to approach this final phase in the relationship between Paddy and George.

Especially as I already know how painful discussing this might be for him.

I have known Paddy for several years now and writing a book together has revealed a man who can come across confidently and effortlessly as 'the man with the answers' in his capacity as a well-respected boxing coach. After all, how many pro fighters are going to listen to a coach who *lacks* confidence in his ability to coach you to success?

It is also true that during the many interviews I have conducted for this book, Paddy has come across as funny, reflective, philosophical, spiritual, emotional – and sometimes, in a dramatic contrast to his coaching persona, even *uncertain* of his own place and purpose in the world. A presentation of himself that is clearly showing a vulnerability I have never seen in the macho world of boxing that he inhabits on a daily basis.

And this is partly why I like him so much.

I know from speaking with Paddy over the years about his relationship with George that there is some significant emotional baggage attached to their split, as I suppose there must be when any close relationship comes to an acrimonious end.

I also know from previous conversations that Paddy *knew* he was going to break with George during their training camp for the Badou Jack world title fight – even though George might well have succeeded in becoming a world champion and bearing in mind what that would have meant for both of them.

I decide that I need to tackle the situation head on and so I ask Paddy, 'How does the relationship with George go from the success of winning the European title, the WBC silver belt and a mandatory shot at the world title, to deciding that you can't work with him any more?'

'Who knows?' says Paddy, looking and sounding exasperated, making me wonder if I have made a mistake in going straight into the story of the split.

'After the Rebrasse fight, George had the monkey off his back. He was able to prove that regardless of the outcome of the second Froch fight, which was so conclusive, that he was justified in challenging for world-level honours.

'Remember, George could have taken easier fights than Christopher Rebrasse at that time. That's what he did after the Badou Jack fight, where he took a couple of fights to allow himself to rebuild before kicking on.

'We might argue that he should have done that after the Froch fights, but you've seen his performance against Rebrasse: confident, controlled, dominant and totally switched on – so I think he proves that he didn't need to do that.'

Once the dust had settled after the Rebrasse fight, you didn't just move to the world title fight against Badou Jack, did you? There was Denis Douglin first on the undercard of Tony Bellew v Nathan Cleverley II in November 2014. Was that an equally comprehensive win for George?

'We had a choice of a couple of opponents. Denis Douglin was a southpaw and we chose him because the WBC world champion who we were scheduled to fight, Anthony Dirrell, was a southpaw.

'Of course, Dirrell had to face Badou Jack before he would face us. But at the time, we knew that Dirrell was the world champion, and while he *might* lose to Badou Jack, you don't train for who the world champion *might* lose to. You train for the world champion. So we trained for Denis Douglin and George won on a stoppage.'

'At that point, I felt that George needed a break. He had hardly had any time off since the first fight with Carl in 2013 and it was now December 2014. So I said to him, "Let's take a break. You need a break from me and I need a break from you. You need a break from boxing, so let's just chill out. We're in a good position. You're guaranteed to fight the winner of Dirrell v Badou Jack so let's chill out, enjoy Christmas and then we'll get back together."

'The earliest I thought that we would be fighting was March 2015, though in the event it turned out to be the September, so we took a break until the end of January.

'The first day back in the gym, I've just got the guys shaking themselves out, shadow boxing, getting loose and getting their bodies working, working on a bit of rhythm. And then George says to me, "I was talking to Sophie [George's wife]."

'And straight away there's this sort of red flag in my mind because I'm not so keen on when any fighter starts off a conversation about boxing with, "I was talking with my wife" or "I was talking with my dad" because what goes through my head is, "OK, you were talking to your dad and let's say he's a plumber. Did you ask him for advice on plumbing? Or boxing? If it's plumbing, I respect that. Your dad's the expert. If it's *boxing*?"

'And I know that it's a person's wife or father, and that deserves respect. But their views on coaching boxing?

'So George tells me that after talking to his wife Sophie, "I think I looked a bit slow in the Rebrasse fight."

'I say, "Well, you threw 1,000 punches, which was a record for super middleweight. You won almost every round and you dominated him, and now you're telling me you looked slow? I don't see it, George." There's no point in me telling him I see it if I don't see it.'

So you weren't seeing events in the same way at this point? Did this signal some kind of change in your relationship?

'Maybe? My opinion was based on the facts. A record of 1,000 punches and George dominated the Rebrasse fight. But now, we were one fight away from our goal and George becoming the world champion.'

But it wasn't all smooth sailing, was it?

'Well, nothing ever is in boxing and instead of facing the southpaw Anthony Dirrell, we were now facing Badou Jack, who had taken the title from Dirrell.

'So the fight goes to purse bids. Sauerland put in a bid because now they're George's promoter. Floyd Mayweather put in a bid because he promotes Badou Jack and Mayweather wins the purse bid.'

What happened after Mayweather Promotions won the purse bid?

'In line with protocol, they gave us a date for the fight. And the date that they gave us was significant because it was the very last Saturday within the parameters of time set by the purse bid that dictates when the fight must happen by – and in this case, I believe it was within 90 days.

'So that would have made the fight happen in August 2015 and the second George gave me the date I said to him, "Look George, I don't think the fight will happen on that date." And then he said, both shocked at me and annoyed with me, "Why? Why are you saying that?"

'And I say, "I just don't think you are. I know how those dudes think. You ain't fighting in August, man."

'And then he raises his voice, "Why aren't I?"

'He's clearly upset so I say, "It's more why *would* you be, not why *won't* you be? You're a ginger-haired white dude from England fighting a black Swedish dude with his roots in Uganda. Tell me why the Mayweathers would have you headlining in Vegas? As far as an audience for this, where is the English crowd? Where are the Swedish Africans? Outside of Britain and Europe, who knows you both? Granted, you're a big name in Britain because of the Carl fights. And it's true that people *in* boxing will know about the Carl fights. But remember, people *in* boxing don't buy tickets.

'But he didn't accept that, and he continued to get annoyed, saying, "Listen, that's the date they gave us, so it's happening."

'I tried again. "Listen George, that's the *very last* Saturday that they are allowed to give us. Why do you think they've done that? They've given us a date so that we have nothing to question. We can't question them until right before that last Saturday, and then when we do, they're going to move the fight. Floyd is fighting in Vegas in September. You're going to fight on that card. You're not fighting on your own card."

'George seemed pretty pissed off. He said, "OK, I'll ask Neil [his lawyer] to look into it."

'So around a week later, George wants to speak to me after training. You know how sometimes, even though you can't quite articulate why in words, you can *feel* that things are going wrong. That's what I could feel then.

'I could feel things weren't how I would want them to be. It was a week later after one of our training sessions and

George says to me, "I spoke to Neil. The fight *is* happening in August and it is happening that day because he's checked. They've even booked the hotel venue."

'I just said, "OK" and waited for the moment when George would say "And here's the proof it's happening."

'But the proof was never presented.

'So I said to George, "Because a hotel in Vegas has been booked for you to fight Jack, you think the fight is going ahead?"

'"Yeah," he says.

'Floyd Mayweather, Mr Vegas, the biggest sports personality in Vegas, period, who lives in Vegas, runs his company in Vegas, do you think the hotels in Vegas treat him like any other man? Do you think that when Floyd calls a hotel to make a reservation they say to him that he better run on down with his deposit to secure the date or lose it? Or do you think maybe, that they say, "Yes sir, Mr Mayweather" and get all excited about having Floyd at the hotel because if they have a big enough event, that's where the money is? Do you think they might just allow Floyd to book it without commitment?

'So I say, "George listen, just because Floyd might have reserved a date, it doesn't mean that much. It's certainly not cast iron proof that you're fighting that date."

'George says to me, "That's the date. It's on." And he says it with such a sense of finality that it's clear what he's really saying is that this conversation is over and that he doesn't want to talk about it any more.

'So I said if he was happy with that, we would plan our training aiming for that date.

'That was it. Straightaway, I left the gym because we were training up in London and I headed home to Swindon. As I was driving home, I called Neil, George's lawyer. I told him that the fight wasn't happening on the day that he had been told and I told him why. He disagreed and said that he had called the Mayweathers and that they had reassured him. I said to Neil that, I wanted *him* to know that I was telling him that everything that I was going to do was to prepare George for a September fight – because that was what was going to happen. I told him that as far as George was concerned, I was going to prepare him for an August fight, but that in reality my preparations would ensure that George peaked in September because the Mayweathers would change the date to make Floyd's show. I made it clear that I wanted Neil to know this and I also made it clear to him that while I was head coach, I was in charge.

'Finally, I made it clear to Neil that in no uncertain terms was he to make any of this known to George. This was strictly for the team to know. George did not need to know because as long as I was able to adjust accordingly when the date fell through, everything would be fine. I also called The Father, George's strength and conditioning trainer, to make sure that he knew the plan to ensure George peaked in September, not August.

'*Everyone* was on board.

'Then, two months before the August fight date, which was three months before the actual fight happened in September, George asked if he could come over to my house in Swindon and see me. What made this something out of the ordinary was that he wanted to see me on a Sunday – so I knew that there must be something wrong. Otherwise, he could have waited until Monday, couldn't he?

'So George gets to my place and I say, "What's up with you that you wanted to come and see me today?"

'"OK," he says, "it *annoys* me that you think Badou Jack is a good fighter."

Paddy draws out and really stresses the verb "*annoys*" to leave me in no doubt about the word he feels stands out as a problem.

'"I said it *annoys* you? Why does it *annoy* you?"

'"I don't know," he says, "It just does."

'"OK," I said. "Well, listen. Jack's got excellent balance; he understands distance; he feints well; and he's got a good jab. Those are the fundamentals of boxing. So he *is* a good fighter. In addition to that, it's not my job to make you complacent. It's my job to help you become world champion.

'So he says, "OK" a couple of times before he brings up what else is on his mind.'

'"Why are you training Duke [Luke Watkins] and Eamonn [O'Kane]? They ain't bringing you in any money?"

'"Let me remind you, George," I said, "that you weren't bringing in big money at the start of your career. *You* turned pro. *You* had to grow yourself. Let me also remind you that I've been in boxing over 18 years. I've been growing fighters for that long, including you, and I believe in Duke and Eamonn and that's how it is." We didn't talk any more then. We just left it.

'A little while after that, George was having a party in the daytime at his place in London and me, Kerry and D.J. – remember that Kerry is pregnant at this time with Casey – we all went up to the party. I ended up in the kitchen with George and his wife Sophie and he says to me, "I want to go to America to get ready for the fight."

'"OK," I say to him. "If you want to go to America to get ready for the date that you're thinking in August, there's no point in going two weeks before."

'"Why?" he says. "Two weeks will be enough time to acclimatise."

'"Well, we're not going to spar in the last week," I tell him. "And we know that the last three weeks of sparring is the most important because that's the intense sparring, the hard grit and the grind. So that's a month before the fight and if we travel two weeks before the fight, then we're travelling right in [the middle of] your most important sparring. Listen, I don't want that. So if we go out, we're going to go out a month before the fight so that we can have our priority sparring out there. We can get everything technically right and sharpened up here and then we can polish everything out there.

'George brought up Kerry then because she was pregnant and asked if she would be OK with us going for a month? I told him that Kerry knew how important his preparation was and that I would have a talk with Kerry.

'I discussed this with Kerry. It was going to be two months, not one, because I knew the fight would be in September. Understandably, Kerry was concerned because Casey was due in August and if I was in the States, then I wouldn't be at home for the birth. I told her, "I can only go by my gut and this fight's not going to happen in August. If I'm away, can you live with that?"

'She knew how much this meant to me. She said that she didn't want me not to do it because I had put too much effort into George and that I had made promises to him. I had given George my word that I would stick by him, so I should stick by him and get the fight done.

'George smashed it in that camp. It was a phenomenal camp. Dan, who does his strength training, recorded personal bests for George in everything. The Father, in his conditioning and his running, recorded personal bests for George too. That's not my statistics; those statistics belong to those men.

'And this was the only camp where George hurt every sparring partner except a guy called Miles, who I sent away early. Miles was a light-heavyweight and not shy of any man but him and George were friends since they were kids and that was evident to me. They would spar like they were friends. I didn't want any hiccups so I said to George, "It's not working out. Miles is the only dude that you're not hurting and he needs to go home."

'George wanted him to stay but I couldn't allow anything to influence the camp unless it was positive. This was our third challenge for a world title and I wanted it to be right. I had a chat with Miles. He wasn't happy but it was what it was. It was absolutely zero reflection on what I actually thought about Miles and he took the news as well as could be expected. It was purely based on the relationship they had with each other, which from my perspective as coach meant that in sparring they weren't being spiteful enough with each other, and that wasn't what I needed.'

So other than that, camp went well?

'George had an excellent camp in every way. And then one day, I come out of the house I was staying in at Big Bear and I see George outside kicking stones around the yard and he looks really pissed off.

'I go up to him and ask what's up and he turns around and his eyes are red. He was really wound up and emotional. He didn't tell me what was wrong at first, so I had to ask him again. When he finally told me what was bothering him, I wasn't surprised.

'"They've changed the date of the fight. I'm fighting on Floyd's card now. That's it. Fuck it. I'm going to purse bids."

'I said, "George, slow down. There ain't no need to go to purse bids. I ain't trying to rub salt in your wounds, dude, but I told you this – that you wouldn't be fighting in August. Now listen, The Father has been told this. Dan has been told this and Neil has been told this. I told them a long time ago when I first thought this out. You're not fighting, OK, but I'm in charge and all of your training has been done to allow us to adjust for you to be ready for a fight in September. This has all been planned. It's only now that you're finding out. The fight will happen when it happens and we'll be ready for it.

'But George wasn't having that.

'"No," George was shouting, "I'm going to purse bids."

'"OK then," I said, "think about this. You go to purse bids. Firstly, you might not win it. Let's pretend you do win it. We are now in August. They will give you a month to renegotiate, bringing us up to the end of September. Then you will be given around 90 days to put the fight on. That takes us to the end of December and we know nothing will happen in January, so the earliest you'll fight is February. With that in mind, assuming that you did win the purse bid, which is in no way certain, do you really want to wait until February, possibly December, for this to happen when I am telling you that you are prepared for September? That we have allowed for the extra month in our planning for you? All you have to do is get out of your own way. The fight's still happening. We're prepared for this eventuality. You'll be ready. If you go to purse bids, you'll be cutting your nose off to spite your face."

'George decided to think it over. Later in the day, he asked to meet with me and The Father and we went for a walk up a country road. After a little while, George says to me, "Listen, I'm going to fight in September."

'"No problem," I say.

'"But you didn't know it was going to be in September, Paddy," he says to me.

'I just let that go and confirmed that we would be fighting in September and we didn't talk about it any further.

'Then, a day later, George comes to me and he tells me his wife Sophie had booked flights out at that time because she thought he was fighting in August and would I mind if she came out anyway so they could spend a few days together.

Normally, I would have said no, but I told George that I could see how hard the fight date change had hit him and as she was booked to come out and all of George's training was completely on point, I agreed that he should take four days off and chill out and then we would get right back to it.

'Everything was going great in training and I felt he deserved a break, especially when I took into account how the date change had mentally crushed him.

'So Sophie came over and after around three days, she left. But on her last day, The Father asked for a meeting with me. He was concerned about George and he told me that Sophie had brought chocolates into George's house and other unacceptable things for this period in his training camp.

'"Did you say anything?" I asked him. He hadn't, but he told me he wanted to. I advised him against confronting George as Sophie would only be with us for three days. The Father wasn't convinced and wanted to say something.

'I stopped him and said, "Listen, is George performing well?" He agreed that we all thought that George was beating all of his personal bests. He was also hurting all his sparring partners, so as a fighter George was in a great place. "It's not going to change anything now," I said to The Father. "Let's keep it where we've got it."

'"I'll tell you what, Father," I said to him then, "I'm leaving in a month."

'The Father asked me what I meant. I said that regardless of what happens after the fight, I'm out. As it stands, though, George is in a good place and on schedule, so why say anything?'

Regardless of what happens after the fight, I think to myself. Which is a way of saying that regardless of whether George wins a world title, and regardless of the possible earning potential and opportunities that being an elite-level world champion could bring George and the team, Paddy had still had enough of working together and he was done.

'At the end of the camp, when we were leaving Big Bear, I went in to see Abe Sanchez and say goodbye because we were staying three doors up from where he was training. I spoke with Abe and then George went in to do the same as I sat in the van and waited for him.

'When George came out, I said, "Are you cool?" and he said, "Yeah, I just had a quick chat with Abel and he told me I'm looking great in the gym and that everything I need to do is done. He said he could see it in me."

'So I thought that it was nice to hear that confirmation from someone like Abel and George says to me, "I knew I was ready to go anyway."'

It was September 2015, like Paddy had predicted, when George contested the WBC super middleweight title against Badou Jack, who held the championship belt after defeating Anthony Dirrell. The fight was at the famous MGM Grand Garden Arena on a show headlined and promoted by multiple world title winner – Floyd Mayweather Jr.

How did you feel going into the fight, I ask Paddy?

'Everything in George's training had gone well. George had done everything and he had given everything; he had hurt every sparring partner and broke all of his personal training bests; he was technically and physically superior to where he had been in the preparation for any other fight.

'Yet, when the fight came with Badou Jack, in the first round George gets dropped and by a fighter it *annoyed* him that I thought was good. And if he didn't rate him, there are likely a few questions going through his head now as he's looking up at him in the first round of a 12-round fight.

'And that ain't a good place to be for a fighter.'

What did you say to George in the corner after the first round?

'I said, "Listen, don't worry about it. It's the first round. Put it to bed." At this point in the bout, you don't worry about it and tell your fighter "we're a round down", in the same way as if we had won the round I wouldn't be telling my fighter that we are a round up. I just asked George to focus on his fundamental strengths and establish what we know is his excellent jab. One simple message, "regain control", and we would build up from there.

'From rounds two to six, I felt good and George was competitive. I'm not saying George won every round, but I had him ahead. I thought that the fight was beginning to shift in our favour. And then in round seven, George is poor. He comes back to the corner and I ask him what's wrong? He tells me he's tired. "You're not tired," I tell him, because remember, I've been in this conversation with George before. "Just get back to what you're supposed to be doing. Focus on the fundamentals."

'But he gives me the same performance level in round eight, while Jack is keeping his workrate high. When I get

George back in the corner I say to him, "That's two rounds we've lost; you're not tired. Get back to your jab and build from there."

'And then in round nine, George gives me the same thing. There's this photograph of George and it reminds me of this photograph of Muhammad Ali when he was close to retiring and his hands are flopped out in front of him like he's just tired, man, and with no shape. George had a picture of himself in the gym in London that showed him in a similar pose. I always hated the picture because it looked like George had no shape and no form in it – which couldn't be further from the truth. I used to say to him that he should take it down. As his coach I really didn't like seeing it, or him seeing it, but it was part of a montage of images that someone had given him, so he didn't want to remove it.

'And that's what George looked like now. After round nine, the third round we'd lost on the bounce, I stood up in front of him and dropped my hands to strike the pose that he and Ali had formed and I disliked so much and I said to him, "Pick your fucking hands up. You're not tired. You posted personal best after personal best for this dude in your fucking camp. Stop acting like this. You're not tired."

'I knew the fight was close again now and with only three rounds left, we needed to finish strong. George re-found himself, got back on top and regained control in the next two rounds.

'When he came to the corner for the final time after round 11, I said to him, "Now listen, you're three minutes away from winning this title. Give me everything that you have. You've got three minutes to become the world champion. You can't coast this. It's tight. Give me everything that you have." And that's what George did. He went out there and gave me a really strong round.

'But in the end, we lost a split decision, in Vegas, to Floyd Mayweather's fighter on one of Floyd Mayweather's shows.'

I look at Boxrec and two judges scored Jack as the winner and one for George. The judge scoring the card in favour of George had it 114-113 in his favour. One of the judges who went for Jack scored the contest 116-111. However, significantly, the other judge who opted for Jack scored the fight 115-112. Had George performed differently in rounds seven to nine, and had only two of those three rounds been won by George, then the scorecard *might* have read more like (actual scorecard in brackets): 114-113 (116-111) Jack, 113-114 (115-112) George, 111-116 (113-114) George. And the MC would have been saying, 'And the *new* world champion "Saint" George Groves.'

What happened then?

'Well, as the scorecards were read out, and the split decision in favour of Jack was confirmed, George was clearly upset and he stormed out the ring.

'So me and The Father collect up all of our things from the corner and walk back towards the dressing room. Just before the corridor that would take us to the dressing room, the promoters had set up a tent where they did the drug testing and George's wife Sophie was standing outside of the tent. I stuck my head in and saw George sitting waiting for his test looking devastated and one of the Sauerlands, George's promoters, was there consoling George.

'I could see that he was physically alright and he was having a moment with his promoter so I didn't want to walk in and disrupt that, so I left the tent to walk back to the changing room, where I would see George shortly.

'Then, as I pass by Sophie, who was still outside of the tent, I hear her say, "Yeah, you walk off."

'I turned round then and looked at her as if to say, "What?"

'And she says to me, "You haven't even checked he's alright."

'"He's fine," I told her.

'"No he isn't," she says. "What do you mean he's fine?"

'"He's physically fine," I tell her. "I can see he's physically fine and I'll see him back in the changing room."

'She got more upset and Nisse Sauerland [the promoter] came out of the tent then. I just shook my head because I was hardly going to get involved in an argument at that point, so I put up my hand to signal that from my point of view the conversation had ended and I went back to the changing rooms.

'Once George had finished in the tent, I knew that he was walking back to the changing room with Sophie and I thought, "I'm not going to stay here for more verbal", so I grabbed my stuff and said to The Father, "I'll catch you later, dude, I'm off."

'And that was the end of the world title fight.

'Later on in the evening, The Father came to see me in my hotel room and asked me what I thought was going to happen?

'"Who cares?" I said. "What happens is that George has lost. You know what I told you a month ago, so now I'm gone."

'When I returned to the UK, I was absolutely resolved that I was done with the whole situation with George. We had had some fantastic times together. But ultimately, I had put two years of my life into George. Because I had committed to George's training camp, my child was born while I was away. I was not at the birth. In all, I was away for two months, right at the end of Kerry's pregnancy, which wasn't easy for her at all.

'In fact, while I was in Big Bear with George, Casey ended up in intensive care for ten days with my wife, three weeks after he was born. So was I committed as a coach when I stayed with him [George] even under the pressure of such conflicting circumstances? At the time, I felt like a committed coach, but you can only imagine what I was feeling like as a father and a husband.

'And the thing is, in order to protect George, I didn't tell him about what Kerry or my son were suffering because I knew he could do without the stress, so I kept the worry to myself. He didn't take it well when he found out the fight was postponed. There was no need to add to that.

'When I returned to the UK, I got a call from an Irish newspaper and they wanted to interview me about the fight. During the interview, they asked me about Kerry and Casey because the reporter knew I had a baby on the way. So I told the reporter how things were and that Casey was born while I was away and that he and Kerry had been in intensive care.'

None of this was revealed to George at the time in order to maximise his chance of success. To my mind, I don't see how much more a coach can do to demonstrate his commitment to his fighter. But by this time, the partnership had reached a point where Paddy knew that he could no longer work with George – and now it was the end of the road.

We stop the conversation there and I can see that Paddy is moved by reliving these episodes in his life. There is sadness about how the relationship with George ended. I wonder whether this experience of the business and personalities in boxing sapped a good deal of his enthusiasm for the sport. At the very least, this must have been one of the 'headaches' that we refer to in the title of the book.

But if the experience with George, which had been soured by its acrimonious end and drained some of Paddy's passion for boxing, was a headache, then the next character who takes centre stage in his story must have acted like an Irish pain-relieving pill.

Now it was time for Paddy to look towards the future with a new king of the ring and a journey that would lead all the way from Swindon to the Mecca of boxing, New York's Madison Square Garden, and the greatest fight you've never seen.

21

A Million Miles an Hour

Eamonn 'King Kane' O'Kane

AFTER TWO hours of training at Paddy's gym, I have a quick towel down to remove the moisture from my hair and body; I change my T-shirt and pull on some tracksuit bottoms; I take a long spray of something to mask the fact I've been perspiring for the whole time that I've been running, punching, pivoting and sparring; and then its straight over into Paddy's house for a cup of tea and the *craic*.

Tonight, we're here to talk about one of the best men that Paddy has been privileged to train and now call a friend – the two-time IBF intercontinental middleweight champion, WBC international silver middleweight champion and Irish national champion Eamonn 'King Kane' O'Kane.

Paddy grins at the mere mention of O'Kane's name, and it is clear from the beginning that he is looking forward to this conversation about a man he affectionately calls 'wide eyes' and who once left the ring at Madison Square Garden, New York, to cheers from almost 20,000 people and the compliment that he was 'The Irish Jake La Motta'.

And that's some praise from a New York audience.

Paddy immediately warms to the subject of when he first met Eamonn as we begin to talk about his first experience of 'King Kane'.

'I first met Eamonn when I went up to Adam's [Booth] to watch George spar for the Paul Smith fight. It was Adam, George's trainer before he worked with me, that invited me to London to watch Eamonn spar. I have always respected Adam's view on boxing and the analytical and detailed way he approaches the science of his coaching. Eamonn was training in a gym under Vauxhall Bridge and as soon as I walked in, I recognised Eamonn's face because he had won the Irish *Prizefighter* competition.

'When I got there, Eamonn was already sparring and the way he was going at it, I could have sworn his life was on the line – but it was just a training session. He was giving everything to what he was doing in the ring and afterwards we got chatting about where we were both from, because Eamonn's Irish too, just I'm from the south and he's from Derry, further north.

'I asked him how many fights he'd had so far and he asked me if I had any tips or advice for him. I told him: stop trying so hard; you're putting way too much effort into your work. Every single shot you make is executed with such a level of intensity – you're putting your heart and soul into each one. You need to relax a bit, slow down, get your jab going, and get a rhythm going with that jab. Use it to distract your opponent and pick your openings. Stop loading up all the time.

'He seemed to be taking some of what I was saying in, so I kept going. I said to him, "Look Eamonn, there's three dudes in the boxing ring, and two of them have got gloves on – so a fight's gonna break out sooner or later. The thing is, the second that first bell goes, you're straight in there and *getting* yourself in a fight. That's gonna be OK for you at a certain level. But at the top level, dudes'll be like 'OK' and they'll just ride your storm for three or four rounds, and then start to find openings in you as you tire. Then they'll break your rhythm. And then they'll start getting tough on you."

'And that was it. We talked for another five minutes about some other stuff and left it at that.'

Eamonn 'King Kane' O'Kane, I say to myself as Paddy starts one of his customary sweeps of the kitchen: shifting, tidying and checking that everything is in its place.

I spoke with Eamonn for a couple of hours, calling him in Ireland as our schedules just couldn't synchronise when I had hoped to meet him in person. I had watched videos of his fights over and again, so I felt comfortable talking with him about his achievements, his fighting style and his work with Paddy.

In advance, Paddy had warned me that if I found his accent a little difficult to tune into, then Eamonn's would be on a whole new level. Added to that, Paddy said, would be the fact that like Eamonn's 'million miles an hour' fighting style, he could talk nineteen to the dozen too.

And Paddy wasn't wrong.

When I called Eamonn, I wanted to have the conversation on speaker phone. I soon found out that wouldn't be possible. I needed to keep the phone as close as possible to my ear so that I could concentrate fully on the words he was saying in a broad Irish accent – and at warp speed.

Immediately, Eamonn put me at ease with a 'Hey Teach' and like Paddy had told me, it was almost impossible not to like him from the get-go. I started the interview by asking him where his fighting name had come from.

'Famous boxers have flamboyant titles, right Teach? And since being young, I wanted one too. There was also the obvious alliterative quality of the hard "K" sounds. And to use the noun "King" suggested a leader of people and a leader is what I wanted to be in boxing.'

What about the name 'wide eyes'?

'That came about from that sort of stare that I have when I'm in the zone and determined to succeed at what I'm doing, I suppose. Maybe like a wild Irishman, I enjoyed the fight and got stuck in. It was Paddy who gave me the "wide eyes" name, so he must have seen that.'

And what are your first recollections of meeting Paddy? You must have had a trainer already at that point?

'Paddy came to watch me spar in London. I was just turning pro then and looking to develop. David Haye was there and Adam Booth. While they were all watching the sparring, there were a lot of comments that were being made – but the most intelligent comments were being made by Paddy. What first struck me about Paddy was that he said things how they were and he wasn't into "blowing smoke up my arse". He seemed to like my approach and attitude to boxing. I loved how he would tell me what I wasn't doing well, as well as what I was. I knew then that the successes I'd had as an amateur might have had people telling me I was great. I didn't need that. I wanted to be better and wanted someone who would tell me what I needed to hear, not what they thought I *wanted* to hear. From what I'd heard so far, I thought that Paddy would tell me the facts and what to do to get better.'

Once he's satisfied with his kitchen, Paddy sits down. What happened with Eamonn then, I say?

'A week or so after George had fought Carl [Froch] the first time, my phone rings and it's Eamonn's adviser [a man called Francie] who tells me that he represents Eamonn O'Kane and that Eamonn would really like to come over to England and work with me, so was I interested?

'"It depends," I said. "Will Eamonn listen to me?"

'"Is that your first question?" his advisor says to me, and I told him, "Yeah. Will Eamonn listen? Because last time I met him, everything that he did was a million miles an hour. And he didn't take the advice I gave him back then because I've seen him fight since and he's *still* going at a million miles per hour.

'"He didn't listen then, will he now?"

'"That was then," his adviser told me. "It wasn't the right time for Eamonn then. But it is now, and he wants you as his trainer. So are you interested?"

'I was, and so he asked me what I wanted out of the arrangement financially. Now, the money's important, but it's not the main thing for me, so I told him to send Eamonn over to England, see if we liked each other first, and then talk about the money if we felt we could go somewhere together.

'So around two weeks later, Eamonn and his dad arrived in Swindon and came to my gym.

'I liked Eamonn from the early stages of knowing him. I called him 'wide eyes' because if you ever see Eamonn he's just so excited about life. It's like his eyes are so wide they're just sucking everything in. He had a great energy that came off him, and I was excited about working with that energy in the gym from the beginning – and man, he *loves* fighting. When he's in the zone, he's got this *look*, you know. But not just fighting. He loves the training too, every aspect of being a fighter – even the discipline.'

I start to think about the talented, but indolent, fighters that I have read about who needed a coach to really push them. In his book *Iron Ambition*, even Mike Tyson describes himself as 'lazy' and explains how he needed a trainer to really motivate him, or he would have looked to avoid training properly.

'You know, there are lots of fighters who just enjoy the fighting itself, and they struggle with the training. James Toney for example, an amazing fighter, would spar his ass off for 24 hours if you ask him to, come in after a night out drinking and put sparring partner after sparring partner through one of the hardest sessions they were ever likely to experience outside of a real fight situation. But training? He didn't like to hit the bags much or go running. Not like Eamonn. He liked *every* aspect of the training – full stop.

'The fact is, when I decided to take Eamonn on as his coach, I wouldn't have worked with him if I didn't think he had the potential to be world level. At the time, Eamonn had already proved he had the ability. He was the IBF intercontinental champion. He was ranked number eight in the world. He had beaten Kerry Hope, who had gone on to win a European title. And he had been the captain of the Irish national team in the amateurs.

'So when I first got Eamonn in the gym, I decided to do a session on the mitts with him, remembering my original comments when I had first seen him spar at a million miles per hour.

'I picked up a couple of things straight away that gave me some clues as to why he was fighting at such intensity. I explained to him my theory on a single jab – touching a dude to be able to know where he is and then doubling up the jab, because if you can land the double jab you're guaranteed the one-two. The fact is, if you can land a double jab, you can easily land the straight one-two because it's quicker to execute. In fact, the double jab opens up the three-punch combination really because the time it takes to land the double jab is the same time it takes to execute a one-two hook attack.

'I wanted to explain these fundamentals to Eamonn to help him understand not to be in a hurry to throw his combinations until he had the time to do it.

'At the end of the first day training together, Eamonn was stood in front of me and he's a real straight talker so he says, "Are we doing this then? Will you work with me?" So I asked him who was managing him right now. Eamonn had an adviser at the time but not a manager. I told him that if I took him on, I would want to be his manager too because I wouldn't want to be doing all the work in the gym and not be able to get him into a position that I feel is warranted after the work he has put in.

'Eamonn and his dad were clearly interested and they asked me what I thought should be their next move. I told them that I was looking to put on a show in Swindon and that I would put Eamonn in as the headliner in a ten-round main event bout.'

I wanted to know from Eamonn, who as a real prospect at the time could have chosen from plenty of trainers, what it was that made Paddy the right coach for him.

'I always thought that hard work was enough to achieve success,' he told me with the benefit of hindsight. 'But Paddy taught me that it was *smart* work and dedication that achieved success. He refined and organised my hard work so it became specific and intelligent. I would describe Paddy as an analyst, not simply a coach. For me, he was a master at this. His gameplans and his boxing savvy are so impressive. He would cover everything with me so that I was totally prepared, you know. He'd be like, "When this happens, do this and when this happens, do this." He left no stone unturned.

'It was a clear progression for me working with Paddy and that's not meant as any disrespect to the excellent coaching I received before working with Paddy. Paddy was always learning about how to improve an athlete physically and mentally. He was his own man and into sports science and nutrition. He wasn't a "fixed in his ways, just go and hit the heavy bags" type of coach. I remember he was really into interval training and lactose thresholds. He really knew how to condition a fighter – and I know it was the excellent condition I was in that got me through some of my toughest fights, especially the full 12 rounds with Tureano Johnson at Madison Square Garden.

'Paddy understood how important the psychological element of the sport is too. He would tell me that everything was an act and how did I want to present myself? Sometimes I needed to present myself as the *baddest* man on the planet, and other times as the *slickest*. We would work on how to do this. He was also really skilled at helping me to achieve a sense of ease when going into battle. I needed to be able to concentrate on the fight, rather than everything else around it, you know, the business. He was a master at that too.

'Paddy's such a great character. He's a heart-warming kind of guy. When I came to Swindon to train, he got people to take me in and care about me. He knew when he needed to be tough with me and when he needed to show me love. He was willing to learn with me too, not just dictate. And he was 100 per cent ready to do whatever it took to make me the best I could be. I appreciated his honesty. He wasn't afraid to tell me things how they were. I needed that. There's also such a good vibe at the gym. Paddy's a humble guy and he gives respect to anyone who comes to train. He might be training three or four pros for upcoming fights and he still makes time for the youth and the novices. He's teaching the same respect to his fighters and coaches too.

'You know, Teach, I wanted to leave a good impression on the sport – make my family, the country and Paddy proud. You say that Paddy really rates me as a fighter, and I'm pleased with that. I'm thankful he was my coach. I don't think I would have made it so far without him. Paddy surely got the best out of me.'

What about the dual role he took on for you? He was your manager too, wasn't he? Was that complicated?

'No – it made sense for me as Paddy needed to know everything in order to get me the opportunities we wanted. He was very smart and knew the boxing game inside out. He knew when to put pressure on promoters and sanctioning bodies to position me effectively, so I was more than happy with the situation.'

I return to Paddy. So you wanted to put Eamonn as the top of a bill in a country, England, where he wasn't all that well known? How did you get the promoters and businessmen on board with that?

'I didn't at first. Rather than go to promoters at this stage, my plan was to make a successful event without promoters in a decent venue, so that we could show promoters that Eamonn *already* had a following. That way, we would have more to sell to interest the promoters because the fact was, at this time, Eamonn wasn't all that well known in England, and good promoters are businessmen after all. If they think that you can sell tickets, then they'll work with you. If not, they won't. My plan would present Eamonn as the main draw. So if we pulled it off, promoters would see that Eamonn could make money, as well as fight. In the end, boxing might be a sport but only the most naive of us would pretend that *professional* boxing is not a business first, and a sport second.

'Eamonn and his dad liked my plan, so we agreed to work together with me as trainer and manager. As quickly as we could, we set up the event in Swindon, with Eamonn on the billboard, the fact that he was the IBF intercontinental title holder splashed all over the posters, and that he was ranked eighth in the world. We called the show *The World Awaits*. I knew that this would be a good chance to get the Eamonn O'Kane ball rolling; keep the costs down by doing it ourselves; get a decent crowd in at the venue; put on a good show with plenty of rounds of boxing; and then look to defend Eamonn's title in the future to raise his profile.

'It would have been in February of 2015 and I set up a Hungarian opponent for Eamonn, a dude called Ferenc Hafner, who had a record of 23-6-0 as a fighter, which tells you that he was decent opposition. I wanted a fighter who was going to stand in front of Eamonn, and stay there. A fighter that would allow Eamonn to show his ability and give the crowd the fight they wanted to see. We needed rounds, so his opponent had to be tough, but I didn't want someone who was going to be life or death for us either at this stage – and risk everything before we had really got going.

'His opponent was a southpaw and from my point of view, this fight was going to show whether we could translate what we were doing in the gym into a fight situation. This fight would be the test to tell me if we were working well together as a coach-and-fighter team.

'Eamonn is an orthodox fighter. So we had been working on how to approach a southpaw with his jab because there's this feeling that orthodox fighters should avoid southpaws like the plague – too much of a risk. So we were working on how an orthodox fighter can turn his thumb up in his lead jab to break the line, or turn the thumb right down to come over the top of his opponent's lead jab, or go straight up through the middle to break his opponent's jab's success. And other ways a fighter can give himself different angles to approach a jab from to overcome a southpaw.

'See, there's this theory that an orthodox fighter shouldn't use his jab against a southpaw and that you have to keep your lead leg outside his in order to control the fight. But to me, that's bullshit. If you don't use your jab against a southpaw, why is it that the best southpaws in the world, like Joe Calzaghe or Pernell Whitaker, why do all these dudes have a great jab? They have to face the same thing against an orthodox fighter as an orthodox fighter against a southpaw. Only difference is that they have to do it more often. And if these dudes all have superb jabs to use against orthodox fighters, why wouldn't an orthodox fighter use a jab against a southpaw?

'The theory is just nonsense to me, so I had been working on Eamonn's jab with him.

'The event was held at the Oasis [Leisure] Centre in Swindon and we sold around 1,200 tickets, which was a very good crowd. Come fight night, the place was rammed and it was rocking. We had another of my other fighters, Luke "The Duke" Watkins [a cruiserweight who went on to secure the Irish and Commonwealth belts], as chief support in an eight-rounder before Eamonn would headline.

'So when it came to the main event, the place was bumping, with a great atmosphere. In order to really sell Eamonn and his Irish heritage, I hired a team of Irish dancers to dance the ring walk out in front of Eamonn, which was really cool – a bit of showbiz to spice up the event. As he walked to the ring, you could see that Eamonn had this zest about him. He was really excited to get in the ring. There was a real focus on the business in hand all over his face that told me he had an "I'm gonna get ya" attitude to his opponent. But you could also see this cheeky grin keep on breaking out that told anyone who could see it how much he loved fighting.

'So the fight started and Eamonn's using the shots we had practised in the gym. And then, less than a minute into the first round, he drops this Hafner dude to the canvas and I'm thinking, "Oh shit!" This is supposed to be a ten-round fight for us, not over in seconds. Looking back now, I just knew what Eamonn was going to do. So when Eamonn's in a neutral corner as the referee's giving the count to the Hungarian, I'm shouting at him, "Eamonn! Hey, Eamonn!" But his eyes are just fixed on the dude who's getting the count. And I'm shouting, "Eamonn! Hey! Look at me when I'm fucking talking to you!"

'I thought if I swore at him, he might just look over because he would be shocked to hear me curse.

'Before the count had ended, Hafner got up and the referee waved the fight on, so both men went at it like this might be the last fight of their careers. This Hungarian guy

Hafner was a tough dude, mind you, who normally didn't get stopped and Eamonn had him down five times over the duration of the fight. Then, not long after that round resumed, and remember this is the *first* round, Eamonn got dropped. He was clipped and fell on his arse. And as he went on his arse, it was crazy. His eyes were wide and alert and he had a massive smile on his face. I remember it really annoying me as he looked over at our corner with this big smile on his face, like he's saying, "Hey coach, we're having fun now!"

'As the round continued, Eamonn dropped the Hungarian again and as the bell sounded for him to come back to our corner, he was doing this little swagger, just so full of joy in his craft, a bit like Conor McGregor – total confidence in his own ability to perform and entertain. And when I get him sat on the stool, and I'm looking directly at him, he's still got this huge smile on his face as I pull out his gumshield and I shout at him, "What the fuck are you laughing at? What did I tell you about being patient? What did we spend 12 weeks working on? Use your jab. Take your time. He's tough. He's gonna be here all night. Use your jab like we practised. Do as I damn well tell you."

'I know he can sense the frustration in my voice because he's saying, "Yes coach, sorry coach." And he's trying not to smile, but he can't help himself. He's just enjoying himself so much.

'So I sent him out for the second round and he had a great fight – lit the place up by dropping the Hungarian dude so many times, even though he had been dropped himself, and we got the win with a stoppage, a technical knockout in round four.

'A great start to our relationship. It was beautiful.'

When we talked, I asked Eamonn what he remembered about *The World Awaits* event.

'I remember everyone would joke that I was fighting Hugh Hefner! The fight was a sell-out – and I'd only been in Swindon for three months. I was really impressed with how Paddy managed that. If I'm honest, I think I got caught up in headlining the whole thing.

'In the build-up to the fight, Paddy had worked with me on how to turn my left hook over and spin out after the punch. To be fair, his plan worked because I caught Hafner that way. It's also true that I was knocked down in the first round, which probably helped the excitement of the show, but I know it didn't make Paddy very happy. I was just carried away, I suppose. I wanted to put on a good show and improve my profile.

'When Paddy got me into the corner he was mad and, excuse the language, tore me a new arsehole. I learned a lot from that fight: firstly, about the business element of the sport, and how to improve my profile. Secondly, about what Paddy called "vibing", which meant how I was getting used to understanding and responding to Paddy's instructions in pressurised situations. It was a good night.'

But just when they felt they had made such a great start together, Paddy and Eamonn were about to face the first serious problem of their partnership.

22

The Title That Wasn't a Title

I DON'T understand what Paddy means, I say to him. How can a title *not* be a title? It either is or it isn't a title, surely? Otherwise it's a meaningless concept. The whole thing doesn't seem to make sense to me.

'It was complicated, Teach. It was a nightmare really. And I didn't find out all the details and facts for a while after Eamonn headlining at the Oasis in Swindon.

'After the win, I sent Eamonn back to Ireland for a rest and I just started abusing the IBF with these constant emails because I wanted to get something big made for us. I was like some insane, possessed boxing stalker.

'When I finally got to talk with them, I told them that I wanted to get Eamonn out fighting again to defend the intercontinental title that he held. And the guy at the IBF says to me, "You want to *defend* the title?" Like as if there's a problem. And I say, "Yeah, defend his title. That's the normal way we do things when you have a champion, isn't it?"

'And then, out of the blue, the guy hits me with the comment that Eamonn's *not* the champion. I'm shocked, and that's putting it mildly; so, I get a bit sharp back and say, "What do you mean he's not the champion because we're happily telling anyone who'll listen that he *is* the champion? That can't be right. Check your facts, man. Eamonn beat Kerry Hope for the title at the Odyssey Arena, Belfast, on Carl Frampton's undercard in October of 2013. The fight went the distance and Eamonn won it on points. That's a fact."

'"Yeah, but Paddy," says the IBF guy, "Eamonn got *stripped* of the title."

'"*Stripped* of the title? How?" I'm probably shouting a bit now because this is hard to believe. "Have you told Eamonn? I ask him." "Yeah," he claims, "we told the people on the shows Eamonn was boxing on. We notified *them.*"'

Paddy shifts to the edge of his sofa, the frustration he experienced for Eamonn back in 2015 still palpable now as I listen to the story. 'I couldn't believe what I was hearing. But the IBF guy told me they had followed all the correct procedures and that if Eamonn didn't make a defence of his title in a specific amount of time, then he'd be stripped of the title. The time limit had expired. So Eamonn was stripped of the title.'

I try to take this in and imagine what it must have felt like for Eamonn to think he was a title holder – and then suddenly he wasn't.

'I was frustrated, Teach,' Eamonn told me. 'I had fought for a WBC title, so without telling me, the IBF had decided

I wasn't interested in the title of theirs that I held – and they stripped me. Fortunately for me, Paddy was like a dog with a bone when he found out.'

What happened next, I ask Paddy?

'I was just amazed that this could be the case and I kept saying to the IBF that Eamonn still thought he was the champion. I knew that the guy wasn't gonna move on this so I said to him, "Is the title vacant at the moment?" It was, so I told him straight that they needed to give Eamonn the chance to box for the title, and regain it. And they were like, "Well, we'll consider anyone in the top ten rankings to fight for it."

'I couldn't accept that and I said to him, "What's to consider? Eamonn doesn't even know you've taken the belt away from him. He wasn't even notified. That can't be right. You've gotta let him fight for it."

'That's when I make my move and I tell him that I'm putting a show on in June, in Ireland. [I said to him] we can make the title fight the headline and as Eamonn's manager I will be happy to accept any fighter that the IBF consider and deem good enough to be an opponent. I told them, "You're the IBF, I need to trust you and I need you to commit to doing this. The title's vacant. There's no mandatory challenger. You've got to give Eamonn his chance. It's the right thing to do."

'As soon as we finished talking, I wanted to be as sure as I could be that I could make this happen. I smashed out an email summarising everything that we had discussed, and ended the email with a statement that pretty much said that the IBF agreed to Eamonn fighting for the vacant title. That way, if the IBF disagreed they would have to get back to me. They didn't, and as far as I was concerned, we were on for making the fight.

'In order to get moving quickly, Eamonn set up his own promotions company called King-Kane Promotions and we got the fight made with Eamonn versus Lewis Taylor for the IBF intercontinental title. His opponent was a nice kid from Derbyshire with a 16-0-1 record at the time. He was a tough kid, as tough as you like, man. He couldn't really punch but boy was he tough. He reminded me a lot of Christopher Rebrasse [who George Groves fought for the European title]. Rebrasse wasn't the biggest puncher in the world and he wasn't the fastest dude in the world. But if you allowed him to get any momentum going, then he was a nightmare. He had a good chin and he could fight. Just like this kid from northern England.

'The fight happened in May of 2015. The day before the title fight, I remember that I had to attend the rules meeting, which is standard practice in boxing.

'I brought Neil Sibley, who was acting as Eamonn's lawyer at the time, into the rules meeting. When we got there, the fight officials showed up – but there was no referee.

'I couldn't believe it. And when the officials told me that the referee wouldn't be able to make it until the day of the fight I asked them, "What was the point of having the rules meeting without the most important person involved?"

'They claimed we were meeting to go over the rules. But I wasn't having that and I told them that the *real* reason we were meeting was to *remind* ourselves of the rules because we had all been in the fight game long enough, and we all *knew*

Ali in Ennis, County Clare, Ireland 2009. Ali receives the key to the city where his Irish great-grandfather was born. It also turns out to be the same place Paddy was born too!

Lamon T. Brewster, Laila Ali and Paddy in the gym in Los Angeles, 2003.

During the good times with George Groves before the first fight with Carl Froch, Manchester, November 2013.

Lamon joyous in victory against Wladimir Klitschko, April 2004, with the WBO belt around his waist, his father to his right, and a picture of former coach and mentor Bill Slayton who had passed away only months previously, above his head.

Paddy expressing his frustration to referee Howard Foster over the controversial stoppage of George Groves in round nine of his world title challenge against Carl Froch, November 2013.

George Groves after winning the European and WBC silver super middleweight titles with a shut-out decision against Christopher Rebrasse, September 2014.

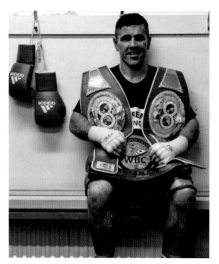

Eamonn 'King Kane' O'Kane (Old Wide Eyes) celebrating winning the IBF intercontinental title for a second time on his own promotion back in Derry, Ireland.

'The Greatest Fight You've Never Seen.' *'King Kane'* digs a right into the body of Tureano Johnson in a final eliminator for the IBF middleweight world title. This fight was brutal and proved the Irish warrior deserved to be on the world stage.

Eamonn "King Kane" O'Kane, Madison Square Garden October 2015, *'Let's have it!'*

'Blackirish' Luke 'The Duke' Watkins becoming the first black professional Irish champion in history in June 2017, stopping the teak tough Dubliner Ian Timms. Also pictured from right to left are Ryan Martin and Luke 'Casper' Kelleher Paddy's assistant.

Three generations of fighters trained by Paddy. From right to left, Robert Lloyd, Taylor, Luke 'Casper' Kelleher Paddy's assistant, 'El Raton Gordo' Lewis Roberts and Luke 'The Duke' Watkins.

Pictured here (right to left) Paddy, Eamonn 'King Kane' O'Kane, Luke 'The Duke' Watkins, Mark Nielson (Paddy's partner in the 'Fight Town' series) and Luke 'Casper' Kelleher.

Paddy with the *real* 'Cobra'. One of Paddy's youth national champions 'The Cobra' Kyle Bains seen winning the national amateur championship for the second year running.

Teach, Ray-Ray and Alex after a sparring session coached by Paddy.

Paddy, Kerry (Paddy's wife), and his sons DJ and Casey (Junior)

Teach, Kate (my wife) and my daughter Evie

the rules. The *real* reason for the meeting was to establish whether our *interpretation* of the rules was the same, and if not, come to some agreement that would make sure we were all singing from the same hymn sheet when it came to the fight. So how could we have this rules meeting without the referee?

'They didn't agree, which I felt was completely inappropriate, and I started to ask Neil Sibley, our lawyer, to note down exactly what was being said so that we had a record.

'The officials carried on and we started going through the rules. Eventually, we came to discuss the rules in the event of a low blow occurring during the fight. Part of the rules is that in the event of a low blow, the guy who executed the low blow must be sent to a neutral corner, and the victim of the low blow should be given up to a maximum of five minutes to recover. I said, "OK, but whose choice is it if the victim gets five minutes?" "Well, the guy that's injured Paddy," is what the officials say with a look at me like they're thinking, "Sure, shouldn't you know that already Paddy?"

'So I say, "If my guy gets hit in the balls, goes down, and gets back up, he has five minutes to recuperate, right? I just wanna know that if my guy is injured, it is his choice if he takes the five minutes," and they said, "Of course, because he's the one that got hit."

'I just wanted them to be clear, and I was happy with that, so I asked Neil to record the fact in writing. And they looked at me like I'm wasting their time – *that* kind of look.'

Paddy pauses at this point as he remembers how annoying, and seemingly disrespectful, it felt to have the rules meeting without the referee present. But what was worse, when it came to the event, was that when the referee was announced – it was *that* referee. A referee from a past fight who had created such a controversial moment that it reverberated through the world of boxing for weeks and months afterwards.

'When I realised that the referee for the fight was going to be Howard Foster, I'd be lying if I said I wasn't affected by the news. I was concerned. The fact was that me and Howard had history from the first Froch v Groves fight.

'Everyone knows what happened in the first fight, don't they? For me, Howard stopped the fight too early and it's as simple as that.'

I nod because everybody does know what happened in Froch v Groves I. And six years on, the rivalry and controversy that existed between these two men at their peak is still drawing big crowds. As I write, the public will tune into Sky Sports to hear these two commentate next to each other, perhaps just as much as watch the bouts on the undercard. It is hard to tell how much of the presentation of their relationship is premeditated and for the cameras, but to the casual observer it seems that there is still plenty of needle between these two gladiators and world champions – even if, years later in May 2019, Carl Froch insists that their two wars of 2013 and 2014 are water under the bridge now and that any suggestion they might come out of retirement for a third and final instalment of their epic struggle is ridiculous.

Maybe, but deep down inside, I think both fighters know that a third fight would sell, though Froch, ten years George's senior, would be unlikely to agree to it. Still, if the volume of interest in these two and their 'An Evening With Froch and Groves' type show is anything to go by, then the public's appetite for their battles has certainly not been sated.

'And now,' says Paddy, 'I was with Eamonn in another title fight and Howard Foster was the referee? It was a déjà vu, man, like it was all maybe going to happen again. I was worried.'

Were you worried about the referee too, I ask Eamonn when we talk about the Lewis Taylor fight?

'Well, there was an atmosphere, to be sure, as there was a lot of emotion surrounding the appointment of Howard Foster as referee for my title fight. There was the controversy surrounding Froch v Groves I that Paddy had experienced and I'd had some history with Howard too when I fought John Ryder.

'But Paddy was strong for me and he dealt with the situation. He didn't portray any concern to me as his fighter, so I'm surprised to hear from you that he was concerned, Teach. But that shows how good he was at his job. He knew that if he showed me he was concerned this would have affected my focus. I remember that a bit of bad blood flared up in the fight but Paddy managed our emotions and instructed me successfully. Paddy had my back. I trusted him totally.'

I return Paddy to the subject of Howard Foster.

'Thinking about it now, me and Howard Foster might not be the best of friends, but I think he was treated disgracefully after the first Froch v Groves fight. He had windows put in at his house and the windscreen of his car too. I found this out from a ref at an event I was working at up in the north of England years after the first Froch v Groves fight, and well after Foster had refereed Eamonn in the IBF title fight.

'At the time of Eamonn's IBF intercontinental fight, though, I had no idea. So, you know, maybe at the time of Eamonn's fight, Howard Foster didn't see me in too kindly a way. I don't know but if he'd been subjected to the kind of abuse he had because of stopping George in the fight, feeling like people were coming to his family home and attacking him, then maybe he saw me a little bit like I was on the other side from him, as part of the problem – as a kind of enemy. It's human nature, I suppose. And perhaps he was a little defensive-feeling at the time too, which wouldn't have helped us get on and perhaps explained his reaction to a big incident in the middle rounds of Eamonn's fight.

'I saw him as a bit of a problem at the time because of the issues in the past and the feeling was reciprocated, I suppose. On reflection, it probably ain't right that we saw each other like that back then, but that's how it was. Shit happens.

'Taking all of this into account, on the night of the fight, when Howard Foster was announced as the referee, we have this history, and he wasn't at the rules meeting – well, of course I'm going to be concerned. Even if in reality there is nothing to be concerned about, the stakes are high for us. And because the facts are that the last fight I was in when he was referee, something happened that I didn't agree with,

I'm going to be anxious about his appointment as referee. Simple as that.

'It's important that I say that I'm not blaming Howard Foster for not being at the rules meeting. There may have been a very plausible reason for him not being able to make the meeting. I don't know. Who I *am* blaming is the IBF because in the interests of fairness and transparency, the board should have replaced him and provided a referee who *could* make the meeting.

'That would have been fair.'

Yeah, I say, it would have been. That seems common sense to me. But I'm learning the more involved I get in boxing that other factors sometimes have a greater influence on the way a fighter's career pans out, at the expense of concepts like common sense and fairness.

Have you seen Howard Foster recently, I ask?

'So at the time Eamonn was fighting Lewis Taylor, me and Howard fell out again. But we've put that to bed now because I saw him at a show relatively recently where he refereed the fight between my guy Duke [Luke Watkins] and Mike Stafford in Leicester, where Duke was defending his Commonwealth cruiserweight title. He refereed the bout impeccably. I went out of my way to shake his hand and he was happy to shake my hand afterwards too. He said some very positive things about Duke. I thanked him and we've moved on.

'But that doesn't change the fact that Howard almost did it to me again with Eamonn that night.'

So tell me about the fight, then. How did it go down?

'Fight night came in Eamonn's home town of Derry, Northern Ireland, at the Lavey Centre. Lewis Taylor was Eamonn's opponent for the IBF intercontinental title in a bout that was topping the bill. This was a fight that if we won, we knew it would position us well in the IBF rankings and allow me to move into the next stage of my plans for Eamonn.

'Eamonn started the fight really well and I could see that he was taking my advice and trying to measure his performance, using his jab to set up combinations and remaining patient. Then, as usual with Eamonn, a fight broke out and they were trading some vicious shots and both giving as good as they got.

'Midway through the seventh round, Eamonn gets hit with a low blow and he goes down. It was an accidental shot. Both fighters were free-trading with each other and there was no malice in Taylor's shot, but it was a hard enough and a low enough shot to put Eamonn down. And the thing is, Eamonn isn't the type to go down easy. He ain't no footballer looking to get the other guy sent off, or get himself a breather, and as he went down he's looking at me to show that he was in some pain.

'Howard starts walking Taylor to the neutral corner and as he's walking him to the neutral corner, I'm screaming at Eamonn to get his attention because Eamonn is folding up on himself. When Eamonn looks over, I put my hand up and shouted to him to take the whole five minutes that was his right as the victim of a low blow, as agreed in the rules meeting the previous day.

'And as I'm doing that, I see Howard Foster looking at me across the ring. And then he leaves the other dude in the neutral corner and comes back and stands *in between* me and Eamonn.

'Now, as Eamonn's trainer, I'm shouting at Eamonn for him to listen to me and he can't even see me because of where Foster has positioned himself. To make matters worse, Eamonn is in the corner on the opposite side of the ring where he went down, so he can't hear me at all, no matter how loud I shout.

'Five or six seconds go by and then all of a sudden, Howard Foster brings both boxers together and they start fighting again. I'm like, "What the feckin' hell?" And as the bell sounds for the end of the round, and Eamonn is walking back to our corner, I jump into the ring and shout at Howard, "You've done fucking wrong there! He's supposed to have five minutes!"'

And Foster?

'He just looked at me and ignored me, so I repeated myself even louder and with the same expletives and added, "Why didn't you give him his five fucking minutes? He got hit in the balls. Give him his five fucking minutes!"

'Foster just stares at me and says, "Shut up!"

'I was furious. I said, "Don't tell me to shut up! You're here to do a job same as I am. Don't tell me to shut up. Give him his five fucking minutes!"

'And that was it. Both of our bloods were boiling over and the fight continued.

'The fight itself ended up being close and it went the distance. But we got the decision. We got the win, the title and the IBF intercontinental belt.

'We were on our way.'

Eamonn's view of events closely matches Paddy's but interestingly he explains why he didn't take Paddy's advice when he was in the middle of the storm with Howard Foster.

'Paddy wanted me to take the five minutes. But I was torn between two emotions. If Howard thought I was hurt, maybe he'd stop the fight? It was playing on my mind because he was giving me the impression that he might stop it. I could hear Paddy shouting at Howard to give me my five minutes but I couldn't get the idea that Howard might stop the fight out of my head. I was also thinking that if I have a go at the ref, who clearly wants me to continue, how might that affect the judges if the fight comes to a decision? Will they back the ref? I had to make a decision in that instant, in a highly pressurised situation, so I just blocked out the pain and fought on.'

I'm learning fast as an aficionado of boxing, I remind Paddy, though I am in no way an expert. As a fan, I am becoming more and more interested in how fighters are managed. I don't think it is unfair to say that the boxing business is not always fair. In the complicated world of manoeuvring and positioning fighters with all the boxing supervisory bodies and these organisations' dealmakers and power brokers, it isn't always fair which fighter gets his or her shot at a world title – regardless of which boxers they might have fought or how many fights they might have had.

How did you make sure that Eamonn was positioned to get the world title shot he deserved?

'Once we won the IBF intercontinental title, if I had been bothering the IBF before, well, I was the biggest pest they had ever had the misfortune to deal with from that point because I knew that the next level for Eamonn would be to manoeuvre him into a position to get a crack at the *actual* IBF world middleweight title that was in the possession of [Gennady] Golovkin at the time.

'That was the level where I thought Eamonn had earned the right to belong, and that was the level where the serious money was. If Eamonn could get his title shot, then he could maybe land the kind of purse that sets a man, and his family, up for life.

'But we had to get there first. And the business of boxing doesn't always make it that easy. Just because a fighter might be good enough, might have earned his chance, and might deserve a shot at the title, doesn't mean he always gets the shot.'

Look at how long it took Jake La Motta to get what he deserved – and what he had to do to get his title shot. And look at what it *did* to him. If you've seen the film *Raging Bull*, you'll know what I'm talking about. The people in charge of boxing make the decisions. But their motivations might not always be the most *noble* element of the noble art.

'After winning the title, I inundated the IBF with emails and calls. I was relentless until they spoke with me. I told them Eamonn was the intercontinental [champion], so where's he going to be in your rankings? They told me what you would expect, that the committee would be meeting to make the decision and I would be informed in due course. But Eamonn was 32 by now and we needed to make progress, so I thanked them and repeated my question, "Where will Eamonn be in your rankings?"

'Eamonn was ranked at number seven at that time, but the dudes at numbers six and five hadn't fought recently, so I told them straight – that means Eamonn should be at least number four now. They say to me, "Well Paddy, it doesn't quite work like that," and they won't budge. But I kept the pressure on them, and between that conversation and the next one someone else lost, and there was a shift in the rankings, so now my argument was that Eamonn should be ranked at number three.

'They tried to put me off again and said that if I was doing my job, which I was, I should leave them alone and let them do theirs. But I knew that I had something special with Eamonn, and I wasn't going to let this opportunity go. So every little thing that happened with any of the fighters in the IBF rankings, I was emailing or calling them to let them know that we were here, we were ready, we were watching them, and we were waiting.

'When the new IBF rankings finally came out, Eamonn was at number three, which was a beautiful thing. Golovkin was the IBF world title holder, and the way the IBF rankings worked, they kept the one and two rankings vacant. So I called the organisation and I said to them that Eamonn wanted a shot at the title and that we wanted to be the mandatory challenger for Golovkin's next defence.'

Eamonn described to me how he felt when Paddy told him of his ranking.

'I was very proud. I was now the highest-ranked contender in my division. It was amazing. I had to work hard not to get caught up in it. If I thought, "Wow, I'm amazing" that could have a negative effect on my training.

'Paddy kept me grounded. I also kept myself determined by visualising how hard I had worked and how I had kept raising the bar from when I started to box at six years old, to winning the Ulster title at 13, to winning the *Prizefighter* tournament, to turning pro. That kept me motivated. Also, the idea of being able to tell my boys Charlie, Oscar and Lewis about my achievements – that drove me too.'

What happened next then, I ask Paddy?

'Apparently, so the IBF said, getting a title shot didn't quite work like I thought. I said, "Look, if Eamonn is ranked at three, and the guy ranked at four, who was a dude called Tureano Johnson, took each other on then surely that would be an eliminator bout for the right to be the mandatory challenger for the world title belt held by Golovkin?

'They could hardly say no when I was using their own rankings logic against them, so they sanctioned the fight and it was put out to purse bids.'

And that's how they went from the Oasis Centre, Swindon, to Derry, to finally fighting at Madison Square Garden, the spiritual home of boxing; of Sugar Ray Robinson; of Jake La Motta; of Jack Dempsey and of Roberto Duran.

'And now, *we* were going over there to fight for the right to contest a major world title.'

23

Putting the Peanuts
Back in their Shells

MADISON SQUARE Garden – to any boxing fan, and even more to any fighter, this is the place where boxing history has been made time and time again; a venue that has been built and rebuilt on legendary fight after legendary fight. Like a young lad obsessed with dreams of scoring the winning goal in the cup final at Wembley Stadium, young fighter after young fighter has dreamed of fighting for a world title shot at the Garden.

I asked Eamonn about his reaction when he found out that he was going to take on Tureano Johnson for the right to contest a world middleweight title.

'I didn't feel like it was true, if that makes sense. It's something you dream about as a kid, isn't it? I was kind of numb. It was hard to digest. I look back now and think, "How did I stay calm?" I mean, even the weigh-in for that fight was sold out! As a boxer, though, you can't focus on the show.

It's about your performance. Paddy helped me control the situation. I was confident, though. My condition, the effects of the nutrition advice I'd had in camp was excellent. I was in fantastic shape – which you can see on the day of the weigh-in. Conditioning was the key for me. I was an intense fighter and great conditioning helped me perform in the style I wanted to.'

Paddy laughs when I tell him about Eamonn's memory of finding out he was going to fight at the Garden. I ask Paddy how the fight was made for such a glamorous venue. After all, Swindon via Northern Ireland to New York's Mecca of boxing was a pretty big leap.

'When I had started with Eamonn, I insisted on becoming his manager because I believed that I had the knowledge and experience to manoeuvre him into a position to fight at world level, and we were almost there.'

Almost – but not quite yet. 'There was still the matter of the purse bids. And the boxing business being the boxing business, nothing ever goes smoothly.

'It was hard to make the fight, especially at this level. We had been trying to get the backing to put in our own bid, but we hadn't got the deal over the line before the purse bid deadline, so we weren't in a position to make any offer.

'But Golden Boy [the promotional company fronted by six-weight world champion Oscar De La Hoya] did – and they gave us a date and made us chief support on the undercard of the world title defence by [Gennady] Golovkin against David Lemieux at Madison Square Garden, New York.

'This was it. The final step we needed to take before getting a shot at GGG and the world title, and for Eamonn, the *serious* money that it was possible to make when a fighter reached that level of status.

'I was already heading to the States at around that time because we had decided to have George's [Groves] training camp for his world super middleweight title fight against Badou Jack at Big Bear, California. So I invited Eamonn to come with us and do his training camp at Big Bear too.

'I recall notifying George that Eamonn would be coming over with us to prepare to fight Tureano Johnson and George seeming uncomfortable with the idea. I told George not to worry, that Eamonn would pay his own way and that he wouldn't be coming over on George's coin – so there was no issue for George. George paused for a few moments and then told me that he was happy enough with this situation, as long as Eamonn was paying his own way.

'I remember thinking at the time that George being "happy" with the situation was a strange response.

'I had told George about Eamonn out of respect for him and our relationship. But ultimately, Eamonn was a fighter in my stable, just like George. And just like George, I was positioning Eamonn for a world title shot. So whether Eamonn trained at Big Bear or not, it was my business, not George's. And as long as Eamonn's training didn't affect George's preparations, which I would not allow, then there shouldn't have been a problem.

'While I was the coach, I was making the decisions – period.

'We arrived in Big Bear and Eamonn was loving the training – he was training like a beast, he wanted this fight that much.

'When the purse bids finally got sorted out, we were still training at Big Bear. We finished the training camp and Eamonn went home to spend a bit of time with his family, while I continued on to Vegas with George, before we were to meet up in October, in New York, for the final preparations for the fight.

'We stayed in this cool retro hotel just across the road from Madison Square Garden. It looked like time had just stopped there in the 1920s or 1930s, and everything from the decor to the furnishings reminded me of that period of time.

'We were over there for five days before the fight but that was a very different set-up and timescale to the one I had planned, which was designed to optimise Eamonn's preparation and ensure that his physical and his *mental* strength were at their peak as he went into the fight.'

Do you think there was something dodgy about the fact that you had less than a week in New York before the fight?

'You see, Teach, this is the fight game – and the fight game is a business, where small advantages taken can mean the difference between winning and losing. I could have been accused of being paranoid at the time. But when you've got some experience of the business, and certain things happen that shouldn't happen, then in my view, that paranoia is probably justified.'

What are your recollections of being involved with Golden Boy Promotions, I asked Eamonn? Things like the flights to New York, your purse and your contract?

'At the time, at least the bits I was aware of like our flights over to New York and that kind of thing, it seemed like Golden Boy were trying to make things as difficult as possible for us.

'I didn't know a lot about it really. Paddy was in control. I trusted him and he had my back. He was a great manager as well as a great trainer for me. He had my best interests at heart and wanted the best for me, which you can see from the actions he took to protect me. I left him to it really. He talked to me about the situation, but told me not to worry about it. He didn't burden me with any of it. I needed to perform on the night and he had me very well mentally prepared.'

Tell me how it all panned out, I say to Paddy.

'I had told Golden Boy that I wanted Eamonn in New York two weeks before the fight. They wouldn't cover that cost and insisted on being responsible for five days only, so we agreed to cover the remaining nine days ourselves and gave them the dates when we wanted to travel. Golden Boy didn't book the flight for the dates we had requested and they told us that there was a problem with Eamonn's visa. I was annoyed with this so I said to Eamonn, "Screw it, let's go over on a waiver," which wouldn't have been the correct type of visa to enter the USA to fight.

'Not long after this, I changed my mind. I kept turning over possible outcomes if we won the fight, and what Golden Boy, or Tureano Johnson's people, might do if we won the fight but had the wrong US entrance visa. It wasn't worth taking the risk and having Eamonn's potential win taken away because he didn't have the right to be working over there. I was worried it would mess with Eamonn's head.

'Some people might think we were putting two and two together and making five. But at the very least, I felt Golden Boy had made things difficult for us. And in my experience, some people in this game would delve to strange depths in order to get what they wanted.

'In the end, Eamonn's visa came in with five days left for us to get over to New York – which, coincidentally, exactly matched Golden Boy's original timescale offer.

'Anyway, we got ourselves there and we did the press conference at MSG. It was nice for Eamonn. Roberto Duran was there as well as GGG Gennady Golovkin, Oscar De La Hoya and Bernard Hopkins – and Eamonn was right there for his big chance.

'But like I said, this was business, so after the press conference, Neil Sibley, our lawyer, tells me that Golden Boy's representative has the contract with him for the money side of the event, and that he wants me to sign it.

'So I took the contract and studied it. The figure we were to receive for our purse was recorded at the bottom of the contract, and in the small print legal language there were caveats and stipulations detailing deduction after deduction that we would have to take from the figure, before we could get to what we would be paid for the fight. All the deductions were bullshit. The way they were going we'd have had next to nothing left. When it came to paying us, the figure would be a *gross* figure, rather than *net*, so we would have to pay the deductions from our purse.'

Angelo Dundee, the world-famous trainer of Muhammad Ali, when asked about how much money he was making in the fight game, said, 'The fighters get paid peanuts, and I get the shells.'

What do you make of that, I ask Paddy?

'I did some quick mental maths. With the deductions that were coming off our purse, it was obvious to anyone with basic arithmetic skills that we wouldn't be getting what we had agreed with them. And what was worse, these were deductions that we were expected to pay according to the contract, and they had never been discussed with us at any point in the negotiations.

'I was fuming, and I wasn't prepared to just let this happen. It was the principle of the matter. But this wasn't just about money we had agreed to. So I decided to play them at their own game.

'From a young age, I try to tell my young fighters that what they are learning in school is hugely important to them and that they should concentrate and study hard. Maths and English matter massively when you consider contracts in boxing. If you can confuse someone with words or numbers, then you are in control of that person. How many people sign contracts without understanding what they are signing?'

Take the difference between a net and a gross percentage. The gross figure is the money a person receives *before* deductions, and the net figure is what a person actually takes home *after* deductions.

'I noticed that the figure that we were being paid didn't have whether it was net or gross printed next to it. Golden Boy's representative had already signed the contract as if it was a done deal and we would just go along with all of the deductions to our purse. So I thought if Golden Boy were going to be like that, then I needed to fight fire with fire. Next to the figure I wrote the word *net*, so that we wouldn't have to pay the deductions, and I signed the contract.

'I took a picture of the contract, with my adjustment on it, as well as keeping my own copy, and sent Golden Boy's copy back to them.

'Ten minutes later, I'm standing there talking with Neil, our lawyer, and you know when your shoulders begin to tense up because you just know that there is someone behind you and he is just about to touch you on the shoulder? Well, that's how I was feeling.

'So this guy from Golden Boy comes over and says, "Hey Paddy – what's this?" And he's waving the contract. So I say, "It's a contract." And Neil is stood next to me, looking more and more uncomfortable.

'And the dude from Golden Boy says to me, "The contract ain't right. You wrote *net* next to this figure. That's not right."

'I said to him, "I can't remember writing that word. But," and I pointed at his signature, "is that your signature?" He says, "Yes" and I say, "Well, that's my signature next to it too. So, to be clear we've got your signature, we've got my signature, and everything above them is agreed to. So we have a contract. I don't see what the problem is.

'He's just shaking his head then and he says to me, "But there are deductions to come off your purse."

'I can feel myself getting wound up so I say, "What are those deductions for, anyway? They ain't fair. You ain't notified us of them. And now you want to tell us? That ain't right. It feels like you made it difficult for us bringing us over here, now you're trying to get deductions off us that we never agreed to, and you're not supposed to. And *now* you're getting upset that somebody allegedly wrote *net* on a contract you have signed? There ain't no deductions for us. Eamonn's purse is *net*. It says so right there – on your contract."

'I can see he's getting angry and he says, "But I signed it first and the word *net* wasn't on there."

'"Sure, that wasn't clever now, was it?" I say to him. "To sign a contract like it's a blank cheque."

'He's definitely angry now, because he starts telling me I can't talk to him the way I am.

'I just keep going and say I'm not talking to him like anything. I'm just saying it how it is. You signed the contract first, not me.

'Anyway, I decide I've had enough then and I tell him that I've got my copy, and a photographic copy that I have emailed to myself. He can do whatever he likes with his copy – and I walk off.

'It's funny now I remember it because at the day of the weigh-in for the fight, there's this video which always makes me smile. Eamonn's on the scales. Bernard Hopkins is stood behind Eamonn and I'm stood over Eamonn's left shoulder.

'To the right of Eamonn, as you're looking at the video, Bernard Hopkins is appreciating how physically great Eamonn's condition is. Then you see Oscar De La Hoya come over to Hopkins, whisper in his ear and then look over towards me. I can see Oscar rubbing his fingers together in the money sign and both he and Hopkins are looking at me and I can't help but think: they're thinking that I'm an asshole because they know what I've done to protect my man.'

And that's how Paddy put their peanuts back in their shells.

'And I love that because like Bob Marley says, "They were playing smart but not playing clever." I was looking after Eamonn and plain and simple, that's my job.

'The thing is, I'm always of the mind that you take a fight for at least one of three reasons: for experience, for opportunity or for financial benefit. In the beginning for a fighter, it definitely ain't about money because you're having to sell tickets and you're busting your ass just to survive. And it ain't about opportunity at this stage either. What opportunities are you going to get when you're not known? It's about experience. You're building yourself and getting experience. You want to fight a southpaw, a tall dude, a short dude, a strong guy, a puncher, a guy with good footwork, an awkward guy who can tie you up. You fight all these guys who have these attributes *individually,* so that after ten to 15 fights you're able to fight a guy who has these attributes *collectively.*

'The next reasons are opportunity and financial benefit. And financial benefit might not come until later in a fighter's career. When a fighter comes to the end of his career, he wants to know he will have enough money to retire on and look after his family – and if he is one of the lucky ones, maybe his kids' families too.

'Eamonn and I knew the money wasn't what it could be, but the opportunity to become a mandatory for GGG was worth the risk.

'Sometimes, it's different, and the fighter might get offered a world title shot earlier in his career, when maybe it's four or five fights, maybe 18 months too early. And the coach needs to know that's *exactly* why the other team are offering you the fight now – *because* it's too early. That's when you have a choice as a fighter. If you have a strong team behind you, and faith that they can steer you well and the chance will come along again, then you can say no. Or, you think, you know what, it might be a bit too soon, but it's a great opportunity and good money – so you take the fight and you roll the dice.

'When you take a fight for the second reason, opportunity, sometimes it might not pay you good money. There's a high risk because if you take this fight and lose, it can set you back. But if you win it, then the next fight could well be the one that opens the door to the big money – so the risk is worth it.

'With me, the fighter makes the decisions. After all, he's the one taking the risks. In my role as a manager, it is my job to position my fighter with the best opportunities I can. When we have had a fight, I go to my guy with two options where possible and I say, "Which way do you want to go?" And this was exactly how I worked with Eamonn.'

Were there any down sides of working with Eamonn, I ask cautiously, as I can see how strong their relationship still is. Anything that you regret?

'My only regret with Eamonn is that we didn't get together earlier than we did. I can only imagine what we might have achieved together if we had started together earlier and worked together longer.'

I move the conversation on to the fight with Tureano Johnson itself, which I have watched over and over again. Paddy once said to me, 'Teach, this is the greatest fight that you've never seen – watch it. It's a war – pure and simple.'

I was sceptical at the time but I can only encourage you to watch this fight. I've shown it to so many people now, friends and students, and I always start off the same way as Paddy did with me: 'Watch this fight. *It's the greatest fight you've never seen.*'

No one who has watched it has disagreed so far.

And this is why.

24

The Irish Jake La Motta

DID YOU know that the fight would be at the Garden in New York when you agreed to the match?

'As far as the Tureano Johnson fight, initially we didn't know it was at Madison Square Garden. It was the opportunity that mattered to us and we took the fight before we knew any of the venue and date details.

'I remember how excited Eamonn was when I told him we would be fighting in New York. He says to me in his broad Irish accent, "Ah Jaysus coach, it's Madison Square Garden. I'd love to fight there. All the greats have fought there." And he knew the money wasn't great, but he understood the plan and where winning this fight could lead us to.

'He was such a good person to coach. Eamonn, old wide eyes, he really is a warrior. He just loves fighting. He would have fought Johnson in a back garden or a phone booth if I asked him to. He'd fight anywhere – just for the pure enjoyment of it.

'Fight night came and this was our third fight together. Eamonn was in great physical and mental shape and he had made weight beautifully. He's giving off exactly the vibes I want to feel from one of my dudes before he goes into the ring for a big fight.

'One of my favourite event images of Eamonn is his ring walk that night. The Irish flags are up over his shoulders, and remember, we're in New York, so there's a lot of Irish interest. The Garden was on its way to being packed when he came into the arena. Eamonn had brought over a decent crowd too – and it's a long way from Ireland to New York. There were Irish flags up around the arena, and you only need a handful of them and the Irish get themselves going and shouting, and it kind of made us feel like we were the home fighter.'

I wondered what Eamonn felt about using his Irish heritage to promote himself as a fighter in the US.

'I'm an Irishman and a Catholic, even though I'm from Northern Ireland. So I was fine with it. I loved the flags and the pipers and dancers. I boxed for Ireland and Northern Ireland, so that helped too as it can be a complicated situation. For our fight in New York, I thought it was a great decision, what with New York's Irish community. Making the most of the Irish connection helped with our support as there were a lot of other nationalities attending, so it was nice to know we had people on our side. We didn't know it at the time but the fight at Madison Square Garden would be my swansong. I'm sure we would have used the Irish connection to promote me well in the future if we had continued fighting.'

Paddy continues the story. 'I was in front of Eamonn on the ring walk because I wanted to get to the ring before him. I didn't want him to get caught up in the whole event. I wanted him to enjoy his ring walk. It was a special thing. But when he got to the ring, ready to take care of business, I wanted him to lock his eyes on me. I told him, "As soon as you see me, just focus on what we talked about, what we've practised and what we're supposed to be doing here."

'His eyes lock on mine as he makes his way to the ring and he's in a beautiful space.'

'My ring walk was unreal,' recalls Eamonn. 'There were mini-explosions of cameras everywhere. The fight was being streamed across the entire US. There were Irish tricolours, pipers and dancers. But I had to make sure that I didn't get caught up in all of that.

'A month before the fight, Paddy had prepared me for this. We scripted how I would complete my ring walk to prepare me mentally for the size of the event. Paddy knew what to expect, but I didn't, and Paddy knew there was a chance it might affect me. I had enough to worry about with the fight and our gameplan. Paddy would already be in the ring when I began the ring walk, so we agreed that I would keep my eyes focused on him as I walked to help me remain calm – and it worked.'

Paddy continues, 'The bell goes. Round one starts. Eamonn goes out to meet Johnson and 30 seconds into the round Johnson lands a lovely left hook. Eamonn gets dropped a minute and a half into the round. He gets up, they go at it, and then Eamonn's dropped again by a clubbing right hook to the back of his head with 40 seconds of the round remaining. If you watch the fight, you'll see that it's more of a cuffing shot that pushes Eamonn off balance – and that's why Eamonn goes down. I mean, this is gonna sound crazy, but bar the two knockdowns, I thought the first round was pretty even, with no one finishing the boss.

'But it's also true that this was not a good start for us and I'm thinking to myself that it was only three weeks ago that George was dropped in the first round in his title fight with Badou Jack – and we know how that ended.

'Our gameplan for taking Johnson on had been clear. I had shown Eamonn how he wouldn't need to go looking for Johnson. Johnson would want to get in Eamonn's face because that was his style. In all of his previous fights, Johnson had barely taken a backward step, always wanting to fight inside. So, rather than use up too much physical energy inside, the plan was to drive Eamonn's lead leg underneath Johnson and then keep bouncing Johnson off him all night with his hip and forearm if he got too close – and then attack him.

'But round one was drastic. When I got him back to the corner, Eamonn was aware of everything. He was OK and we weren't in severe trouble. I said, "You've got to start relaxing, man. Just relax and get a little bit of a rhythm going. Don't get into a fight just yet. Establish your rhythm to get yourself going."

'In round two, I think that Johnson had just about blown himself out a bit trying to kill Eamonn in the previous round. Halfway through the second round, Eamonn took an excellent left hook from Johnson – and he didn't even budge. They were both trading punches freely and evenly. In my opinion, you could've given that round to Eamonn as he stole a few good shots off at the end.

'When I got Eamonn back to the corner, he had picked up a small cut above his left eye. But it was nothing to worry about. Even so, I was deliberately as slow as possible leaving the ring just to pinch a few extra seconds for Eamonn, and to let the adrenalin do its work on the cut.

'If you watch the fight, it's in the third round when you can first see Eamonn starting to drive his lead leg underneath Johnson and then bump him with his hip to try to keep his opponent off balance and keep him on the back foot. And that's something you see Eamonn doing throughout the fight.

'The fifth round went to Eamonn, who was the busier fighter this time, even though Johnson landed some decent right uppercuts. What I remember most in this round, though, was how Eamonn walked back to our corner beckoning the crowd to make even more noise, and they responded to him brilliantly.

'In my opinion, the sixth round was Eamonn's best round. Watching it again, you can see how Eamonn bullied Johnson the whole round. Eamonn answers everything that Johnson throws at him – and more. He's busy, busy, busy the entire three minutes, and he never seems to let Johnson off the ropes – pressuring and pressuring him. Eamonn has Johnson backing up throughout the round, which wasn't Johnson's usual style. So, he's either doing something that is technically different to what he has done before as a fighter, or Eamonn has him doing something that he isn't used to doing. And Eamonn's letting his shots go in numbers too, with powerful and hurtful combinations. He had a beautiful sixth round.

'In the seventh, we were a little shocked. Johnson starts the round on the outside and he's popping his shots off, using lateral movement. In all the fights we had studied, Johnson had never moved like this. It seemed against his style. You could see that both fighters were beginning to feel the pace by now. It was a fairly uneventful round, but Johnson probably did enough to win it. In saying that, I did have to get the ref's attention for allowing Johnson to keep punching Eamonn behind the ear, which he did repeatedly, and anyone can see this who watches the video of the fight.

'Eamonn came out for the eighth round re-energised. During the previous minute in our corner, the house doctor had been called to check Eamonn over because it had been such a brutal fight so far. I think Eamonn's enthusiasm when he came out of the corner was for the doctor. He wanted to show him that he was still well in this fight.

'It was a close round, with Eamonn keeping Johnson against the ropes for much of it. Johnson's head shots were good and very visible for the judges. Eamonn was working on the inside and producing some decent shots, but maybe they were harder to see than Johnson's more obvious form of attack. Eamonn kept to the fight plan and I could see him driving his lead leg into Johnson's stance to keep him from settling. But Johnson was just as stubborn as Eamonn and with each of Eamonn's shoves, Johnson shoved right back.

'When Eamonn came back to the corner, the doctor was up on the apron checking him again. And to be honest, I was beginning to have some concerns of my own at this point. But regardless of the punishment he was taking, Eamonn was still showing that he deserved to be in this fight.

'Round nine passes with Eamonn starting beautifully, landing damaging body shots and some beautiful combinations. Johnson knew by now what Eamonn could do and sensibly he was on the move. He didn't want to hang around too long and allow Eamonn to get to work on the inside. For me, Eamonn controlled that round, dictating where and when the action took place. In fact, the round finishes with Johnson against the ropes and Eamonn almost running his hands into his opponent.

'And then came round ten.

'Eamonn took some serious shots in that round, to add to the punishment he had absorbed in the previous rounds. Eamonn was a warrior, man, that's a fact. But like every real warrior, he might not show his opponent that the shots were hurting him, but that doesn't mean they weren't doing damage. I've got the towel in my hand in that round and I'm looking for an excuse to stop the fight because Eamonn is taking some serious shots without significant reply and I'm not sure it should go on.

'The thing is, it was one of those fights where both men were taking a load of punishment. But I have the responsibility of looking after my man and I don't want the fight to go on unless Eamonn's eyes are clear and his legs are steady. As a coach, if it's a brutal fight, I'm gonna let it go on if I see those things, because I'm the coach of a *fighter*. If we don't allow a brutal fight to continue, then you would never have had *The Thrilla in Manila*, or Gatti v Ward or Morales v Barrera – you just wouldn't have had those amazing fights if they weren't allowed to go on. But you have to justify your reasons for allowing these fights to continue.

'And at the end of each round, as soon as Eamonn heard the bell, he turned, walked back and locked his eyes on me – totally in control of himself.

'But as round ten ended, the doctor was up on the apron expressing his concerns – and silently I had to agree.

'Eamonn had taken some hellish strong shots to the head and when we were in the corner I said to him, "If the next round looks like that, I'm pulling you out."

'And he says, "You can't, coach! There's only two more rounds."

'He knew how many rounds it was. He was there. He was aware. He was present. I told him, "Eamonn, you took too many shots to the head. You need to jump on his ass and change the momentum of this fight. If I get the same round in the 11th, I'm stopping the fight. So if you don't want that, you need to give me something."

'In the 11th round, Eamonn went out and jumped all over Johnson. And I'm thinking, "God damn you, Irishman!" because he took my reasons to stop the fight away and we were back on again.

'Then it came to round 12, the last round, so I surely wasn't going to stop the fight then without a great reason, and it was a hard-fought final round.

'At the end of the fight, I knew we had lost it. But it was also true that Eamonn had set down a marker for the world to see which said he deserved to be at this level. At Madison Square Garden, he had made his mark. I knew we were going to get more big fights, regardless of this loss, because he fought like a warrior.

'At the end of the fight, he gave me a big smile and said, "What do you think, coach?" And I said, "You fought your ass off. I'm proud of you, brother." And I think Eamonn thanked me for not stopping the fight.

'The announcement was made and we had lost the fight. But this was Madison Square Garden and a knowledgeable boxing crowd. And as we're climbing out of the ring and walking down the aisle, Eamonn is getting cheered the whole way out through the arena, and I mean cheers and applause so loud it was almost ear-splitting. It was amazing.'

What do you remember about the fight, I ask Eamonn?

'I remember going down in the first round – which wasn't how we had wanted the fight to start! In that round, I couldn't really work out where I was getting hit. In reality, I was getting hit on the ear by Johnson's clubbing shots. It was a good gameplan from him. He would circle out to my side and then hit me on the ear, which caused me to be off balance.

'It's a very strange feeling. It's the same as if you have an ear infection. If you get up too quickly, you're off balance and it affects you. That's how this was. He hit me like this twice. I got up off the canvas no problem, but my balance was causing me issues.

'At the end of round one, I got to my corner and as I sat still my centre of gravity came back. We only had one minute but Paddy got me composed and refocused. The thing is, the shots Johnson was hitting me with weren't that big. So I couldn't understand why I was feeling like I was. I know now that the ear is the weakest connection point to the brain. Seems to me that Johnson, or his team, knew their science. You could argue his strategy (if this is what it was) was a good one – but it's dangerous. Hitting the ear and the back of my head is illegal and maybe the ref should have done something about it? We had a gameplan too: step forward with my lead leg and use my hip and shoulder to shunt him back, which had some success. But often, his method of circling me kind of nullified it.'

What about after the fight, I ask Paddy?

'When we were backstage, there are people constantly stopping Eamonn, slapping him on the back and complimenting him. And even though he's been through 12 brutal rounds of a pure war of a fight, he's smiling and bouncing up on his toes. And suddenly, Eamonn stops, and he looks at me and he says, "Shall we do it again, coach?" I just shake my head because he's just gone through such a brutal war, and I smile and think, "What a man I'm working with here – crazy Irishman!"

'And things were fine until we had been in the dressing room for a while. The doctor came and started checking Eamonn. But I already knew things weren't quite right because Eamonn just wasn't himself, and it had happened quickly. The energy he'd had had completely changed in him, like it was suddenly sapped out of his body.

'The doctor finished his checks and told me Eamonn was all fine. I remember saying to the doctor, "What do you mean he's all fine? He needs to go to the hospital. I'm concerned for him." The doctor just repeated that he'd checked Eamonn over and everything was fine.

'I wasn't having that. I said, "You need to put him in an ambulance and get him to a hospital. I'm telling you he's not right. He's *not* alright. He's just been in a war. Weren't you in there watching it? You might *think* he's OK, but he's not. And you need to get us an ambulance."

'Then that man, that *doctor*, he says to me, "If you want to get him to a hospital, then you need to take him in a cab."

'I was furious, and I say, "Are you fucking joking me? To a hospital across the other end of New York, on a Saturday night, and you want us to get a cab? I want an ambulance. Get us a fucking ambulance! What's your fucking problem? You're the doctor here, so look after him."

'The doctor was disgruntled, turned away from us and left the dressing room. Then he comes back after a few minutes and says that there's an ambulance on the way.

'They come to get us, put Eamonn in a chair and I get in the back with him. Eamonn's wife Nicola came with us in the ambulance and his other family and friends followed behind in cabs. It was a long way downtown to the hospital, even in an ambulance with its lights flashing and its horns blaring. I don't know what the hell the doctor was thinking of wanting us to travel in a taxi. Who would have given a shit about us in the Saturday night New York traffic in a taxi?

'We arrived at the hospital eventually and when we got out of the ambulance, Eamonn's head was all swollen up like a coconut. It was big, like *cartoon big*, and I was worried. They got him upstairs quickly and got him into a bed. Pretty swiftly, they got on to the urine tests and when Eamonn passed his sample, it was black. Black as a pint of Guinness.

'The doctors put Eamonn in a bed and settled him down. Then they told us that he had been through such an ordeal during that fight, and he had used so much of his strength, that his body was beginning to break down his muscle just to survive – and that's why his urine was black.'

And what about Eamonn? How did he remember feeling after the ordeal of such a fight?

'I couldn't tell there was something wrong,' he told me. 'Maybe it was the adrenalin? But now, when I look at pictures of myself after the fight, when I see the swelling, I can see the change in myself in pictures from when I was in the taxi going compared to the journey to the airport to come home. Even then, when I was coming home, my whole body was still swollen – just not as bad as straight after the fight. I had been so lean on the night of the fight, and now I looked fat, like I'd put on four or five stone in a couple of days.'

So it was bad then, I say to Paddy.

'Yeah,' he says, 'it was bad. Over two days, the medical staff had to give Eamonn over 14 litres of fluid intravenously. We knew that Eamonn was going to need some time in hospital for observation, and to recover. His wife Nicola, his dad, his brother and Neil, our lawyer, went back to the hotel. But I asked the nurses for permission to stay with Eamonn.

And as luck had it, it happened that there was a bed free on the ward, right next to Eamonn. The nurses told me that it was unorthodox, but they let me stay with him, and I slept in a bed next to Eamonn for three nights.'

You must have been really worried for him, I say.

'Yeah, I was *really* worried for Eamonn. I had gone through this experience earlier in my career when I was coaching Sammy Stewart, my first pro, in the late 1990s. It was my first title fight with him in Takoma, Washington when he fought for the NABF bantamweight title against Pedro Pena and they just had a war. Sammy got a bad cut in the first round.

'After the fight, me and Sammy had separate rooms at our hotel, but I felt so concerned for Sammy's welfare that I sat in a chair next to his bed watching him breathe all night – just in case anything happened.

'And that was what it was like now: nurses and doctors coming in and out to check on Eamonn. He was in a bad way. His head and face were badly swollen. And one night, during the three days, he got really upset and he says, "I'm sorry if I let you down, coach."

'I couldn't believe what I was hearing when he said that. I said, "You should have heard the crowd cheering you as you left the ring. You think that you let me down? No way, man."

'Eamonn was just a fighter – a pure fighter. And his upset was his pride coming out. He didn't just fight for himself. He fought for me. He fought for his family. He wanted to make everyone proud of him. He was fighting for everyone. And now he felt he had let himself, and us, down. He couldn't have been more wrong.

'After three days, we were given the all-clear that Eamonn would be OK to leave the hospital soon, and one of the nurses comes in with the hospital paperwork for signing. She goes over to Nicola motioning for her to sign it. I said, "Excuse me, what are you doing? You don't take paperwork on this fighter to anyone but me. Nicola is his wife, but I'm his manager, and I deal with everything. She's worried and she has enough to deal with, so you talk to me, OK?"

'The next day, me and Eamonn were chatting away to each other, and eating food, because he's improving quite a bit now. Then Eamonn gets a text. He picks up his phone, reads it, and then he says, "Coach, I've got a text here and I think I should show it to you, but you're probably not gonna be happy about it."

'I say, "Why do I need to see your texts?" because it's his personal phone and none of my business. He tells me it's from George Groves. I told him it was still his business, but he wanted me to read it and he handed me the phone. The text to Eamonn from George said, "Saw your fight. You fought like a warrior. But you need better people around you."

By this time, you and George had parted ways, right?

'Yeah, I had let him know the week we came home from Vegas.

'I just said to Eamonn, "classy dude" and handed him back his phone.

'Eamonn told me he wanted to reply to George but I was like, "Don't reply just for me. What's the point? Leave it alone. Don't water the weed if you don't want it to grow. If you feel you want to respond for yourself, go ahead. But if you're gonna do it on account of me, then don't bother.

'So he didn't, and we left it at that.

It turns out that due to the severity of his injuries, Eamonn could only remember snatches of the whole hospital experience. I told him the story, trying to deliver it as best I could in a style Paddy might think was about right.

'To be honest,' Eamonn said, 'I didn't really know what was occurring exactly. Paddy had been intercepting paperwork and dealing with the situation, so that I could recuperate effectively. I was in no state to even know how bad I was really.

'It's lucky I selected Paddy as my trainer and manager because he had my back then too.

'In this game, your health is your wealth. It's as simple as that.'

I think about what must have happened when they returned to the UK after the fight. Eamonn hadn't won, but he had earned a lot of respect. Respect that would get him more chances to achieve his dream.

But he had been hurt too – badly. And that must have been playing on everyone's minds.

'When we were back in England,' Paddy went on, 'Eamonn went home for a rest. I told him after a month or so we'd get back together and start just cracking at the mitts to see how he felt.

'But in the meantime, I would start trying to get something in place, to see how he wanted to move forward. The Johnson fight had been a hard one, and the injuries would take quite a bit of time to heal. We just didn't know what the effects would be for a few months to come.

'What I did know was that Nicola and Eamonn's family were worried for him, and that some serious decisions were going to be made over the next few weeks.

'I had been busy over the weeks where I had not seen Eamonn and had been in discussions about a good fight for Eamonn in Belfast.

'But Eamonn's family had some big concerns and rightly so.

'They were all worried about him, and Eamonn's family are very close-knit. They had supported Eamonn all the way and put up with a lot in order for Eamonn to make it in boxing.

'But now, they were very concerned. They felt he had been on a great journey. He had fought at Madison Square Garden. He had got his shot. But there had been a price too, and now something had to change.

'Eamonn's point of view was that he had proved he was world-class level – and he was right. He had.

'It was hard for Eamonn and it was hard for his family. Eamonn loved boxing. But his wife was pregnant now and Eamonn decided to retire at 33.

'In the end, it turned out that Eamonn made the right decision, even if at the time there were opportunities presenting themselves because of the Johnson fight.'

It seems that Eamonn agrees with Paddy's assessment, even if a day does not go by when the decision to retire pains him a little bit.

'Teach, retiring from boxing is still a decision that I think about every day, four years on, now I'm 37.

'I competed as a boxer and gave it everything. I was a successful athlete. I'm still a fighter. I'd go back tomorrow if it were just for me. But I have to think of my health and of my family. For me alone, no problem, I would go back tomorrow. But would that be the right decision for my family? No, not for the people whom I love. But I'd be lying if I didn't say that I think about the *what-ifs*.

'That's the hardest thing to deal with. Not being big-headed or anything, but I was so close to fighting for that world title. It's not something that you can just forget. Someone who has a determined personality like mine will always be thinking that I could have done more, and done it better. You know, maybe if I had have won a world title, I would have kept going, but would that have been right for my health? I'm not sure.'

'Eamonn's got three boys now,' Paddy tells me. 'So Nicola's got four boys, including Eamonn! I saw him recently at an event, and I could see that old "wide eyes" mischief in his eyes. I sometimes say to him, "Eamonn, if you come back I can get you one more fight," and he shouts, "Do it, coach. Do it!" But he knows I'm joking.

'He still calls me "coach". I was speaking to him only a few days ago on the phone and he starts with, "Hey coach, what's the craic?"

'That's Eamonn "King Kane" O'Kane – a complete warrior, and my friend.'

I think we're finished for the night, and then Paddy waves his hand at me.

'Teach, there's just one last thing that really sticks in my mind about the fight, and that's a conversation I had in a hotel lobby after the hospital experience.

'It must have been when we were checking our stuff out of the hotel that we were staying in before we left New York. I was standing, minding my own business, when this dude comes up behind me and he taps me on the shoulder.

'Were you in the corner of that Irish dude the other night at Madison Square Garden?' he says to me.

'I said to him, "God, you've got some memory my friend, haven't you?"

'And he says to me, "It's the hat. I remember your hat."

'So I say, "Yeah, guilty, it was me."

'"Man," he shouts, "that Irish dude was so God-damned tough. He was like *Jake La Motta*!"

'And then there were other people around the hotel lobby who started going, "Yeah, that kid was a lot like Jake La Motta." And someone else shouts, "Yeah, the *Irish* Jake La Motta! That was something."

When we talk, I ask Eamonn about whether he knew that he had been re-christened in such a flattering way?

'I didn't know that, but it makes me feel very proud. I love that. It's lovely to hear that the New York fight crowd compared me to one of their own, and one of the hardest men and most obvious warriors in boxing too. I'm grateful to everyone who trained me to help me get to this position. I know that Paddy's training allowed me to achieve all of this. He's a special character to be sure.'

As I'm driving home, I think about that last comment comparing Eamonn with one of New York and the world's best. What more can be said about Eamonn O'Kane than that compliment from a knowledgeable New York fight crowd? How many fighters will go to New York and leave being compared to, and described as, one of their heroes?

Not many, is the answer, I think.

Not many.

25

Fight Town

2 September 2019

THE BILLBOARD posters and all the social media advertising describe this as the biggest boxing event in the South West.

My favourite is opposite a major roundabout in the centre of town. Luke 'The Duke' Watkins is dominating the majority of the advertisement. He is bare-chested, his hands balled into fists, tensing his substantial muscles while his face is locked in an expression like a war cry. He looks mean and ready to take care of business. The strapline on the poster reinforces this, screaming out, *'The Duke is back and he's in beast mode!'*

Except, as with everything in boxing, this isn't quite true. Less than 24 hours before Luke is expecting to headline the event, his opponent pulls out with an injury and regardless of Paddy's efforts, a suitable replacement can't be found.

I catch up with the Duke when the frustration of his fight falling through has subsided. Luke, for those of you interested in what a fighter does when he is not training, is learning to speak Spanish – and progressing *very* rapidly.

'I love learning and the process of learning is really fun to me,' he tells me. 'The last time that I was obsessed with something the way I am with the Spanish language was when I got into boxing.'

The last time I spoke with Luke we barely touched on boxing, spending most of our time discussing the Spanish language, culture, history and philosophy. So this time I will make sure we stick to boxing.

Having spent some time with Luke, it is clear that he is a deep thinker and I'm interested to know if this cerebral way of approaching the world translates into his boxing.

'When I first arrived at Paddy's gym,' he says, 'I was 19 and I progressed through the amateurs and into the professional ranks with Paddy. He understands that my brain, when it comes to boxing, works on the levels of tempo and maths. He quickly understood that and whenever he spoke with me, he was able to explain effectively in a way that makes logical sense. I've worked with other coaches but they don't explain *why* I'm doing something, and that doesn't sit well with me. When a man is trying to smash you in the face, you want to know *why* you are doing what you're doing and *how* it will work best.'

Has boxing given you any sense of direction and purpose, I ask him? I know from previous conversations that his teenage years were a little turbulent.

'When I started at Paddy's gym, I just loved fighting. I was a big lad. I wouldn't back down from conflict and so trouble found me more often than not. Looking back on my life, I would talk to Paddy. It's hard to talk to your parents at 19, isn't it, and these chats helped me to do the right thing.'

As a pro, Luke has won the Irish national and Commonwealth cruiserweight belts in his time with Paddy. What has been the achievement you have been most proud of so far, I ask him? His response is not what I expect to hear.

'The friendship outside of boxing that I have developed with Paddy,' he says with conviction. 'It's something that I will have for the rest of my life. I love boxing but it is only a part of my life. You know, it's more a relationship with Paddy than a friendship. We're more like family. What Paddy practises, he preaches. I respect that.'

I know that Luke hasn't cited the Commonwealth belt that he won in 2017, but I am interested to know how it felt to win this.

'At the time, it felt amazing. I'm obviously happy I achieved that. But now, I'm more like, "OK, we did that." For some boxers, it's all about belts and bragging about achievements. But for me, I like the whole process of boxing. I think in some ways, winning the Commonwealth title was more for other people than for me. I was pleased for Paddy too because he started me pretty much from scratch, controlled my career for me, and this is recognition of our work. For him to see someone he coaches grow and develop to this extent – that's something special. And he must be continuing to feel that excitement with his new fighters too.'

Paddy's your manager too, isn't he?

'I'll be honest, Teach, I hate the business side of boxing. It's shit. There are a lot of crooks out there in business – and boxing is full of them. I can't stand that bit. So I leave the business side to Paddy. I just want to fight.'

I tell Luke about Vatche's view that he fell out of love with boxing for a long period of time because he felt that the business didn't treat him fairly because of his ethnic background.

'Boxing is one of those businesses where you have to really ingratiate yourself with people who are powerful. If you're one of those people who sucks up to people, then great, you're in. I am not that guy.

'Boxers have to be realists too. This is a business and it's not just about how good you are as an athlete. I know fighters who aren't the best fighters, but man they are loved, they give the business what it wants, and they keep getting opportunities.

'People have no idea how hard this business can be. There have been times on fight night where I have had to borrow money just to pay a promoter for the privilege of fighting. I have actually *paid* to fight.'

Moving from struggling to make ends meet at one end of the boxing spectrum to 80,000 spectators at a packed Wembley Stadium for George Groves' rematch with Carl Froch, you were around it all, weren't you?

'I went to every single thing. That's what I mean when I say I love boxing as a whole and the places it has taken me. Being around something of that size was amazing. I've seen some really famous people. I loved it.'

You sparred with George, didn't you?

'I don't know how many rounds I've sparred with George because he was with Paddy for two years and we started working together straight away. But it was a lot.'

How did you find sparring a top fighter who became a world champion?

'I remember it clearly being a step up but nothing that I couldn't handle. That's when I *knew* I could fight, working with George like that, because even though I'd had good experiences with opponents before, this was *George Groves* and I coped with it well. I was a bit star-struck too, to be fair,' he says laughing.

It is testament to his ability and talent that Luke is still ranked in the top ten British cruiserweights as I write, despite the fact that in the last year he has had horrendous luck with fights being cancelled.

I hope that this year Luke gets some better luck. I will definitely be at his next fight when it happens.

But with or without 'The Duke', tonight's show must go on and I have arranged to meet Paddy at the venue, the Oasis Centre, Swindon, for the weigh-ins. I have access-all-areas tonight so that I can observe Paddy in action as a coach.

When I arrive, the fighters have already entered the venue with their coaches, managers and the event promoter.

A security guard escorts me to the weigh-ins. 'They're down here,' he says as he takes me through some double doors. 'Lady Luck' Bec Connelly sees me and says, "Hey Teach", followed quickly by Paddy, who just shouts "Teach" as he observes the weight of one of his fighters' opponents.

The weigh-ins are a low-key affair, attended by the fighters, trainers, managers and the promoter – plus the odd family member and hanger-on. The usual ritual of stripping to underwear is observed for the male and female fighters, followed by medicals. Soon enough, the waiting begins for the fighters as they step off the scales. They all seem pretty calm but there must be tension that they are not showing.

I notice that Casper is in the room and I gravitate towards him.

'Will the fighters eat now?' I ask him.

'Yeah, they need to.'

'What will they eat?' I ask as I notice 'Sir' Bradley Townsend pull out an egg and cress sandwich from his kit bag.

'They normally eat slow-release energy type foods like nuts, so that they don't have an energy spike that might disadvantage them when it comes to their turn to fight.'

I test Casper's theory and see the fighters eating nuts, as he had said, and plenty of salad, sweet potatoes and broccoli. They're saving their real food cravings until after they have performed.

Once the weigh-ins are completed and the fighters head off to their dressing rooms, I chat to Paddy and get the wrist band that gives me the access I need. We are in the venue a couple of hours before the first fight and it is empty except for a few event staff making some final touches to the VIP tables.

The venue holds around 1,500 spectators, which is a decent size for a small hall event. I walk around the venue, taking in the layout. The ring is in the middle of the hall, with a cordoned-off area stretching from a corner of the ring to a corner of the room to allow for the ring walks. There is a podium at the beginning of the ring walk to announce the arrival of the fighters and allow them to stand and take in the venue for a few moments before their walks to the ring. Surrounding the ring are the four rows of ringside seats and behind these are VIP tables where food and drink will be served to the tables as the fighters exert themselves.

Walking between the tables and the ring apron, I calculate that it would be unlikely that sweat, saliva or blood could travel the distance. Unlikely, but not impossible, I think, as I imagine the distance that fluid might travel propelled by the force of a powerful right cross or crushing left hook.

Behind the tables is the standard seating.

When I walk back to the centre of the hall to look more closely at the ring, Paddy is already inside. He is wearing his fedora and standing in the home corner looking towards the centre of the ring. He looks serious, like he's thinking about something hugely important. Then he starts walking, slowly pacing every inch of the ring canvas. He uses the balls of his feet to test the surface, like he's pressing down a divot of grass on a football pitch. Now and again, he grinds the ball of his foot into the canvas. He's testing how taut the canvas is. The tauter the canvas, the better for those fighters with good footwork and a preference for fluid movement around the ring. The spongier the canvas, and the more the feet sink into it, the slower the fighter's movement, which is a disadvantage if your style is to outmanoeuvre an opponent.

At around 5pm, an hour and a half before the doors open, Paddy gestures to me that we're heading to the dressing rooms. The dressing room area is through a series of corridors passing squash courts where the away fighters are housed, and into what at first glance looks like a sort of function room.

I feel privileged to be given this opportunity to be involved so intimately with Paddy and his fighters. I know that this is a big deal. Over the years, I have developed a relationship with Paddy and several of the fighters at his gym, and I know that they feel that they can trust me.

Even so, I am not taking this trust for granted and I am keen to make sure that they know this.

In the dressing room, its walls lined floor to ceiling with mirrors, are Sam 'The Sniper' Smith, 'Sir' Bradley Townsend, Casper and Natty, one of the coaches at Paddy's gym, who is also a two-fight pro whose real name is Jensen Irving.

Glamorous this is not. But it is functional and will do the job. 'The Duke' isn't headlining because his opponent pulled out at such short notice. This means that the order of the evening's fights needs to be rearranged – which Paddy does. This is more complicated than I might have expected and requires some delicate negotiation. The fighters have sold a lot of their tickets to friends and family. Each fighter had a specified time to fight and babysitters have been booked to cover these times. Paddy can't please everyone as he drafts and redrafts the order of events, trying to accommodate requests to fight at certain times so supporters will still be in the venue.

He seems slightly frustrated, but in a good humour, as he tries to meet the needs of his fighters while reminding them that in boxing, the only constant is change. He won't be able to accommodate everyone's preferences. Even I get roped into scribing the re-jigged fight order, on account of the fact I have pens that can be located quickly.

Once we have established the running order of the night, Paddy sets up the table where he will wrap the fighters' hands.

The table is organised meticulously, like a medical professional, and everything is exceptionally neat. There are two pairs of medical scissors, rolls of tape and bandages. Fringing the table's perimeter, Paddy cuts strip after strip of identical lengths of tape. There are pads to warm up the fighters later and some bottles of pills.

Paddy sits down and gestures for Sam to join him as his fight is on first. Sam offers Paddy his right hand and Paddy begins wrapping carefully and precisely – talking to everyone in the dressing room but never taking his eyes from the repetitive motions of binding his fighter's fist.

I have often wondered how a coach uses the intimate moment when he wraps his fighter's hands. It seems to me that this is an opportunity to connect with each other.

Once Paddy begins wrapping Sniper's left hand, his jab hand, he takes his opportunity. He asks Sam to imagine the fight that is about to happen. Sam is fighting at super middleweight, but he has weighed in at the lower end of the weight category and could have made middleweight while his opponent has tipped the scales on the limit – making him significantly heavier than Sam.

As Sam's opponent is larger than him, Paddy focuses on how Sniper can curb his opponent's momentum. He uses the pebble and the train analogy. Talking ever more quietly as he aims his words only at Sam, he talks about not giving an opponent the distance to build up his momentum and how Sam should use his jab to disarm his opponent and neutralise his weight advantage.

As he instructs Sam, Paddy wraps the hand he is referring to – reinforcing and embedding his ideas through the action. He tells Sam to make sure he moves effectively and to break down his opponent with his jab.

I'm impressed with the clarity, the simplicity and the delivery of his instruction.

There is a lot of waiting for the fighters, and their personalities are reflected in how they manage this time. Bradley whistles to himself and seems relaxed in this action as he stretches out on one of the sofas. 'Natty' eats and drinks before shaking his muscles out, which seems to me to be a way of controlling the nervous energy that must be coursing through him. Later he withdraws into himself, listening to music on his earphones with his eyes closed. Sam moves around the room, occasionally shadow boxing.

At around 5.45pm, Phil Williams, a heavyweight who trains at Paddy's gym, arrives in the dressing room. Phil is a journeyman, a boxer who travels up and down the country appearing as the away fighter, often at short notice and often not winning against up-and-coming prospects. It is considered common knowledge that the job of a journeyman is to be paid by a promoter to fight his home-crowd ticket sellers, put on a good show but ultimately to fall short. Phil's 3-21-1 record is evidence of his role.

Unusually for Phil, he is the home fighter and the ticket seller on this occasion – so the outcome could be different.

Phil's preparation hasn't been ideal today. As the home fighter, he has been running around collecting ticket money and delivering fight tickets even on the day of the fight. He looks distracted by it.

That doesn't sound like the best preparation, I say.

'Teach, it's not. I've been all over running around today – even to the Swindon Town match. When you're the home fighter, and there's promotion and social media to do, it's hard.'

Do you prefer being the away fighter? I ask this knowing that Phil has travelled all over the country to fight this year, with 19 fights in only 13 months.

'I love boxing at home,' he says. 'But I don't like the ticket selling. When I'm the away fighter, it's less stressful. I get a call saying will I box in a week for £1,500. I turn up. I box. It's simple. I don't want to be a prospect,' he says, shaking his head.

While I have been talking with Phil, Paddy has been wrapping Natty's hands in the same methodical way as Sniper's. The atmosphere is slightly different. It's more relaxed with Natty. There are jokes. Paddy checks the comfort level of his hands, which are wrapped with gauze across the knuckles for added support. Tonight he is fighting at welterweight, 10st 7lbs, and he looks trim. There is no wasted flesh on his body. Natty begins to move around the dressing room bobbing, weaving and rolling from side to side. He shadow boxes effortlessly in front of the mirrors lining the walls.

I enjoy watching Natty move around. He is both fluid and graceful as his sinuous body glides around to some internal choreography as he imagines he is slipping his opponent's punches and pivoting around his stricken adversary.

It strikes me that boxing, like bullfighting, encourages the aficionado to really invest in its participants – something the great Ernest Hemingway, an aficionado of both, explains brilliantly. I am really looking forward to watching Natty compete this evening. I suppose I should be objective but like most fight fans I am not. I like Natty as a fighter, a lot, and I hope he performs well tonight.

At 6pm, the Bob Marley music that is an obligatory part of any boxing experience with Paddy begins. At the same time, 'Lady Luck' Bec Connelly arrives. She looks fit and strong, bigger than normal, which I find out is because she has moved up a weight division to take this fight. Her boxer plaits are tight and she looks like she means business.

This is in a direct contrast to this morning at the gym.

I trained and sparred a few rounds this morning at Paddy's gym, where Becs spent most of the session sipping Lemsip on the ring apron. She talked about feeling like she had flu, the potential of her experiencing a panic attack and how she was feeling more fatigued than she had for any other fight.

She shadow boxes as Bob Marley's 'Buffalo Soldier' plays, bouncing around on the balls of her feet as she feints and jabs.

Paddy sings along to the track loudly.

I *really* want Becs to get a result tonight. I know how hard she works to be a pro boxer and how challenging her personal circumstances are. I also remember how tough her last fight was against a high quality Olympic silver medal-winning fighter. Becs was courageous and full of heart and determination. She refused to give in and took some serious punishment. The fight was stopped, but she tried – and we all really wanted her to win.

I focus on the act of wrapping a fighter's hands, creating the protection for the fist with bandages and tape and sculpting them to fit the fighter's hand perfectly. It seems like an art to me – something that a man learns to do well over years of practice. There's clearly a method to it and I'm sort of meditating while watching the almost hypnotic quality of the wrapping when a near-empty bandage cartridge hits me in the head and breaks the spell.

Paddy laughs and winks at me.

He is wrapping Becs' hands now and she insists I take a picture of them. She asks me to take the picture from 'her good side'. I haven't got the courage to ask a fighter which is her 'good' side, so I just guess and hope that I get it right.

When she sees the image, she smiles – so I guess my instincts were right.

Paddy is making Becs laugh and in the picture that I take they are both smiling and laughing, which is a deliberate ploy of Paddy's as we all know that Becs can feel the pressure of an event, so the best thing that he can do for her is try to relieve it.

I speak to Becs and ask her if she's happy with her weight.

'No,' she says, 'I'm the heaviest I've fought at. It's all muscle but it's not me.'

She reflects for a moment and then says to me, 'You can cut the tension with a knife in here, right Teach?'

I think this might be her personal view, rather than a representation of all of the other fighters' feelings in the room. And this is normal, I imagine, because the other fighters are behaving differently in their conversation and body language.

When I manage to get a minute with Paddy and ask about the importance of the hand-wrapping process, he tells me, 'It's an opportunity to bond. A chance to find out how my fighter is feeling and quell any nerves that they might have. For some fighters, I need to provide them quiet words and positive affirmations. For others, it's a chance to provide some clear instruction.

'For others still, like Becs, it's when I'll make jokes to release her tension. And still for some others, I might need to be firm with them and trigger their motivation. Each fighter needs different things and it's my job to know that.'

Does the way you design and create wraps change from boxer to boxer?

'Some prefer tighter than others, Teach. But the important thing from the coach's perspective is how I use the time.'

At 6.30pm, half an hour before the event begins, the gloves for the night arrive.

Sniper has been skipping and shadow boxing to keep himself loose. I watch him jab with his long reach, imagining his opponent as he catches phantom body shots with his right elbow and counters with strong jabs and right crosses to his imaginary opponent's chest and face.

Paddy is inspecting the gloves for the night. He checks their weight and then the security of the padding and the laces. To make sure, he puts the gloves on himself to feel that they are right for his team. I hear him tell the officials for the night that the gloves need to be softened up.

At 6.40 pm, as we near the time for Sniper to fight, Paddy takes the time to usher him to one side and speak quietly, but intensely, with him. As they talk, Paddy physically demonstrates what he wants Sam to achieve when he is fighting.

By 6.45pm, Paddy has Sniper working with him on the pads in order to help him stay loose and feel confident in the actions and reactions of his body. The punches that strike the pads are concussive and come with professional force in their delivery. I know that if he lands a shot like that, it will hurt.

They work on controlling power: 25 per cent, 50 per cent, 75 per cent and fully loaded shots selected for the right purpose and at the right time. They work on Sniper using a combination then sliding to the right of his orthodox opponent before delivering a decisive blow. They work too on speed and Sniper attacking then sliding out of range and re-setting his attack.

At 6.55pm, Sam is pacing around the dressing room like a caged animal. He is ready and his mind is clearly on the fight. Paddy begins to apply vaseline to his face.

The mood in the dressing room has changed now. Paddy is standing in front of Sam and giving him some final instructions that only he can hear as Bob Marley's 'Exodus' provides a suitably serious and percussive soundtrack.

At 6.58pm, Paddy brings all the fighters together for some final words.

'You've done everything,' he tells them. 'Your opponents are there to ask you questions, of course. But you have the answers to all of their questions.'

Sniper stands alone in the middle of the dressing room, his signature touch, a wide-brimmed fedora cocked at an angle on his head. No matter how many of us are around, it must feel lonely for the fighters. Who can *really* help them once they are in the ring?

Sam is ready and I can see the concentration in his face. His eyes seem to almost harden and drain slightly of colour, like his personality is changing in order to become what will be necessary to do his job tonight.

I walk through the veins of the building linking the dressing room to the auditorium just in front of Sam, Paddy and the cornermen. There is no talking now and as we reach the entrance to the auditorium where Sam will take his position on the podium for his introduction. I step through the door and head with the cornermen to our allotted positions.

I walk down the same route that Sniper and the other fighters will take for their ring walks. I take my seat, which is at a table against the ring apron, right on the home fighter's corner. To my left is the fight promoter; to my right are the officials from the British Boxing Board of Control; and opposite me is a writer from *Boxing News* who I recognise.

The lights dim. Sniper's raucous friends and family are making plenty of noise. His ring music plays and he walks to the top of the podium to begin his ring walk. He is flanked by Paddy to his right. Sam is tall, his black hat contrasting with his red gown, and cuts quite a figure. He looks across at the audience full of confidence and dignity and then makes his walk slowly and assuredly to the ring.

Paddy walks a pace behind Sam, at his shoulder, making it clear that he is there for his fighter and that they are a team. But the way he positions himself also makes it clear that this is his fighter's night and Paddy is simply here to help him succeed. Like Sam's, Paddy's face is set in an expression that clearly means one thing: *it's time to go to work*.

Sam steps into the ring and the referee issues the final instructions and his list of rules and warnings for clarity. Sam's Latvian opponent looks strong and bigger than him.

As the bell for the first round signals, Paddy ducks out of the ring and positions himself on the ring apron, watching the opening action in forensic detail.

I am so close that I can see the beads of sweat on the backs of the fighters glistening under the ring lights. I can hear the impact of gloves against bone, every exhalation with a thrown punch, every grunt of recognition when a shot lands cleanly and the creaks and groans of the ring canvas as the fighters shuffle and pivot.

Sam's is a four-rounder and during the first round, Paddy encourages him to 'watch your distance', 'slide back', 'move to the side', 'don't let him get momentum' and 'meet him when he comes'.

I'm not sure that Sam can hear Paddy, although Paddy has assured me he trains his fighters to be able to hear his voice above other noises. That's why he makes sure that the only voice his fighter can hear on the night is his own.

I notice when Sam executes a move that Paddy approves of, Paddy recognises this with a 'there you go', just like he does in the gym during sparring and training.

The corner at the end of the round is calm and quiet. Paddy leans in close to Sam ensuring they both have eye contact and speaks softly and carefully, reinforcing his message that the key strategy for the second round is to 'meet him and slide back straight away'.

I watch closely and notice that Sam is communicating subtly with Paddy during the second round. Sam raises his eyebrows or nods almost imperceptibly as Paddy instructs him to be 'sharp when he comes and stop the momentum'.

Round three passes with some jabbing and moving to score points and manage his heavier opponent.

'It's close,' Paddy tells him before instructing Sam that when he ties up his opponent, he must be 'ready to come out and stick him' to secure the points in the final round.

Sniper comes out for the fourth and final round full of intent. 'Thirty seconds to go,' shouts Paddy's second, who times each round for him.

Sam extricates himself from a clinch and Paddy shouts, 'Straight to the stick. I want a double jab – right. Finish strong.'

When the result is announced it *has* been close, with a 39-38 win for Sam setting up the chance of a Southern Area title fight in his next outing.

'It was a hard fight,' Paddy admits, 'but we won.'

The next fight on the card is heavyweight Phil Williams, fighting out of the home corner this time, against the brilliantly named 'One-Punch' Miles Willington, who I imagine at a poorly conditioned 19 stone might not live up to his ring name.

Before he goes to fight, Paddy works the pads with Phil. They focus on the fundamentals: jabs, power jabs, one-twos and hooks. While they circle each other, Paddy keeps his eyes on Phil and quietly coaches him on how to manage the fight to avoid allowing the heavier man an advantage on the inside.

I have talked to Paddy about how he coaches and motivates each fighter and he has told me that each individual needs an approach tailored to his or her personality if a coach wants to get the best out of the fighter. What George Groves needed to perform was different to Eamonn O'Kane, or Laila Ali, or James Toney – and a coach had to work out what each fighter needed in order to win.

I hope to see this difference in his coaching and corner direction tonight. Having watched him with Sniper, it didn't seem like Sam needed much motivation. Paddy provided Sam with direction so that Sam could channel his intensity and then, at the right time, Paddy spurred his fighter on to a strong finish to impress the judges.

Just before we move off for the ring walk, I notice that Phil is still talking to officials about a mistake with ticket sales.

I can't help thinking that none of this can be of any help to an athlete's preparations – preparations for a very dangerous game in which switching off or losing focus for a second or two can have *serious* consequences.

But this is the reality of selling tickets for a boxing show, I suppose.

It's hard work and I am beginning to understand what Phil was telling me about preferring to be the away fighter and earning a fee to fight rather than a percentage of the ticket sales. This is probably *not* what fighters dream of when they turn pro.

The first thing I notice about the heavyweights in the ring is that they are truly big lads, and they seem physically less well-conditioned than the fighters in lower weight divisions on the card. But I remind myself how unwise it is to make a judgement on a boxer's chances of success based purely on his physical presentation. Former world heavyweight champion Andy 'The Destroyer' Ruiz, for one, might take issue with that.

After all, like Phil's opponent's ring name reminds us, at this weight it really does take only *one punch* to win a fight.

But not this one.

During round one, Paddy directs and motivates Phil in equal measure. 'Stick him,' Paddy reminds Phil. 'Don't get bored of the simple things. Stay switched on. Back on the stick, Phil. A bit more work, Phil. Listen to me Phil, walk around him, make space.

'*Listen to me.*'

Unlike Sniper, Phil is not responding immediately to Paddy. Some of this is probably to do with how Phil's career works. Phil fights anywhere at very short notice, often without Paddy and using cornermen he doesn't know. He's used to relying on himself and may be finding it hard to re-adjust to a coach who is invested in his success.

In the corner after round one, Paddy advises Phil. He is firm, clear and speaks more loudly than he did with Sniper.

'When he's on the ropes, meet him, slide back, and meet him again and then move away. You're standing there for him to hit.'

Presumably, Paddy isn't convinced that his instructions are being received by Phil as he asks him, 'Are you gonna listen to me? Meet him with the stick. Stop leaning in on a 19-stone dude. It's costing you more energy than him.'

Unfortunately, round two pans out much the same as round one with Phil not moving enough to create openings for angled attacks and staying on the line in front of his equally immobile opponent.

When Paddy gets him back in the ring after round two, his tone and approach change. He looks Phil in the eye and says with slight menace in his voice, 'You're not listening to me. Do you want me in your corner?'

'Yes,' says Phil, taking on water.

'Well listen to me, then. Because if you give me another round like that last one, you'll come back and I won't be here.'

Phil responds to Paddy in round three, moving around his opponent, who by now has landed a lot more than 'one punch' without really putting a dent in Phil.

Phil is also sliding back after his attacks to draw the slowing unit of his opponent on to his shots. Paddy consistently delivers loud and firm basic instructions to Phil throughout the round. The instructions are easy to follow and delivered almost aggressively.

When Phil sits down on his stool, Paddy is clearly happier. 'You listened that time and you won that round. Remember, your feet are more important than your hands. Your feet deliver the shots. You won that round, so let's make it clear in this last round.'

In the fourth round Paddy gets what he has asked for from Phil and he is adjudged the winner of the bout 39-37.

The third fight of the night involves Jensen Irving, or Natty as he is known at the gym, in a welterweight contest. Natty's record is 2-0 and he is a fighter I have enjoyed watching spar. In fact, Natty's story has intrigued me from the beginning.

Natty, by his own admission, was not in a good place before he came to boxing – neither for himself nor his family. Through boxing, however, Natty has transformed himself and improved his life – and the lives of those he loves. Every week he supports people like me, who he coaches so effectively at Paddy's gym.

I also know that Paddy derives a great deal of satisfaction from Natty's successes. Natty's opponent is already in the ring. He looks fit and strong and very well conditioned, so this should be a good test for Natty.

When the lights dim to let us know that the home fighter is about to enter, Bob Marley's 'Natty Dread' starts to play. This isn't your typical ring walk song. It's not bombastic. It's not hardcore. It's not upbeat and designed to get your heart pumping but it is packed with significance and meaning.

Everyone knows how Paddy feels about Bob Marley at the gym. It is a constant soundtrack to training. Bob's lyrics are tattooed on to Paddy's arm. Natty has been given his nickname because of Bob. As the lights come up to reveal Natty on the podium, he is wearing shorts that are half Union Jack and half the green, yellow and black of the Jamaican flag. There is a cheer immediately.

As Marley's reggae music plays, Natty walks calm and cool along the route of his ring walk. He is exceptionally well conditioned for this fight. As he nears the corner where I am sitting, I turn to face him and he nods at me in acknowledgement before he enters the ring.

I know what Hemingway meant by investing in a fighter, and the dangers associated with this. This is not a *financial* investment. It is more risky than that. The fact we follow an individual in this sport makes a big difference to the experience – the highs are high, but the lows? I am becoming intellectually and emotionally invested in Natty's success and also the success of the fighters at Paddy's gym.

The crowd are clearly with Natty and the noise outside the ring contrasts with the calm, almost serene way Paddy and his fighter are quietly talking.

During round one, Paddy comments on Natty's work and offers mild instruction. 'Answer everything,' he says. 'Stop any momentum. Speed kills. Shift the space. Beautiful – you're reading him.' He even reminds Natty to work with speed, shouting, 'Da-da, da-da' to remind Natty to deliver quick one-two combinations. Natty is strong, intelligent and quick. Like all good fighters he hits without being hit, frustrating his opponent. While in range and landing his own shots, he moves his head on and off the line, slipping and shifting his shoulders and using his strong core to roll effortlessly under his opponent's attacks. He leans back to force his opponent to miss by a small margin before punishing him with a stinging counter. Natty pivots and turns effectively to position himself at awkward angles to his opponent and deliver clean shots to the body.

This is exactly the kind of boxing I want to watch, like a game of chess played out in the form of combat sport.

I suspect that Paddy feels the same as I can't help but think that the tone in which he is commenting on Natty's work while he leans on the ring apron is, like mine, appreciative.

In the corner after round one, Natty is composed and Paddy gets straight to the point, 'Everything he does he pulls his head off the line to the right – catch him there.'

This is exactly what Natty needs. If he has recognised this himself, then he has reinforcement. If not, he knows what to execute.

Round two goes to plan and Natty dominates, exploiting Paddy's advice. As Natty sits in the corner between rounds, Paddy simply smiles at him before asking, 'How are you feeling?' Natty is feeling good and so Paddy decides that the gameplan will now allow him to fire some combinations he has been working on.

Round three continues strongly for Natty and the more successful he is, the more boisterous the crowd become. Paddy is aware that Natty has controlled the fight and won each round so far. To win the fourth and final round, Paddy advises Natty to 'break his attacks up with your jab – and then drop your shots on him. Most importantly, ignore the hype of the crowd, keep your focus, and win this'.

At the end of round four, having followed Paddy's advice throughout and dominated each round to the extent that *Boxing News* describes Natty as exhibiting 'a lot of quality', Natty wins every round – resulting in a 40-36 decision.

Paddy returns to the corner for the next bout with one of his welterweights, 'Sir' Bradley Townsend. Bradley is a skilful and entertaining boxer. His opponent for the evening, a guy called Des Newton, looks fit and tough – and he's grinning at the crowd as if he might be a showman and a bit of a handful.

Paddy keeps his advice from the ring apron simple as the rounds go by, such as, 'Don't get bored doing the simple things' and 'stay small in the exit'.

He also shows psychological awareness as he recognises that while Bradley is clearly the more skilled and technically proficient fighter, his opponent is soaking up punishment and appearing not to be too affected by Bradley's shots. This, in turn, is frustrating Bradley and could result in poor decision making and shot selection. 'Toughness is not a skillset' he shouts to Bradley, who acknowledges with a nod and keeps tight and measured in his approach.

Perhaps recognising some tension in his fighter's shoulders Paddy shouts, 'Have fun in there, just like you and Natty in the gym' to release some of the pressure. And it seems to work as Bradley pivots on his left foot, making his opponent miss and look clumsy at the same time, before he spins away to re-set his attack.

In the corner, Paddy talks in a low, calm voice to Bradley. He also uses more words than he did with some of the other fighters, speaking for much longer. I wonder if this is on purpose. Can Bradley take in more information in a pressurised situation than some other fighters?

Paddy is aware that the other guy is showboating – pulling faces at Bradley and gesturing to him with both hands down by his sides, like Roy Jones Jr did in his fight with James Toney.

Only unlike Roy Jones, Des Newton keeps getting hit for his trouble.

Paddy can see that the showboating is affecting Bradley.

'He's showboating because this fight is going your way,' he tells him. 'He's trying to draw attention away from the fact that your shots are hurting him.

'Creep to him and edge towards him with your jab,' Paddy urges Bradley. 'Use your stick – don't let him build any momentum, because that's all he's got. Be ready to let go when you see the shot is there.'

Which Bradley does, winning his bout with a convincing 40-36 points victory.

I enjoyed this fight and as much as it might annoy the boxing purist for me to say it, I enjoyed watching Des Newton and all his silliness, winding up Bradley and playing up to the crowd. He is good natured in defeat too, smiling like he's had a good time and shaking everyone's hand.

Next to fight is 'Lady Luck' Bec Connelly.

Everyone likes Becs – and I mean *everyone*. She's a full-time mum of five, runs her own businesses and is the first official female rifleman in the British Army – oh and she's a professional boxer too. And for the record, you read the army bit right – *female* rifleman. And the army is out in force to support their sister tonight.

The first time I stepped nervously into Paddy's gym, Becs took me on a pads session. I didn't know what to expect. I had no technique or understanding, but I actually understood what she was telling me. She was clear, patient and most of all welcoming – which played a big part in me coming back.

I know that she is nervous tonight. It's one of her things. Becs gets nervous. And she was nervous this morning when I saw her at the gym, telling anyone who talked with her how she was feeling coldy and a bit panicked.

I tried to do my little bit to help and reminded her of how well she had done in her previous fights. And even though the last one had been a decisive defeat, it had been against a really strong opponent. She just needed to believe in herself.

In the dressing room, she was putting on a brave face but we all knew how she would be doubting herself deep inside.

'You can't allow Becs' insecurities in,' says Casper as we wait for her ring entrance. 'You can't allow her to focus on her weaknesses. She needs a coach who is firm with her, focuses on the positive and tries to take away the pressure she puts on herself. Paddy knows what to say, and crucially how to talk to Becs.' Paddy has told me that if Becs is relaxed, she performs so much better. So he has two jobs: to ensure that Becs stays relaxed and keeps her belief, and to make sure that she is focused with the right direction – because if her nerves take over, then she will be a lot less successful.

On the ring walk, Paddy stays close to Becs and keeps talking to her, and this continues in the ring as the announcer speaks to the audience. Paddy talks quietly in Becs' ear to ensure she stays calm.

Just before the bell sounds, he says to Becs, 'Stay in that headspace.' She smiles as she walks out to meet her opponent.

As Becs returns to her corner at the end of round one, a little red in the face and her tight boxer plaits fraying a little, Paddy takes out her gumshield laughing, 'Don't bite my finger off now.'

Then he pulls a funny face at her. Becs laughs, her tense shoulders relax and she takes on some water. When her breathing has regulated itself, Paddy offers one piece of advice, 'Keep your right hand tidy as you slide out.'

Then, as he is putting Becs' gumshield back in her mouth, he tells her to hit 'the girl with the three eyebrows'.

Becs is smiling as she leaves her corner to attack round two.

The humour is contrived and Paddy has told me that he needs to do this or the tension Becs feels and the pressure she puts on herself can start to control her.

During round two, Paddy mixes instruction with affirmation. 'Good girl. Double the stick. Keep working.' Becs needs to hear his voice as an anchor.

As Becs returns from a close round two, Paddy does a silly dance as she takes her stool, before choosing the right time to explain to her, 'I need those sharp feet.'

And Paddy is right because Becs' opponent is increasingly smothering her work and not allowing Becs to get her shots off.

At the close of round three, it is clear that Becs is frustrated by her opponent's strategy. Paddy senses this, and he must also realise that this is a time when Becs could lose her focus.

'Now,' he says firmly, 'what do you think is allowing her in so close?' forcing Becs to engage with his question. Then he follows with urgent, imperative instructions to ensure total clarity, 'I need you to hit her and move. Hit her and move with crisp, straight shots.'

And that's what Becs does as Paddy keeps reminding her in single words, 'Straight! Straight!'

Even though the fight has been a bit messy and Becs' opponent has spent the whole bout smothering her work, the judge scores the fight 39-38 and Becs celebrates with the Swindon crowd.

Keeping Becs calm, happy and focused with clear direction has probably made the difference here.

There is a longer pause in the proceedings now as the ring announcer and promoter conduct a charity auction. I find this part of a typical boxing card exceptionally dull – but it is what it is, I suppose. I just look over my notes and the programme of the night to make sure I am clear on who Ryan Martin is fighting in the night's headline bout.

Ryan's opponent is a welterweight called Ohio Kain Iremiren, and as he walks to the ring he looks tall to me and very well conditioned. His arms look long too, like he's going to have a decent reach.

Ryan is a hometown favourite who is building himself up to a serious title challenge. Paddy really believes in him and has told me that Ryan has what it takes to challenge for something really significant.

When the lights go down in the venue, Ryan is illuminated and the atmosphere of the evening changes. There is chanting and cheering, but there is something else too, something that tells us that even though everyone fighting tonight meant business, these two fighters *really* mean business.

Ryan makes his ring walk with Paddy just set back slightly behind him, and he looks impressive underneath the lights as they enter the ring.

I notice that Paddy's expression has changed. He seems more intensely focused with Ryan and it's like his face is set in its expression like a Japanese mask. There is little conversation between Paddy and Ryan. They both stand upright as the ring announcer does his job. Perhaps Paddy is expressing his confidence in his fighter *because* he's saying so little to him? If Ryan is ready, what does Paddy really need to tell him at this stage?

During the first two rounds of the fight, Paddy says little but he observes Ryan's work intricately. When Ryan returns to the corner, he sits on his stool and unlike with his other fighters, Paddy kneels down directly in front of him. He speaks with Ryan quietly and then whispers in his ear – something so quiet that even from as close as I am, I can't make it out.

I wonder if Paddy says less with Ryan than he does with his other fighters simply because Ryan doesn't need it?

As Ryan sits down on his stool at the end of round three, Paddy says to him, 'You didn't give me that one-two slide,' rather than, 'Why didn't you one-two slide?'

I imagine that Paddy is choosing his words carefully as the latter seems accusatory, like a challenge, whereas the former is more conciliatory and almost suggests that the fighter is providing his coach with a kind of gift as he *gives him* the right moves.

As the minute counts down, Paddy continues, 'You did beautiful. I just need to see a little bit more. Wrap around him and go to the body.'

As the fight continues, we can all see that Ohio can fight and he has come to win.

Ryan is acting on Paddy's advice and trying to wrap around his opponent before digging a short hook into his ribs. But Ohio is not accommodating Ryan's strategy and frustratingly for Ryan, he is caught with a counter as Ohio predicts one of his pivots.

When Ryan returns to the corner after round five, I can see frustration on his face. Ohio is awkward. Ryan's strategy isn't quite paying off yet. Both fighters are landing shots and both are absorbing each other's punishment. Both are clearly working hard, and at a decent pace, as the sweat is glistening on both of their bodies.

I can see that Ryan is frustrated. He is shaking his head and I am sure Paddy can see it too. Paddy stays calm, kneeling in front of Ryan. 'I need that little bit underneath, like this, *bap, bap*,' he says, demonstrating the action he wants. 'Don't load up on him yet.'

The fight has its fair share of controversy – caused by a series of low blows. By round five, Ohio has hit Ryan low twice. The referee addresses each of these fouls with a 'keep your punches up' but while he looks towards Ohio, I don't hear him use Ohio's name. After the third low blow, the referee speaks to Ohio. When a fourth one lands, Paddy remonstrates with the referee from the ring apron. After the fifth infraction, Paddy shouts directly at the referee. When the round ends, Paddy confronts the referee and asks why he hasn't deducted a point from Ohio for the consistent infringements?

'Because he hasn't hurt your boy,' is his response.

'How can a man repeatedly hit another in the balls and go unpunished?' Paddy asks the referee.

'It doesn't matter if he hit him in the balls if he didn't hurt your boy,' is the referee's response.

The temperature seems to rise now as Paddy explains vigorously to the referee why his responses are unacceptable.

After a few more seconds, Paddy gives up and returns to his corner. When Paddy's back is turned, I see the referee shrug his shoulders and then do a *yap-yap-yap* gesture with his hand. I don't think his responses are fair, or his actions dignified.

I wonder what the Board of Control officials think of his conduct?

Both fighters do everything they can to secure a win in the final rounds in what *Boxing News* describes as 'a grandstand finish' with 'ferocious exchanges'. When the referee Lee Every announces the final result, the controversy continues. 'Welter-War Ends in a Draw' is how *Boxing News* alliteratively reports this battle. Ryan is understandably frustrated with the 77-77 result in front of his home crowd. It's written all over his face.

At the announcement of the draw, the usual barking, growling and simplistic comments in support of Ryan can be heard from the partisan and increasingly drunk crowd.

I sympathise with them, even though I think the fight was close and Ohio did enough to push Ryan in the decision.

It's also true that Ryan sustained several low blows and if the referee had punished even one of them with a point deduction, Ryan would have won.

Back in the dressing room after the fight, the medicals have all been completed, Paddy has had a fruitless conversation with the referee and he takes a frustrated Ryan aside for a private chat.

I keep my distance when Ryan returns. He speaks with people he trusts far more than me. He's talking with 'The Duke' and Casper when I hear him say about Ohio, 'He was tougher than I expected and he was doing some things where I thought I was safe, but I wasn't.'

Ryan also says he felt mentally flat against Ohio, which resulted in him not landing the final, closing punctuation mark of the last punch in the exchanges – important for the judges.

As Ryan continues his conversation with 'The Duke' and Casper, Paddy and I decide to leave for final orders at his local pub, which isn't far away.

We don't say a lot on the way over to the pub and as we walk into the bar, one of the drinkers asks, 'How did it go tonight, Paddy?'

With a tired smile, and a Guinness in his hand, he replies, 'All won, but one of them was a draw.'

We sit down and I ask Paddy to reflect on the evening's events. Understandably, he is thinking about Ryan.

At first, Paddy is involved in two dialogues. One of these is physical, with me, and the other is through text with Ryan, who is feeling like things haven't gone his way tonight.

Paddy reflects on the referee's decision not to deduct a point from Ryan's opponent, even though Ryan was on the painful end of five low blows. I know this is a problem because if just one point had been deducted from his opponent, Ryan would have won the fight by a 77-76 margin.

Will you contest the decision, I ask Paddy?

'I've requested to see the scorecards,' says Paddy as he drinks half a pint in one go. 'It was a close fight. The opponent was strong. But I had Ryan two rounds up. *If* I get the scorecards, I can look at them and see if there are any grounds to contest.'

His last statement is clearly punctuated with the emphasis on a mighty '*if*'.

It wasn't a loss, though, I say. Ryan was very competitive. He hit the other lad with some big shots that rocked him. For the neutral, I thought it was a really entertaining and skilful fight.

He nods, appreciating and considering what I am saying.

'The other guy was really composed, especially when Ryan landed those big shots,' he says.

Paddy imitates Ryan landing his biggest shots and then locks his face in an emotionless expression to imitate how Ryan's opponent barely reacted to the hits.

'He's a good fighter, that Ohio. I thought that it was a chess match, more than an exciting fight as such. A fight between two skilled and talented fighters: move, counter-move, set up and attack.'

Then Paddy grimaces slightly. 'Ryan wasn't quite himself in the exchanges tonight. He wasn't getting off that final punch to catch the judge's eye.'

I tell Paddy that I overheard Ryan saying as much to 'The Duke' after the fight.

'I told him in the corner, "Remember Frampton v Santa Cruz? The second one Frampton lost? Frampton was strong in the exchanges, but slightly less skilled at making sure he had the final shot of the exchange and caught the judges' eyes." I wanted Ryan to make sure he did that.'

Is it important to both land that last shot of an exchange and finish the last ten seconds of a round in an eye-catching way, I ask? 'One hundred per cent, Teach – it's human nature that you're accepting here. If the exchange, or round, is equal, then the judges will be influenced by the last impression in their memory. For a points win, it's key.'

It turns out that Paddy's belief and confidence in Ryan is well placed.

In his next fight a couple of months later, Ryan takes on a strong competitor in the South African welterweight champion, an ambitious and superbly conditioned boxer named Mziwoxolo Ndwayana (don't ask me how to say this), and I am at ringside for this too.

The fight is an eliminator for the opportunity to compete for the Commonwealth welterweight title and the snap and intensity in both men's punches are testament to this fact.

Regardless of the pedigree and exemplary condition of the South African, the fight does not last long – less than six minutes in total.

After a sharp and focused first round from Ryan, in which he scores with powerful right hands and rolls under heavy-handed hooks from his opponent, Ryan moves up several gears in the second round. Working on the inside in the gaps between his opponent's spells of pressure, Ryan mixes a variety of damaging hooks to head and body that connect with his target each time. When the final hook to the right side of his opponent's lower ribcage finds its target, the South African is left writhing on the canvas in agony, unable to beat the referee's count.

I speak to Will Hale of *Boxing News* after the fight. He is impressed with Ryan, having seen him several times before, and tells me that he rates Ryan's one-punch power and likes him as a fighter who can box and punch.

According to Will, Ryan is going to go somewhere. Though Will doesn't specify the destination, from his positive response to Ryan's performance I imagine he is referencing somewhere worth going.

But it's getting late now, well after midnight, and I hear the pub's owner telling us all that we've got to leave and I realise that I've been in fight town for over eight hours.

It's lashing down when we leave the pub, so I give Paddy a lift round the corner to his place.

I don't say much as he gets out. I just smile, shake his hand and thank him for allowing me to be such a close part of the event. And I ask him if he wants to come over to mine and eat Spanish food.

The truth is, I feel privileged to have been so close to the fighters and to Paddy as he worked tonight. It has meant a lot to me to be accepted and trusted like this.

But I don't put it like that because I can see that he's tired, and now that we've wound down a bit from the event, I'm feeling tired too.

26

Final Thoughts

I INTEND to finish the book where I started it – at Fitzpatrick's boxing gym. To the different characters frequenting Paddy's gym, it's a special place – more than just a boxing gym. I'm sure that other gyms are special too, and possibly in a very similar way, but this one is ours.

I want to finish by talking with the youth who have in many ways made Paddy's gym a second home. I speak with 18-year-old professional boxer Lewis Roberts, known in the gym as 'Chubbsy' and just about to make his professional debut as *El Raton Gordo*.

Lewis is everything you might expect of a dedicated young professional. He is lithe and muscular – without a single ounce of fat on his body. He is exceptionally fit and agile as he enters into the profession he has been training for with Paddy from six years old. Lewis trains most of the week at the gym and has been coaching youngsters too. Speaking a little Spanish myself, I'm interested in his fighting name, *El Raton Gordo*.

It means fat mouse. But there's no fat on you at all, so how did you get that name, I ask?

'It all started off because we had travelled to a fight around four hours from Swindon,' he tells me. 'When we got there, I weighed in too heavy and I wasn't able to fight. "Chubbsy" as a name has stuck with me ever since and I rarely ever hear my actual name in the gym!

'Before "*El Raton Gordo*" my name had been "*El Gordito*", which translates to "fat boy" in Spanish. This is because some people who have seen me fight comment that I box with a bit of a Mexican style. I've been sparring with pros who are training for titles since the age of 13, just like a young Canelo! And that's why we bought the Mexican hat that I will be wearing to the ring on my debut fight night.

'You don't get noticed in this game for being your average Joe, so having something different about you just gives you some advantages over everyone else when it comes to the business side of boxing. I've got talent *and* a name, which sets me out from the rest when it comes to promoting myself as a fighter.'

So you've come to this gym since you were six years old. What is special about *this* gym, I ask?

'So many things in the gym make it special for me. Paddy is a world-class trainer but mostly it's the vibes that the gym gives off. No matter what's happening in the world, there is always a good vibe around the gym.'

It is clear from Lewis' response that Paddy's gym is a stabilising refuge in an uncertain world, rather than somewhere to simply train and learn how to fight.

'Boxing at Paddy's is all I have ever known,' continues Lewis. 'I have never known any different than the morals I've learnt in and around the gym. If I hadn't come to Paddy's gym, I don't think I would be the man I am today. That is why I think boxing can do wonders for kids in schools. I've seen first hand people coming into the gym who have changed their lives around for the better.

'Paddy is like an older brother to me – a much wiser older brother. He's taught me so many lessons, not just about boxing but for my life. I feel privileged to be taken on what has been so far, and what will be, a great journey that has only just begun after a 12-year apprenticeship with Paddy.'

Kyle Bains, one of Paddy's younger national amateur champions at 17, tries to sum up his experience for me.

'Paddy's gym isn't only a boxing gym, it's a community; a family of people trying to better themselves. Paddy pushes you physically and mentally whilst at the same time making sure that you enjoy yourself and have fun with many others. The vibe and character in the gym is like nothing I had experienced before: from Bob Marley being blasted out of the speakers to the photos of previous champions on the gym walls. There is a constant feeling of positive energy. It is a place where people of different backgrounds can come together and help each other grow.

'Paddy's a great coach,' he continues. 'Anything that Paddy tells you to do has a purpose. He won't ever get anyone to do anything without telling them why they are doing it and how it will benefit you. He describes things in many different ways, so that it's easy to understand. Every day in the gym is different. He plans out what part of boxing we are working on in order to make us complete fighters.'

So would you say that rather than just improve your fitness and your skills as a boxer, Paddy has changed you as a person in a positive way, I ask Kyle?

'Before coming to Paddy I was overweight, unfit and not in a positive state of mind. I never thought I would be where I am today, and I owe that to Paddy. He's not only a coach but like a family member, teaching me lessons in boxing and in life that I hold close to my heart. He's made me into a young man and an all-round better person. Paddy cares for his fighters. He helps take youth off the street and give them something to strive for. As long as you enjoy Bob Marley you're sure to fit right in the gym, and if not Paddy will soon change that!'

Of course, Paddy runs a professional boxing gym. But like Kyle says, it's so much more than that. Paddy uses boxing as a vehicle to inspire young people to become a positive influence in their community. And not just the youth either. There are many people who come to his gym whose previous lives have included dark thoughts – and possibly even darker actions.

Paddy is not just offering boxing as a sport. This is boxing as hope. Boxing as a way to find peace and begin to love yourself and other people. Boxing as a tool to bring the community together. And in some cases, boxing as the road to a form of personal redemption.

It's powerful stuff.

In fact, as I write this, Paddy is seriously planning on building a community hub out of his gym, with a significant expansion into what he is thinking of calling, 'The Community Sports and Wellness Centre', which would mean that he would support the community with boxing, exercise for fitness, yoga, counselling, health and nutrition – and even a small school for students struggling with mainstream education.

For me, writing this book started as a journey into Paddy's life in boxing. But what I initially expected to be an experience that taught me a lot about the business of boxing and offered me an insider's perspective into this sometimes murky and confusing world, has become so much more than that. I have enjoyed learning and I have had real fun listening to the stories about the greats Paddy has worked with.

But that will not be the lasting legacy of this book for me.

When I first went to Paddy's gym, I was looking to make some positive changes in my life. Paddy helped me to do that. As we talked more, I became interested in his career and philosophy around coaching and teaching – so we agreed to write this book.

The lasting legacy will be friendship.

It has been a privilege to be trusted and allowed into another person's life as deeply and honestly as this book has allowed me to be. I have known Paddy for three years now. Writing his story has meant that we have spent a lot of time together, talking at least once a week for 18 months.

More than anything, I have appreciated the times when we have switched my voice recorder off and just talked as friends about coaching, teaching, philosophy or anything else that a couple of pints of Guinness might encourage us to discuss. Times when we have talked as friends and the subject of boxing, as much as I enjoy it, has just slipped away on to the conversational horizon.

Boxing on its own can be two-dimensional. It is, after all, just a sport in the end. Paddy the man has been more engaging for me, and that has been what has held my interest throughout writing this book.

There is a slight sadness as I write this because while it is exciting, we have come to the end of this project. And unfortunately, the bottle of Islay single malt that I have opened on my desk to celebrate this milestone will only be drunk by me. Because we are in lockdown, Paddy's face is grinning at me through my mobile phone screen. He has a drink in his hand too, but it's not the same. This is not how I had planned to finish our work together.

I ask Paddy what are his final thoughts having completed his book?

He begins with what he considers the 'dark' periods of his life. He reminds me that in his 51 years, he has had four periods where the 'darkness' has almost overwhelmed him.

'To anyone reading this, it's a book about boxing and I'm sure people will like reading about greats like Laila Ali, James Toney and Lamon Brewster. I think boxing fans will enjoy the "insider" perspective of my stories too, whether it's learning about what went on with George Groves behind the scenes or because they just love to hear about the great Muhammad Ali.

'But for me, this has been a constant conversation with myself. Because we have spoken at least once a week for 18 months, I have had my 51 years constantly in my head to chew over. That has been both enjoyable and difficult. No one enjoys every second of their life. Some parts are fantastic highs, like in boxing, and some bits are almost unbearable lows that we have to get through.

'I remember, even before we started this book, saying to you that when you are lonely, you could be in a room with a thousand people and still feel empty. Yet when you're in a good place, you can be totally on your own and be quite content.

'There have been four really down times for me, Teach. The first time was from the ages of 12–15. It was really dark. It doesn't mean every day for me was dark, but that period overall was dark for me. I had some good times, of course, but it was a period when I wanted to take my own life. I just didn't have the balls to do it.

'The second time was when I was 20 and I just thought to myself, "I'm not going to keep going through this." This time I gave it a really good shot but I guess it wasn't my time.

'The third time, I was 26. I'm going through this darkness again and I think to myself that the solution this time is to go somewhere where the choice will be taken out of my hands. So that's when I decide to join the Foreign Legion. It's exactly at that time that Freddie Roach offers me an opportunity that I know immediately I want to take.

'Look, my *plan* in life wasn't to commit suicide. My plan was the same as anyone else's growing up. It was to enjoy as much as I could, create goals and keep moving forward. I absolutely wanted to work with Freddie when that opportunity presented itself.'

We have talked several times over the last year or so about Paddy's experience of what he calls the 'darkness' and about his attempts at 'suicide'. These are facts of his life, challenging experiences that he has had to contend with as well as he could. But he is absolutely clear that his openness to talk about the 'dark' times he has experienced should not be taken as flippant, or that he is in anyway advocating or encouraging suicide to anyone experiencing difficulties in their lives.

In our conversations, it has been the exact opposite in my experience. Paddy's desire is to help others who might learn through his story that there is light at the end of our darkest tunnels – even if at the time we can't see where it is. It's also to encourage anyone who may be feeling the way he himself has felt to seek out the help they need – and talk to someone, because talking is at least a start.

'The fourth time I experienced the darkness,' Paddy continues, 'has been the most recent. It lasted two years, throughout most of the time we have been writing this book, in fact, and I came out of it New Year's Day 2020. It was as dark as any time. But this time, I knew I had bigger responsibilities. I have Kerry and my children. I also knew that there was a way out, because I had been through this before. Even if I couldn't find the answer at this point in my life, I knew that the answer was there.

'For the first 12 months, I didn't tell anyone.

'It's hard because when I walk in the gym, there is a certain type of energy expected of me. Most people see me as being the person who is always having a laugh and mostly that's what people get. But at the same time as presenting this on the outside, I would be seeing people that I knew and I would avoid them if I could so that I didn't have to talk to them. That wasn't them, it was me. That's not nice.

'You know too that my gym is only ten feet from my house, right? I would walk out my door, pause between the house and the gym, fall apart for 30 seconds, shake myself out, walk through the door of the gym, and start singing Bob Marley really loudly so that people would shout, "Hey coach, what's happening?"

'No one had any idea I was feeling like I was for two years.'

This is clearly about mental health and well being so I ask Paddy, 'Do you think that reading your story might benefit anyone who is facing the same challenges?'

'A friend has given me Tyson Fury's book as a present and I can relate to what he says completely. If people can read Tyson's book and think, "If he went through this and came out the other end, then I can too," that's cool. I hope that whoever reads my book gets to know a bit more about the Irish dude with the hat on his head, of course. But I hope even more that whoever reads this book can also see that I went through the darkness, but I have come out the other side – and been able to write this book.

'I didn't realise how deep this book would get. We decided to write a book on boxing together, except it has become a lot more than that and I have opened up my soul a lot more to you than I have to most people.

'In fact,' he says laughing, 'there are people in my family who are going to find things out that I have never told them when they read this.

'I would love my book to help a lot of people. But even helping one person is enough. If one person re-writes his or her script and says, "No, I'm not going to hurt myself", then hasn't this book served a purpose?

'In fact, there are people out there who could help you and they don't know how important what they did was. Take Freddie Roach, for example – he gave me the light I needed.

'In the last ten years or so, I haven't spoken much 'to Freddie at all. People might think it's strange that I'm not close to Freddie in the way I am with Laila, Vatche or Lamon. For me, that doesn't matter. Whether Freddie knows it or not, he saved my life back then. I was suffering and he gave me a reason to cling on.

'People don't realise that to turn on 1,000 lights in a warehouse, you can do that with one switch. One word at the right time, for the right person, can have an impact.

'Freddie saved my life, Teach, but Kerry, my wife, saved my soul. I also have a sister who has stood by me through every mistake that I have made in my life. Most people know the dude in the gym. A few people know the man who these two women have helped to mould.'

Frustratingly for me, as we have written this book, it has often been difficult to get Paddy to comment on his achievements and successes in boxing. He will talk about what his fighters achieved but he becomes more reticent when I ask him to explain what he feels *he* achieved. It is significant for me that when Lamon Brewster talks about winning the world heavyweight championship, he does this in the first person plural, 'we'. That 'we' is referring to himself – *and Paddy.*

I know Paddy is really conscious he doesn't want to come across as bragging. In his opinion, humility is an important quality. But I ask him anyway, 'What have been your greatest successes and achievements?' There is a long pause before he says, 'The fact that I am still here and I *want* to be here and that even in a smaller way, like with the youth in my gym, and sometimes in a big way, like with "T" [Lamon Brewster], I am managing to make a difference for others in the same way that Freddie did for me.'

What do you think makes a good coach, Paddy?

'A good coach is not about what a man knows, it's about what a man can *pass on*. The art of a good teacher is to simplify and pass on knowledge.'

Almost 40 years in boxing, I say, how do you feel about the sport now?

'I love it because I always relate life to boxing. To me, boxing is like life concentrated. Things can be going your way. Then you get hit with something that you don't see coming. You're on your ass now and what are you gonna do about it?'

What has given you the most satisfaction over your career as a coach, then?

'When you know someone has given you their complete trust,' Paddy says without hesitation. 'When I'm working with somebody, I will go to the wall for them. For any individual to give you their complete trust is more honourable and more satisfying than any amount of money on earth. When a man or a woman gives you something like trust that makes them vulnerable, then he or she has given you something of *unmeasurable* value.

'I was speaking to my son D.J. last night and explaining to him that to have real and true friends is so valuable and I don't think most people realise how valuable it is.'

We are nearing the end of our conversation, so I ask Paddy what the future holds for him. If this book were to end in a traditional way, then Paddy would talk about the British and Commonwealth titles that he is positioning Ryan Martin and 'The Duke' to fight for before they potentially move on to something even bigger.

But typically, Paddy doesn't really mention boxing.

He exhales loudly. 'Boxing is my profession, Teach. I just want to be someone who can be relied upon,' he says calmly.

'I've been extremely blessed in my life,' he continues. 'To get the opportunity to work for the last 24 years as a coach in something I love, and to work with men like Freddie Roach, Buddy McGirt, Roger Mayweather and Adam Booth is something I completely appreciate.

'I'm still trying to make sense of how to live my life and honour the blessings that my parents, my loved ones, the coaches I've learned from and the fighters have given me. Ultimately, it's working with the youth that makes most sense to me. I need them and they need someone to believe in them 100 per cent, which I do.

'I know they only trust me if my actions match what I am teaching them – and they help to keep me straight. It eats me up if I mess up or say something without giving thought to how it might be received by the listener. I still dwell on things like that from years ago.

'I appreciate everyone who has shown me love, kindness or given me their time.'

And then, with a self-deprecating laugh, he adds, 'And that's it. Sorry Teach, no Hollywood ending.'

But I'm happy with that, because this is what I expect from Paddy. His last thoughts and hopes for the future are to be a good man – as simple and as profound as that.

I don't want to but I know that this is the right point to end the story – *for now.*

So as a final act, I ask Paddy to give me a line from his favourite musician and philosopher, Bob Marley, that he would like to leave with the reader.

He responds quickly with a line from Marley's song 'Heathen' that goes, *'As a man sows, so shall he reap.'*

Peace to all and keep smilin', as Paddy would say!

Thanks for reading.

Paddy and Teach
April 2020

Also available at all good book stores

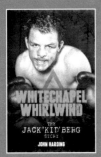

9781785314438

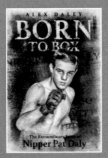

9781785313684

9781785312984

9781785313196

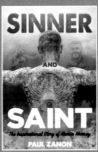

9781785313851

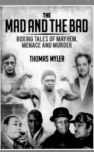

9781785313950

9781785314018

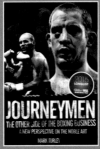

9781785311444

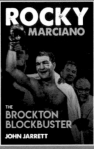

9781785313813